Healing Psalms

Other books by Joshua O. Haberman

Philosopher of Revelation: The Life and Thought of S. L. Steinheim
The God I Believe In: Conversations about Judaism

Healing Psalms

The Dialogues with God That Help You Cope with Life

A Reader's Companion to the Book of Psalms

JOSHUA O. HABERMAN

WILEY

John Wiley & Sons, Inc.

Published by John Wiley & Sons, Inc., Hoboken, New Jersey
Published simultaneously in Canada

Design and production by Navta Associates, Inc.

For general information about our other products and services, please contact our Customer Care Department within the United States at (800) 762-2974, outside the United States at (317) 572-3993 or fax (317) 572-4002.

Wiley also publishes its books in a variety of electronic formats. Some content that appears in print may not be available in electronic books. For more information about Wiley products, visit our web site at www.wiley.com.

ISBN 0-471-26474-1

Printed in the United States of America

10 9 8 7 6 5 4 3 2 1

To Maxine,
the Love of my Life

Contents

ACKNOWLEDGMENTS

I am grateful to Maxine, my wife and wise partner throughout the years, for sharing her keen insight into human nature and helping me claify my thoughts. Thomas W. Miller, Executive Editor, had a major role in determining the basic pattern of this book. John Simko, Senior Associate Managing Editor, was unfailingly on target with numerous suggestions of textual corrections and changes. Phillip J. Ratner, whose art glorifies the Bible, prompted me years ago to do a commentary on the Psalms for which he drew illustrations. I am indebted to my literary agent, Muriel Nellis, for her confidence in this work.

INTRODUCTION

The first book printed in America was *The Whole Book of Psalms*, in 1640. However, many of the Pilgrim Fathers did not need the printed text. They knew the psalms by heart, having sung them at worship services since early childhood. Among Jews, the daily reading of psalms has been an established practice since time immemorial.

Countless people, deeply moved whenever they hear the 23rd Psalm, wonder if other psalms might touch them as much. However, after browsing through the Book of Psalms in search for something that might speak to them, they soon put the Bible back on its shelf. The message of the psalms is not always clear; some texts are obscure, even incomprehensible.

This reader's companion to the psalms is a commentary designed to lead the reader quickly to the core message of each psalm. It focuses on the psalms' relevance to our own life situations. Only minimal attention is given to the historical setting of each psalm, the dating of its composition, and the many theories of authorship. The psalmists were not professional theologians. They were people like you and me, not very different from us in their needs, virtues, faults, and follies. The Psalms, the world's first prayer book, speaks to the human condition openly and honestly. It had many authors, some known and famous like King David, others unknown. All of them freely pour out their feelings. The psalmists speak from the heart. Knowing that there are no secrets before God, they give a true account of their thoughts and situations and are quick to confess wrongdoings. God is just, they believe, and no one escapes His judgment. But God is also loving and forgiving. Repentant sinners are dear to God.

The psalms reflect many different moods: joy and sorrow, pride and shame, love and hate. They tell of sleepless nights, fears, and the flow of tears. The psalmists also glory in a sense of blessedness and thanksgiving for all the good that has come into their lives and for being in God's presence. In other books of the Bible, it is mostly *God speaking to man* through visions, seers, and prophets. In the Psalms, it is *people speaking to God*. As you keep reading, you, too, may find yourself talking to God.

With few exceptions, the psalms are autobiographical, marked by soul searching and confessions. They reach out to God, believing that God cares for His creatures and hears and answers prayer. For the psalmists, prayer is a dialogue with God.

When healthy and well off, you are likely to lull yourself into a false sense of security. You don't think, or don't *want* to think, that the props upholding your life might be knocked out at any moment. Few of us face the fact of our total dependence on powers other than ourselves until this truth dawns upon us when going through a crisis. Illness, the death of a dear one, financial reverses, being targeted by enemies, and all sorts of troubles expose our weakness and need of help. Many a psalm illustrates the adage "Man's extremity is God's opportunity." Trying to cope with life, the psalmists turn to God for help. You are bound to find in the psalms situations with which you can identify. Often the words of the psalmist will echo your own feelings, even as the words of God, spoken to the psalmist, will strike you as a personal message.

On the assumption that most psalms are spiritual autobiographies, *Healing Psalms* tries to reconstruct the life situation that prompted their composition. Bear in mind that the psalmist does not always tell his story in the order in which things happened. Often the psalmist opens up with the outcome of his case or the conclusion he reached and then goes into some detail, recalling what had happened earlier, elaborating on his feelings at various stages of the experience. Accordingly, our commentary does not always proceed line by line, but focuses on different parts of the psalm that will help the reader understand what happened and how the psalmist reacted to the events.

Biblical passages quoted in this commentary are my own translation. The full text of the psalms is taken from *The Holy Scriptures*, which retains "the admirable diction of the Authorized Version," made more accurate through a remarkable fusion of Jewish and Christian biblical scholarship, issued by the Jewish Publication Society of America in 1917.

Five Suggestions for Reading the Psalms

1. Read the psalms regularly, at least one a day.

2. Set a fixed time, morning or evening, for your psalm reading.

3. It is best to read the psalms in numerical order. At times, however, you may want to choose a special psalm to meet a particular need. (See the Guide to Topics in the Psalms.)

4. Read your daily psalm aloud and then read it again. You will be surprised how often you will discover new meaning the second time.

5. Read with a notebook at your side. Jot down any phrase or sentence that impresses you and the thoughts that come to you upon reflection. As you keep reading the psalms, their authors will become old friends, and like them, you will be in dialogue with God.

GUIDE TO TOPICS
IN THE PSALMS

Happy is the man that hath not
  walked in the counsel of the wicked,
Nor stood in the way of sinners,
Nor sat in the seat of the scornful.
2 But his delight is in the law of the
  LORD;
And in His law doth he meditate day
  and night.
3 And he shall be like a tree planted by
  streams of water,
That bringeth forth its fruit in its
  season,
And whose leaf doth not wither;

And in whatsoever he doeth he shall
  prosper.

4 Not so the wicked;
But they are like the chaff which the
  wind driveth away.
5 Therefore the wicked shall not stand
  in the judgment,
Nor sinners in the congregation of the
  righteous.
6 For the LORD regardeth the way of the
  righteous;
But the way of the wicked shall perish.

❧

Two Ways of Life

The First Psalm sets the tone for the entire Book of Psalms: God is not
neutral with regard to human conduct. In the order of the world, as
designed by God, the way of the righteous will prevail and the way of
the wicked will perish. Every person is challenged to choose between
right and wrong. You make choices all the time. Often it doesn't make
much difference what you choose. But *one* choice can change your life:
the company you choose. Shun evildoers. The author of Psalm 1
believes that your associations become your destiny. "Happy is the one
that has not walked in the counsel of the wicked, nor stood in the way
of sinners, nor sat in the seat of the scornful" (v. 1).

Bear in mind the moral standards taught us by God's law. The
more you think about them, the more likely you will keep them.
Strengthened in goodness, you will be as steady as "a tree planted by
streams of water" (v. 3).

Not so the evildoers. Rootless and restless, they will be driven away
by the storms of changing fortune as the wind blows away the chaff.
(See v. 4.)

❧

Reflection: The Two Ways

If daily reports of crime and violence make you wonder if there is such
a thing as "moral order" in this world, be reminded by Psalm 1 that
there is a right way and wrong way and that each has predictable

consequences. God is involved in our lives. He knows which way we choose. And God wants right to prevail and wrong to be destroyed.

The psalmist warns against association with evildoers. Shun those who sneer at the laws of God. Evil is contagious. But so is good. Seek out the company of those who lead righteous lives. The good within us is strengthened when we study the Bible. Its benefits are maximized if we do so regularly, especially in the company of fellow students and a teacher, in keeping with the psalmist's suggestion to meditate on God's law "day and night" (v. 2).

❧ PSALM 2 ❧

Why are the nations in an uproar?
And why do the peoples mutter in
vain?
2 The kings of the earth stand up,
And the rulers take counsel together,
Against the LORD, and against His
anointed:
3 "Let us break their bands asunder,
And cast away their cords from us."

4 He that sitteth in heaven laugheth,
The LORD hath them in derision.
5 Then will He speak unto them in His
wrath,
And affright them in His sore
displeasure:
6 "Truly it is I that have established My
king
Upon Zion, My holy mountain."

7 I will tell of the decree:
The LORD said unto me: "Thou art
My son,

This day have I begotten thee.
8 Ask of Me, and I will give the nations
for thine inheritance,
And the ends of the earth for thy
possession.
9 Thou shalt break them with a rod of
iron;
Thou shalt dash them in pieces like a
potter's vessel."

10 Now therefore, O ye kings, be wise;
Be admonished, ye judges of the
earth.
11 Serve the LORD with fear,
And rejoice with trembling.
12 Do homage in purity, lest He be
angry, and ye perish in the way,
When suddenly His wrath is
kindled.

Happy are all they that take refuge in
Him.

❧

Rejoice with Trembling

Never forget that we are subject to overwhelming forces. As creatures we are dependent on the Creator Who made us. No combination of powers can defy God's judgment. Therefore, revere God at all times.

This psalm pictures God in heaven laughing at the boastful pretensions of political or military leaders. Whatever their power, it will vanish even as today's rulers will vanish.

You may be puzzled by verse 11: "Serve God in awe, and rejoice with trembling." Why tremble? Even when you are happy, let there be an ever-so-slight undercurrent of trembling as you realize the fragility of your life. You could not live a moment if not sustained by a power other than yourself.

❦

Reflection: Do Not Follow the Crowd

Picture the psalmist, a proud son of Israel, visiting neighboring nations and seeing throngs of people crowding their idolatrous temples. He and his people are the only ones who, in defiance of the rest of mankind, cling to belief in the invisible, one and only God. The psalmist is unimpressed by numbers and speaks with contempt of "the uproar" of nations and their "empty muttering" (v. 1). Don't numbers count? What about the saying "Fifty million Frenchmen can't be wrong?" Indeed, they *can* be wrong; even hundreds of millions of people have been carried away by mass hysteria, superstitious panic, and blind fanaticism to commit terrible crimes against humanity. The German poet Friedrich Schiller said it well: "The opinion of the majority is not the final proof of what is right." A popular American painting shows a huge herd of buffalo stampeding toward the edge of a canyon. They keep following the lead animal and then all plunge down the canyon to their deaths. If the human race ever destroys itself, it will be in this way, in disregard of a biblical warning voiced 3,000 years ago: "Do not follow a multitude to do evil" (Exodus 23:2). Infected by mob psychology, people stop thinking for themselves and become blind followers. Running with the crowd can turn into a death march.

❧ PSALM 3 ❧

A Psalm of David, when he fled from Absalom his son.

2 LORD, how many are mine adversaries become!
Many are they that rise up against me.
3 Many there are that say of my soul:
"There is no salvation for him in God."   Selah

4 But Thou, O LORD, art a shield about me;
My glory, and the lifter up of my head.
5 With my voice I call unto the LORD,
And He answereth me out of His holy mountain.   Selah

6 I lay me down, and I sleep;
I awake, for the LORD sustaineth me.
7 I am not afraid of ten thousands of people,
That have set themselves against me round about.

⁸ Arise, O LORD; save me, O my God;
  For Thou hast smitten all mine
    enemies upon the cheek,
  Thou hast broken the teeth of the
    wicked.

⁹ Salvation belongeth unto the LORD;
  Thy blessing be upon Thy people.
                                    Selah

❧

Down but Not Out

What a shock when someone you love turns against you! It happened to David when his son Absalom tried to destroy him. Forced to flee by the initial success of Absalom's rebellion and abandoned by many he had trusted, David was widely regarded as finished. He, however, would not give in to despair. God was not through with him. In the end, David recovered victoriously from the terrible blow he had suffered.

Never say about a setback, "This is the end." Overnight all can change. So we are told in this psalm: "I lie down, sleep, and wake again because the Lord sustains me" (v. 6).

❧

Reflection: Coping with Fear

Being disliked or hated by someone cannot hurt you nearly as much as your thinking about it. You wonder, What is my enemy up to? Is he spreading lies about me? How is he trying to harm me? Your fears, mingled with resentment, become obsessive. You no longer function normally. How can you cope with such feelings? Consider the wisdom of two statesmen-philosophers. The ancient Roman Seneca said, "We are more often frightened than hurt; our troubles spring more often from fancy than reality." One of America's Founding Fathers, Thomas Jefferson, agreed: "How much pain have cost us the evils which have never happened!" The fears in your head may not correspond to reality. They may never materialize. Try a spiritual approach to the mastery of fear. Realize that neither you nor your enemy are the only players in your life. Countless unexpected happenings could occur, with or without your doing—and change the situation you now fear. When the would-be peacemaker Terry Anderson went to Lebanon to arrange a peace deal, he was kidnapped and held captive for years by Muslim fanatics. It was during that cruel captivity that Anderson discovered a new source of faith: "Faith is what you find when you're alone and find that you are not alone." The psalmist, through prayer, gained the reassuring sense of God's presence. Leaving matters, at least for the moment, in God's hand, he was able to say: "I lie down, sleep and wake again because God sustains me. I am not afraid of ten thousands of people who have set themselves against me round about" (v. 6–7).

❧ PSALM 4 ❧

For the Leader; with string-music. A Psalm of David.

2 Answer me when I call, O God of my righteousness,
Thou who didst set me free when I was in distress;
Be gracious unto me, and hear my prayer.
3 O ye sons of men, how long shall my glory be put to shame,
In that ye love vanity, and seek after falsehood?   Selah
4 But know that the LORD hath set apart the godly man as His own;
The LORD will hear when I call unto Him.

5 Tremble, and sin not;
Commune with your own heart upon your bed, and be still.   Selah

6 Offer the sacrifices of righteousness,
And put your trust in the LORD.

7 Many there are that say: "Oh that we could see some good!"
LORD, lift Thou up the light of Thy countenance upon us.
8 Thou hast put gladness in my heart,
More than when their corn and their wine increase.
9 In peace will I both lay me down and sleep;
For Thou, LORD, makest me dwell alone in safety.

❧

Listen to Your Heart and Be Still

What can you do when people tell lies about you and go out of their way to embarrass and shame you?

Stop fretting. Listen to your own heart and conscience: "Tremble, sin not; think it over silently in your heart, upon your bed" (v. 5).

If you have done no wrong, trust that you will regain your good name. By God's law righteousness is rewarded. Lie down to sleep and let God watch over you in safety: "I will lie down in peace and sleep because You, God, let me dwell alone securely" (v. 9).

❧

Reflection: Security under God

You can't relax. You have too many things on your mind. Demands at home conflict with those at your workplace. You worry about debts and deadlines. You have trouble sleeping at nights.

Do you see yourself in this description? Are you beset by all kinds of tensions? How do you deal with your anxieties? Do you look for escape in the movies, the world of make-believe? Do sports activities take your mind off the things that bother you? Do you seek relief in drink during the so-called "happy hour"?

How does the psalmist cope with anxiety? It is clear from Psalm 4 that its author had plenty to worry about. He tells us: "When I was in distress, you relieved me" (v. 2). The psalmist turns to God as his best friend.

God, he believes, singles out the upright for a special relationship: "God has set apart the righteous as His own" (v. 4) The sense of closeness to God gives him "more joy than a rich harvest of corn and wine" (v. 8). Knowing he is in God's presence makes him feel safe and secure: "I will lie down in peace and sleep" (v. 9).

❧ Psalm 5 ❧

For the Leader; upon the Nehiloth. A Psalm of David.

2 Give ear to my words, O LORD,
Consider my meditation.
3 Hearken unto the voice of my cry, my King, and my God;
For unto Thee do I pray.

4 O LORD, in the morning shalt Thou hear my voice;
In the morning will I order my prayer unto Thee, and will look forward.
5 For Thou art not a God that hath pleasure in wickedness;
Evil shall not sojourn with Thee.
6 The boasters shall not stand in Thy sight;
Thou hatest all workers of iniquity.
7 Thou destroyest them that speak falsehood;
The LORD abhorreth the man of blood and of deceit.
8 But as for me, in the abundance of Thy lovingkindness will I come into Thy house;
I will bow down toward Thy holy temple in the fear of Thee.

9 O LORD, lead me in Thy righteousness because of them that lie in wait for me;
Make Thy way straight before my face.
10 For there is no sincerity in their mouth;
Their inward part is a yawning gulf,
Their throat is an open sepulchre;
They make smooth their tongue.
11 Hold them guilty, O God,
Let them fall by their own counsels;
Cast them down in the multitude of their transgressions;
For they have rebelled against Thee.

12 So shall all those that take refuge in Thee rejoice,
They shall ever shout for joy,
And Thou shalt shelter them;
Let them also that love Thy name exult in Thee.
13 For Thou dost bless the righteous;
O LORD, Thou dost encompass him with favour as with a shield.

✎

God Is Not on the Side of Evil

How can you cope with those who are out to get you? Surrounded by people of insincerity, deceitfulness, and vicious talk, you wonder what to do. The psalmist suggests that they will fall by their own devices. The weight of their own transgressions will cause them to break down: "Hold them guilty, O God; let them fall by their own counsels" (v. 11).

God will surely deal with them: "You destroy liars; God abhors the man of blood and deceit" (v. 7).

Just make sure that you keep *yourself* clean. Go the way that is pleasing to God. Those who trust in Him will see happy days: "For You will bless the righteous. O God, You will surround him with favor as with a shield" (v. 13).

✎

Reflection: God Cares

When slighted, insulted, or mistreated, our immediate impulse is to strike back. Often we suppress that urge but cannot help resenting the person who treated us badly. Resentment is a poisonous, self-punishing feeling. How can we get rid of it? Psalm 5 shows the way. If you have been wronged, don't say, "No one cares." God cares. The psalmist is confident that wrong will be punished and wrongdoers destroyed: "You hate all workers of iniquity. You destroy those who speak falsehood; God abhors the man of blood and deceit" (v. 6–7). Three times in a single verse, the psalmist speaks of the joy experienced by those who put their trust in God: "So shall all who take refuge in You rejoice, they shall ever shout for joy, . . . let also those who love Your name rejoice" (v. 12).

✎ # PSALM 6 ✎

F or the Leader; with string-music; on the Sheminith. A Psalm of David.

2 O LORD, rebuke me not in Thine anger,
Neither chasten me in Thy wrath.
3 Be gracious unto me, O LORD, for I languish away;

Heal me, O LORD, for my bones are affrighted.
4 My soul also is sore affrighted;
And Thou, O LORD, how long?

5 Return, O LORD, deliver my soul;
Save me for Thy mercy's sake.
6 For in death there is no remembrance of Thee;

In the nether-world who will give
  Thee thanks?
7 I am weary with my groaning;
  Every night make I my bed to swim;
  I melt away my couch with my tears.
8 Mine eye is dimmed because of
  vexation;
  It waxeth old because of all mine
  adversaries.

9 Depart from me, all ye workers of
  iniquity;

For the LORD hath heard the voice of
  my weeping.
10 The LORD hath heard my
  supplication;
  The LORD receiveth my prayer.
11 All mine enemies shall be ashamed
  and sore affrighted;
  They shall turn back, they shall be
  ashamed suddenly.

❧

"I Soak My Bed with Tears"

You feel you are falling apart. You are sick. You are wasting away. You are terrified. How much longer must you suffer? You cry your eyes out. On top of it, enemies are gloating over your misery. Don't be ashamed to cry out for God's help. There is comfort in the thought that God does not want the death of His believers: "For in death there is no remembrance of You; who will offer You thanks in the netherworld?" (v. 6).

The psalmist speaks as a witness to the power of prayer. He remembers a time of despair: "Every night I soak my bed with tears" (v. 7). When things turned around, he was certain that it was God's response to his cry for help: "The Lord has accepted my prayer" (v. 10).

❧

Reflection: God Heals

When illness or misfortune strikes, we wonder, What have we done to deserve this? Is it punishment for some offense? Is God angry at us?

If our suffering is indeed an affliction decreed by God, then recovery may be taken as a sign of God's forgiveness, compassion, and love. If God metes out punishment at times, He also forgives the repentant sinner.

Could God have created life without evil and made us immune against suffering? We have no answer, but we may believe that for every affliction there is a remedy. If in some way God exposes us to suffering, He is also our helper. The hand that wounds is the hand that heals.

❧ PSALM 7 ❧

Shiggaion of David, which he sang unto the LORD, concerning Cush a Benjamite.

2 O LORD my God, in Thee have I taken refuge;
Save me from all them that pursue me, and deliver me;
3 Lest he tear my soul like a lion,
Rending it in pieces, while there is none to deliver.

4 O LORD my God, if I have done this;
If there be iniquity in my hands;
5 If I have requited him that did evil unto me,
Or spoiled mine adversary unto emptiness;
6 Let the enemy pursue my soul, and overtake it,
And tread my life down to the earth;
Yea, let him lay my glory in the dust.
Selah

7 Arise, O LORD, in Thine anger,
Lift up Thyself in indignation against mine adversaries;
Yea, awake for me at the judgment which Thou hast commanded.
8 And let the congregation of the peoples compass Thee about,
And over them return Thou on high.

9 O LORD, who ministerest judgment to the peoples,
Judge me, O LORD,
According to my righteousness, and according to mine integrity that is in me.
10 Oh that a full measure of evil might come upon the wicked,
And that Thou wouldest establish the righteous;
For the righteous God trieth the heart and reins.
11 My shield is with God,
Who saveth the upright in heart.
12 God is a righteous judge,
Yea, a God that hath indignation every day:
13 If a man turn not, He will whet His sword,
He hath bent His bow, and made it ready;
14 He hath also prepared for him the weapons of death,
Yea, His arrows which He made sharp.
15 Behold, he travaileth with iniquity;
Yea, he conceiveth mischief, and bringeth forth falsehood.
16 He hath digged a pit, and hollowed it,
And is fallen into the ditch which he made.
17 His mischief shall return upon his own head,
And his violence shall come down upon his own pate.

18 I will give thanks unto the LORD according to His righteousness;
And will sing praise to the name of the LORD Most High.

❧

He Will Fall into the Trap He Made

Will evildoers ever get their due? The psalmist, threatened by enemies, seeks refuge with God. Unaware of any wrongdoing on his part, he puts his case before the Almighty: "Judge me, O God, according to my uprightness and integrity" (v. 9).

He counts on God to render fair judgment because God knows what is inside us. God examines your heart: "The righteous God examines the heart and conscience" (v. 10). God knows who is good and who is not. God will judge you according to your righteousness. The one who plots mischief and digs a pit to entrap others will himself fall into it. Evil ultimately destroys itself: "He has dug a pit and hollowed it, and is fallen into the ditch he made. His mischief shall return upon him and his violence shall come down on his own head" (v. 16–17).

Look to God, the deliverer of the upright, and praise His righteousness.

❧

Reflection: Evil Destroys Itself

I cannot believe, O God, that You do not care if justice is done. You are a righteous God and help good overcome evil. Often associated with the biblical doctrine of God's retributive justice is the belief that evil is self-destructive: "They sow the wind and they shall reap the whirlwind" (Hosea 8:7).

Emerson gave us a graphic description of the doctrine of retribution and of evil punishing itself: "Crime and punishment grow out of one stem." It is in keeping with the Bible: "Whoso sheds man's blood, by man shall his blood be shed" (Genesis 9:6).

Again and again, we have seen liars caught in the web of their own deceits, and those who set out to destroy the innocent destroyed by their own devices. As several psalmists say of evildoers: "He has fallen into the ditch he made" (v. 16) and "Nations are sunk into the pit they made. . . . The wicked is snared in the work of his own hands" (Psalm 9:16–17).

❧ PSALM 8 ❧

For the Leader; upon the Gittith. A Psalm of David.

2 O LORD, our LORD,
How glorious is Thy name in all the earth!
Whose majesty is rehearsed above the heavens.

3 Out of the mouth of babes and sucklings hast Thou founded strength,
Because of Thine adversaries;
That Thou mightest still the enemy and the avenger.

4 When I behold Thy heavens, the work of Thy fingers,

The moon and the stars, which Thou hast established;

5 What is man, that Thou art mindful of him?

And the son of man, that Thou thinkest of him?

6 Yet Thou hast made him but little lower than the angels,

And hast crowned him with glory and honour.

7 Thou hast made him to have dominion over the works of Thy hands;

Thou hast put all things under His feet:

8 Sheep and oxen, all of them, Yea, and the beasts of the field;

9 The fowl of the air, and the fish of the sea;

Whatsoever passeth through the paths of the seas.

10 O LORD, our LORD, How glorious is Thy name in all the earth!

Does Your Life Make a Difference?

When you are worried and dread what lies ahead, gain a perspective on your place in God's world. Lift up your head. Look at the countless stars by night or the bright blue sky that expands into infinity and ask yourself, What is my place in the universe? Compared to the immeasurable vastness of the cosmos and the billions of years it has been evolving, you are a speck of dust, and your life is just a flicker. How important can the things you worry about be when man, in fact all of mankind, amounts to no more than the tiniest drop in the bucket?

The psalmist, overwhelmed by the immensity of creation, asked why God would even notice or pay attention to man: "What is man that You are mindful of him and mortal man that you take notice of him?" (v. 5).

An answer is implied in his exclamation: "Yet You have made him but little less than divine and adorned him with glory and majesty! You have made him master over Your handiwork" (v. 6–7).

By elevating man above all other creatures, God showed His preference and concern for man. The sentence "From the mouths of infants and sucklings you have founded strength" (v. 3) is somewhat puzzling. The problem is the last word, "strength." What kind of strength? The difficulty can be overcome if one translates the original Hebrew word in its alternate meaning of "glory" or "praise." This might be a reference to the miracle of human development when the babbling sounds of infants become rational speech, even praise of God. The power of speech is one of God's greatest gifts to man, by which we are enabled to share thoughts and feelings, learn from one another, form closer relations, and cooperate for our mutual good. And most important, words are the channel of God's communication with us for revelation and guidance.

❦

Reflection: The Grandeur and Misery of Man

Whenever horror stories make us think that humans are, after all, just another variety of wild beasts, we may find comfort in Psalm 8. Measured against the cosmos, the human being is as nothing. But among the creatures of Earth, man is supreme. He has been endowed with powers to rule over all other creatures. Will the time ever come when man will gain control over his own ferocious urges and overpower his evil impulses? Someday humans will recognize the folly of mutual destruction in war and fulfill the prophecy: "They shall beat their swords into plowshares and their spears into pruning hooks. Nation shall not lift up sword against nation, neither shall they learn war any more" (Isaiah 2:4). Then it will be possible to speak of man as the crown of creation, even as the psalmist put it: "You have made him but little less than divine and crowned him with glory and majesty" (v. 6).

❦ PSALM 9 ❦

For the Leader; upon Muthlabben. A Psalm of David.

2 I will give thanks unto the LORD with my whole heart;
I will tell of all Thy marvellous works.
3 I will be glad and exult in Thee;
I will sing praise to Thy name, O Most High:

4 When mine enemies are turned back,
They stumble and perish at Thy presence;
5 For Thou hast maintained my right and my cause;
Thou sattest upon the throne as the righteous Judge.

6 Thou hast rebuked the nations,
Thou hast destroyed the wicked,
Thou hast blotted out their name for ever and ever.
7 O thou enemy, the waste places are come to an end for ever;
And the cities which thou didst uproot,

Their very memorial is perished.

8 But the LORD is enthroned for ever;
He hath established His throne for judgment.
9 And He will judge the world in righteousness,
He will minister judgment to the peoples with equity.

10 The LORD also will be a high tower for the oppressed,
A high tower in times of trouble;
11 And they that know Thy name will put their trust in Thee;
For Thou, LORD, hast not forsaken them that seek Thee.

12 Sing praises to the LORD, who dwelleth in Zion;
Declare among the peoples His doings.
13 For He that avengeth blood hath remembered them;
He hath not forgotten the cry of the humble.

14Be gracious unto me, O LORD,
  Behold mine affliction at the hands of
    them that hate me;
  Thou that liftest me up from the
    gates of death;
15That I may tell of all Thy praise in
    the gates of the daughter of Zion,
  That I may rejoice in Thy salvation.

16The nations are sunk down in the pit
    that they made;
  In the net which they hid is their own
    foot taken.
17The LORD hath made Himself
    known, He hath executed judgment,

The wicked is snared in the work of
  his own hands. Higgaion.   Selah

18The wicked shall return to the
    nether-world,
  Even all the nations that forget God.
19For the needy shall not alway be
    forgotten,
  Nor the expectation of the poor
    perish for ever.
20Arise, O LORD, let not man prevail;
  Let the nations be judged in Thy
    sight.
21Set terror over them, O LORD;
  Let the nations know they are but
    men.   Selah

~

God Does Not Abandon Those
Who Turn to Him

Reading your morning paper, you may think the world is going to rack and ruin. So much crime and violence, and abuse of the weak and innocent! Does God know? Does God care? The psalmist insists that "God has not forgotten the cry of the humble . . . the needy shall not always be forgotten nor the hope of the poor perish" (v. 13, 19).

How does the psalmist know all this? He speaks from his own experience: "You have maintained my right and my cause. . . . You have lifted me up from the gates of death that I may tell of all Your praise" (v. 14).

As a witness to what he has seen in his own life and in world events, he reassures us that the harm nations inflict on others will boomerang: "Nations sink into the pit they have made; their own feet are caught in the net they have hidden" (v. 16). The same judgment applies to individual evildoers: "The wicked is snared in the work of his hands" (v. 17).

The psalmist feels confirmed in his faith that "God is enthroned forever; He will judge the world in righteousness" (v. 8–9).

~

Reflection: Prayer

Those of us who pray know that many of the things we pray for are denied. Does the nonfulfillment of prayer render it futile? When I pray to God, I do so without guarantee of the effectiveness of my prayer. I approach God with a sense of dependency on Him for the gift of life and His sustaining power, and assume that there must be a continuing channel between God, my Creator, and me, His creature. But I only know my side of the prayer experience. God's side is a mystery. Does God hear me? Does God know my need and my pain? Does God react to my prayer?

The author of Psalm 9 waited the longest time for God's help. Were his prayers in vain? He did not think so. No matter how long the delay, he still believed that God would answer: "They who know Your name put their trust in You, for You, O God, have not forgotten those who seek You. . . . For the needy shall not always be forgotten, nor the expectation of the poor perish" (v. 11, 19). Prayer, whatever its content, is an expression of trust in God. It passes through the channel that connects us with God. What God does with our prayer we cannot know.

❧ PSALM 10 ❧

Why standest Thou afar off, O LORD?
Why hidest Thou Thyself in times of trouble?
2 Through the pride of the wicked the poor is hotly pursued,
They are taken in the devices that they have imagined.

3 For the wicked boasteth of his heart's desire,
And the covetous vaunteth himself, though he contemn the LORD.
4 The wicked, in the pride of his countenance [,saith]: "He will not require";
All his thoughts are: "There is no God."
5 His ways prosper at all times;
Thy judgments are far above out of his sight;
As for all his adversaries, he puffeth at them.
6 He saith in his heart: "I shall not be moved,

I who to all generations shall not be in adversity."
7 His mouth is full of cursing and deceit and oppression;
Under his tongue is mischief and iniquity.
8 He sitteth in the lurking-places of the villages;
In secret places doth he slay the innocent;
His eyes are on the watch for the helpless.
9 He lieth in wait in a secret place as a lion in his lair,
He lieth in wait to catch the poor;
He doth catch the poor, when he draweth him up in his net.
10 He croucheth, he boweth down,
And the helpless fall into his mighty claws.
11 He hath said in his heart: "God hath forgotten;
He hideth His face; He will never see."

12 Arise, O LORD; O God, lift up Thy
    hand;
  Forget not the humble.
13 Wherefore doth the wicked contemn
    God,
  And say in his heart: "Thou wilt not
    require"?
14 Thou hast seen; for Thou beholdest
    trouble and vexation, to requite
    them with Thy hand;
  Unto Thee the helpless committeth
    himself;
  Thou hast been the helper of the
    fatherless.

15 Break Thou the arm of the wicked;
  And as for the evil man, search out his
    wickedness, till none be found.
16 The LORD is King for ever and ever;
  The nations are perished out of His
    land.

17 LORD, Thou hast heard the desire of
    the humble:
  Thou wilt direct their heart, Thou
    wilt cause Thine ear to attend;
18 To right the fatherless and the
    oppressed,
  That man who is of the earth may be
    terrible no more.

❧

Is God on the Job?

Faith, like love, is in constant fluctuation. You may love someone deeply, but not the same way all the time. Yesterday your love had a passionate intensity. You could think of nothing else but your lover. Today you are absorbed by some urgent business and your mind is on other things. Or you are irritated by something said or done by the one you love and your feelings temporarily cool to indifference, even anger. So it is with faith in God. Things happen that temporarily shake your confidence in God. You, too, may be infuriated, as was the psalmist, by the power and success of some of the worst characters. The wicked arrogantly say of God: "He will not hold us to account. All his thoughts are: 'There is no God'" (v. 4).

The psalmist wonders, Is God absent? Where is God when most needed? "Why do You hide Yourself in time of trouble?" (v. 1). The psalmist waits impatiently for God to act and, as though the Almighty needed awakening, he exclaims: "Rise, O Lord! Strike at him, O God. Do not forget the lowly" (v. 12).

Despite his impatience with God, the Psalmist holds on to faith. Even though today's events may confuse and trouble him, he now sees things in the larger perspective of history: "God is king forever and ever" (v. 16). In His own good time and in His own way, God will have a reckoning with evildoers. He will listen to the lowly and champion the downtrodden.

❧

Reflection: God's Justice

Does God know what the troublemakers and transgressors are up to? Does He care? The wicked act as though there is no judge and no judgment. They are not afraid of divine punishment. The psalmist, however, is unshaken in the belief that the day of reckoning will come: "God hears the yearning of the humble" (v. 17).

❧ PSALM 11 ❧

For the Leader. [A Psalm] of David.

In the LORD have I taken refuge;
How say ye to my soul:
"Flee thou! to your mountain, ye birds"?

2 For, lo, the wicked bend the bow,
They have made ready their arrow upon the string,
That they may shoot in darkness at the upright in heart.
3 When the foundations are destroyed,
What hath the righteous wrought?

4 The LORD is in His holy temple,
The LORD, His throne is in heaven;
His eyes behold, His eyelids try, the children of men.
5 The LORD trieth the righteous;
But the wicked and him that loveth violence His soul hateth.
6 Upon the wicked He will cause to rain coals;
Fire and brimstone and burning wind shall be the portion of their cup.

7 For the LORD is righteous, He loveth righteousness;
The upright shall behold His face.

❧

God Is Watching!

Imagine that you are listening to an excited conversation and you will better understand Psalm 11. Well meaning friends warn the psalmist to make a run for his life because enemies are out to destroy him: "The wicked bend the bow . . . to shoot the upright in the heart" (v. 2).

However, the psalmist disregards the warning. He puts his trust in God: "In God I take refuge" (v. 1). Unfazed by threats, he trusts that God knows what is happening and will protect him together with all the righteous: "His eyes behold and observe mankind" (v. 4).

God distinguishes between the righteous and the wicked. He examines the righteous and punishes the wicked. Therefore, "the upright shall behold His face" (v. 7). Do not misunderstand the phrase "behold His face." It just means "being in His Presence," so close that if God had a face, you would see it. If sin separates us from God, good deeds bring us closer to Him.

❧

Reflection: Escapism

The sanctity of life is being trampled upon by terrorists. They kill the innocent without batting an eyelash. They are plotting the destruction of whole cities, mass murder on a scale comparable to the Nazi Holocaust. It is an assault on our fundamental values. Like the psalmist who also faced massive evil in his time, we ask: "When the foundations are being torn up, what can the righteous do?" (v. 3). The psalmist rejects the counsel of some to escape from all problems by "flying away to the mountains like a bird" (v. 1). We, too, must remain steadfast and trust that God knows what is happening: "He hates the one who loves violence" (v. 5). God will make sure that "the upright shall behold His presence" (v. 7).

❧ PSALM 12 ❧

For the Leader; on the Sheminith. A Psalm of David.

2 Help, LORD; for the godly man ceaseth;
For the faithful fail from among the children of men.
3 They speak falsehood every one with his neighbour;
With flattering lip, and with a double heart, do they speak.

4 May the LORD cut off all flattering lips,
The tongue that speaketh proud things!
5 Who have said: "Our tongue will we make mighty;
Our lips are with us: who is lord over us?"

6 "For the oppression of the poor, for the sighing of the needy,
Now will I arise", saith the LORD;
"I will set him in safety at whom they puff."

7 The words of the LORD are pure words,
As silver tried in a crucible on the earth, refined seven times.
8 Thou wilt keep them, O LORD;
Thou wilt preserve us from this generation for ever.
9 The wicked walk on every side,
When vileness is exalted among the sons of men.

❧

When You Can't Trust Anyone

The author of Psalm 12 deplores the moral decay of an entire generation: "They speak falsehood everyone with his neighbor; with flattering lip and hypocrisy do they speak" (v. 3).

People of integrity seem to have disappeared. In such an age of general corruption, society has lost the will and the possibility of reforming itself. A single liar among your acquaintances could make you miserable. Imagine how the psalmist felt when everyone he knew turned out to be dishonest and a hypocrite. There was no one he could trust. In despair he calls for God's help: "Help, God, for the faithful are no more" (v. 2).

However, he is comforted by the thought that if humans fail to act for truth and decency, God will: "Now *I* will act, says God" (v. 6).

※

Reflection: The Two-Front War against Corruption

The psalmist deplores widespread lying, cheating, and violence. Evil-doers seem to escape punishment. The psalmist invokes God's help, counting on God to heed the cry of victims of foul play and to bring wrongdoers to justice. In an environment of corruption, you are challenged to act in two ways: on one hand, confronting evildoers; on the other hand, trying to preserve your own integrity despite the corrupt practices of many others. Either response demands sacrifice. If you preach morality, you run the risk of alienating others. But keeping yourself clean is no easy matter, either. Honesty may be the best policy, but it will cost you. Take the example of truth-telling. You take your child on a train ride. If you lie about your child's age, you could take advantage of the cheaper child's fare. Will you sacrifice for honesty, or cheat? The way you act in this situation will teach your child an important lesson. The story is told about a little girl who, before boarding the train, was instructed by the parent not to tell her true age of eight but to say that she was only six years old. When the conductor came around and asked, "How old are you?" she answered: "At home, I am eight, but on the train, I am six."

When children are taught to lie to others, they will, in time, also lie to their parents. Small lies lead to big lies. Begin cheating a little, and in the end you'll cheat in a big way. Keeping your own integrity often requires sacrifice. But setting the right example is the best you can do in the struggle against evil.

❧ PSALM 13 ❧

For the Leader. A Psalm of David.

2 How long, O LORD, wilt Thou forget
  me for ever?
  How long wilt Thou hide Thy face
  from me?
3 How long shall I take counsel in my
  soul,
  Having sorrow in my heart by day?
  How long shall mine enemy be exalted
  over me?
4 Behold Thou, and answer me, O
  LORD my God;

Lighten mine eyes, lest I sleep the
  sleep of death;
5 Lest mine enemy say: "I have prevailed
  against him";
  Lest mine adversaries rejoice when I
  am moved.

6 But as for me, in Thy mercy do I trust;
  My heart shall rejoice in Thy
  salvation.
  I will sing unto the LORD,
  Because He hath dealt bountifully with
  me.

❧

Godforsaken?

Earlier psalms deal with troubled and aggrieved persons who turn to God for help and reassurance that good will prevail. What can you do when you see no change for the better? When your prayers are unanswered? When God is silent?

The psalmist's way of coping with adversity and gnawing doubts is to search his soul. He overcomes the sorrows of his heart by remembering the deliverances he experienced in the past. Despite all his troubles, he remains steadfast in his faith, trusting that God, who helped before, will help again: "I will sing to the Lord for He has been good to me" (v. 6).

❧

Reflection: Prayer

The first and foremost object of prayer is to connect with God. Often my prayer brings my needs to God's attention. But it is not for me to give God orders. He is not bound to grant my wishes. The hope for a favorable response from God is based on trust that God welcomes prayer and cares about the well-being of His creatures. When and how God will answer, we cannot know.

❧ PSALM 14 ❧

For the Leader. [A Psalm] of David.

The fool hath said in his heart: "There is no God";
They have dealt corruptly, they have done abominably;
There is none that doeth good.
2 The LORD looked forth from heaven upon the children of men,
To see if there were any man of understanding, that did seek after God.
3 They are all corrupt, they are together become impure;
There is none that doeth good, no, not one.
4 "Shall not all the workers of iniquity know it,
Who eat up My people as they eat bread,
And call not upon the LORD?"
5 There are they in great fear;
For God is with the righteous generation.
6 Ye would put to shame the counsel of the poor,
But the LORD is his refuge.

7 Oh that the salvation of Israel were come out of Zion!
When the LORD turneth the captivity of His people,
Let Jacob rejoice, let Israel be glad.

❧

Who Has the Last Laugh?

If you believe in God, you will feel challenged by those who don't share your faith and won't live by your standards. Sometimes it may seem to you that there are no more decent people around. You resent those cheats and lawbreakers who think they can get away with it. They laugh at the notion that God is watching and judging human behavior. The psalmist calls these corrupt and arrogant unbelievers fools who say in their hearts, "There is no God" (v. 1). But the psalmist maintains his faith that God is aware of human misdeeds and of the suffering of the humble: "For God is with the righteous generation" (v. 5).

Could you share the psalmist's confidence that nothing escapes the judgment of God? The day of reckoning is sure to come when evildoers will be "in great fear for God is with the righteous generation" (v. 5).

Note that Psalm 14 is duplicated with minor changes in Psalm 53.

❧

Reflection: Dependence on God

I must not let cynics and nonbelievers shake my faith that there is a God Who knows what His creatures are doing and Who will hold them to account.

The psalmist calls him who denies God a "fool." What is the folly of the unbeliever? It is his total misjudgment of the human condition. My destiny is not of my own design; neither am I on Earth of my own will or by my own doing. The bravado of William Ernest Henley's poem *Invictus*, ending with the words "I am the master of my fate; I am the captain of my soul," sounds hollow in the light of the human condition. The fundamental fact of my existence is that I am not the master of my fate, but subject to powers other than my own. I am a creature. My "creature feeling" points to the Creator. When I pray, I acknowledge my dependence upon God, my Creator.

❧ PSALM 15 ❧

A Psalm of David.

LORD, who shall sojourn in Thy
    tabernacle?
Who shall dwell upon Thy holy
    mountain?
2 He that walketh uprightly, and
    worketh righteousness,
And speaketh truth in his heart;
3 That hath no slander upon his tongue,
Nor doeth evil to his fellow,
Nor taketh up a reproach against his
    neighbour;

4 In whose eyes a vile person is despised,
But he honoureth them that fear the
    LORD;
He that sweareth to his own hurt, and
    changeth not;
5 He that putteth not out his money on
    interest,
Nor taketh a bribe against the
    innocent.
He that doeth these things shall never
    be moved.

❧

God's Favorites

If you have read the previous psalms, you will be struck by the different mood of this one. It is all positive. Instead of agonizing over corrupt contemporaries, the author of Psalm 15 has a vision of the ideal person who is close to God. That person stands out by moral virtues. The Talmud remarks that all of the 613 biblical commandments are contained in the five verses of this psalm. The message is clear: You come near to God by your moral excellence. The same thought is expressed in Psalm 24.

❧

Reflection: What Is Righteousness?

What difference does my conduct make beyond the relatively small circle of family and friends, and the community where I live? Surely Earth will continue in its orbit, the sun will go on shining, and the stars will keep moving in their courses whether I lie, cheat, or harm my neighbor or not. Why should God care how I behave? I don't know. The Bible tells us *what* God wants of us, not *why*. However, God's commandments strike an affirmative echo in our hearts. Psalm 15 summarizes in a few sentences the essential qualities of an upright person who is welcome in God's presence.

❧ PSALM 16 ❧

Michtam of David.

Keep me, O God; for I have taken
  refuge in Thee.
2 I have said unto the LORD: "Thou art
  my LORD;
I have no good but in Thee";
3 As for the holy that are in the earth,
  They are the excellent in whom is all
  my delight.
4 Let the idols of them be multiplied
  that make suit unto another;
Their drink-offerings of blood will I
  not offer,
Nor take their names upon my lips.
5 O LORD, the portion of mine inheritance and of my cup,
Thou maintainest my lot.

6 The lines are fallen unto me in
  pleasant places;
Yea, I have a goodly heritage.
7 I will bless the LORD, who hath given
  me counsel;
Yea, in the night seasons my reins
  instruct me.
8 I have set the LORD always before me;
Surely He is at my right hand, I shall
  not be moved.

9 Therefore my heart is glad, and my
  glory rejoiceth;
My flesh also dwelleth in safety;
10 For Thou wilt not abandon my soul
  to the nether-world;
Neither wilt Thou suffer Thy godly
  one to see the pit.
11 Thou makest me to know the path of
  life;
In Thy presence is fulness of joy,
In Thy right hand bliss for evermore.

❧

The Happiness of Knowing God's Presence

Few joys can match release from pain, escape from danger, or recovery from a loss. Your life tastes so much sweeter after you have overcome a crisis. It was some such good turn of fortune that may have inspired the composition of Psalm 16. The opening sentence suggests that the worst is over: "Keep me, O God; for I have taken refuge in You" (v. 1).

A deep sense of contentment speaks out of the sixth verse: "The lines have fallen unto me in pleasant places" (v. 6). The key to such contentment is the sense of security inspired by the knowledge that God is near: "I have set God always before me; surely He is at my right hand. I shall not be moved" (v. 8).

According to the sixteenth-century Jewish law code, *Shulchan Aruch*, this sentence should be the motto of every God-loving person. The constant awareness of God's presence may keep us from wrong-doing, move us in the right direction, and make for a happier life: "You make me to know the path of life; in Your presence is fullness of joy" (v. 11).

※

Reflection: Joy in God's Presence

There are those who love God, those who fear God, and those who are happy with God. "I have set God always before me, . . ." says the psalmist, "therefore my heart rejoices and I am happy" (v. 8–9). Why does knowledge of God's presence make the psalmist happy? The psalm gives three reasons. The first is gratitude for God's guidance: "I praise God Who gives me counsel" (v. 7). The sense of security derived from the presence of God is next: "My flesh shall rest in safety" (v. 9). Finally, with God in his mind, the psalmist can cope with the fear of death: "You will not abandon me to the grave" (v. 10). The psalmist concludes with the joyful message that knowledge of God makes one fully alive and happy: "You make me know the path of life. In Your presence is fullness of joy" (v. 11).

✤ PSALM 17 ✤

A Prayer of David.

Hear the right, O LORD, attend unto my cry;
Give ear unto my prayer from lips without deceit.
2 Let my judgment come forth from Thy presence;
Let Thine eyes behold equity.
3 Thou hast tried my heart, Thou hast visited it in the night;
Thou hast tested me, and Thou findest not
That I had a thought which should not pass my mouth.
4 As for the doings of men, by the word of Thy lips
I have kept me from the ways of the violent.

5 My steps have held fast to Thy paths,
My feet have not slipped.

6 As for me, I call upon Thee, for Thou wilt answer me, O God;
Incline Thine ear unto me, hear my speech.
7 Make passing great Thy mercies, O Thou that savest by Thy right hand
From assailants them that take refuge in Thee.
8 Keep me as the apple of the eye,
Hide me in the shadow of Thy wings,
9 From the wicked that oppress,
My deadly enemies, that compass me about.
10 Their gross heart they have shut tight,
With their mouth they speak proudly.

11At our every step they have now
    encompassed us;
  They set their eyes to cast us down to
    the earth.
12He is like a lion that is eager to tear in
    pieces,
  And like a young lion lurking in secret
    places.

13Arise, O LORD, confront him, cast
    him down;
  Deliver my soul from the wicked, by
    Thy sword;

14From men, by Thy hand, O LORD,
  From men of the world, whose por-
    tion is in this life,
  And whose belly Thou fillest with
    Thy treasure;
  Who have children in plenty,
  And leave their abundance to their
    babes.
15As for me, I shall behold Thy face in
    righteousness;
  I shall be satisfied, when I awake, with
    Thy likeness.

❧

When God Is Your Best Friend

How intimate can you be with God? Reading this psalm is like listen-ing in on a conversation between the psalmist and God, his best friend. The psalmist is sure that his every thought and every step are known to God. In contrast to the author of Psalm 73, whose envy of the pros-perity of some sinful persons nearly destroyed his faith—"my steps had almost slipped" (Psalm 73:2)—Psalm 17 affirms: "My feet have not slipped" (v. 5).

The psalmist is on speaking terms with God: "As for me, I call upon You, for You will answer me, O God; listen to me, hear my speech" (v. 6). He declares his steadfastness in following the ways of God. All he asks for is protection against enemies. He does not crave their wealth. For his part, he is satisfied to greet each morning with a clean conscience, knowing that God is present: "As for me, I behold Your Face in righteousness, satisfied to awaken with the vision of You" (v. 15).

❧

Reflection: Prayer

If only we could be as sure as the psalmist that God receives our prayers and knows what is in our hearts: "I pray to You because You answer me, O God" (v. 6). The essence of the religious experience is knowing you are connected with God. The object of all worship and religious ceremonies is to maintain that connection. Could you watch without envy and resentment the success and prosperity of villains? The psalmist was physically threatened by such evil characters, "whose belly You fill with Your treasure, who have plenty of children and who build up rich estates for their infants" (v. 14). Nevertheless, the psalmist would not lash out in anger against God. He is merely asking for God's help. Such help may not be granted, but that would not shake his conviction that God is present in his life: "As for me, I shall behold Your presence in righteousness. I am satisfied when, upon awaking, I find You present" (v. 15).

❧ Psalm 18 ❧

For the Leader. [A Psalm] of David the servant of the LORD, who spoke unto the LORD the words of this song in the day that the LORD delivered him from the hand of all his enemies, and from the hand of Saul; 2and he said:
I love thee, O LORD, my strength.
3The LORD is my rock, and my fortress, and my deliverer;
My God, my rock, in Him I take refuge;
My shield, and my horn of salvation, my high tower.
4Praised, I cry, is the LORD,
And I am saved from mine enemies.

5The cords of Death compassed me,
And the floods of Belial assailed me.
6The cords of Sheol surrounded me;
The snares of Death confronted me.
7In my distress I called upon the LORD,
And cried unto my God;
Out of His temple He heard my voice,
And my cry came before Him unto His ears.

8Then the earth did shake and quake,
The foundations also of the mountains did tremble;
They were shaken, because He was wroth.
9Smoke arose up in His nostrils,
And fire out of His mouth did devour;
Coals flamed forth from Him.

10He bowed the heavens also, and came down;
And thick darkness was under His feet.
11And He rode upon a cherub, and did fly;
Yea, He did swoop down upon the wings of the wind.
12He made darkness His hiding-place, His pavilion round about Him;
Darkness of waters, thick clouds of the skies.
13At the brightness before Him, there passed through His thick clouds
Hailstones and coals of fire.
14The LORD also thundered in the heavens,
And the Most High gave forth His voice;
Hailstones and coals of fire.
15And He sent out His arrows, and scattered them;
And He shot forth lightnings, and discomfited them.
16And the channels of waters appeared,
And the foundations of the world were laid bare,
At Thy rebuke, O LORD,
At the blast of the breath of Thy nostrils.

17He sent from on high, He took me;
He drew me out of many waters.
18He delivered me from mine enemy most strong,
And from them that hated me, for they were too mighty for me.

¹⁹They confronted me in the day of my calamity;
But the LORD was a stay unto me.
²⁰He brought me forth also into a large place;
He delivered me, because He delighted in me.
²¹The LORD rewarded me according to my righteousness;
According to the cleanness of my hands hath He recompensed me.

²²For I have kept the ways of the LORD,
And have not wickedly departed from my God.
²³For all His ordinances were before me,
And I put not away His statutes from me.
²⁴And I was single-hearted with Him,
And I kept myself from mine iniquity.
²⁵Therefore hath the LORD recompensed me according to my righteousness,
According to the cleanness of my hands in His eyes.

²⁶With the merciful Thou dost show Thyself merciful,
With the upright man Thou dost show Thyself upright;
²⁷With the pure Thou dost show Thyself pure;
And with the crooked Thou dost show Thyself subtle.
²⁸For Thou dost save the afflicted people;
But the haughty eyes Thou dost humble.
²⁹For Thou dost light my lamp;
The LORD my God doth lighten my darkness.
³⁰For by Thee I run upon a troop;
And by my God do I scale a wall.
³¹As for God, His way is perfect;
The word of the LORD is tried;
He is a shield unto all them that take refuge in Him.

³²For who is God, save the LORD?
And who is a Rock, except our God?

³³The God that girdeth me with strength,
And maketh my way straight;
³⁴Who maketh my feet like hinds',
And setteth me upon my high places;
³⁵Who traineth my hands for war,
So that mine arms do bend a bow of brass.
³⁶Thou hast also given me Thy shield of salvation,
And Thy right hand hath holden me up;
And Thy condescension hath made me great.
³⁷Thou hast enlarged my steps under me,
And my feet have not slipped.

³⁸I have pursued mine enemies, and overtaken them;
Neither did I turn back till they were consumed.
³⁹I have smitten them through, so that they are not able to rise;
They are fallen under my feet.
⁴⁰For Thou hast girded me with strength unto the battle;
Thou hast subdued under me those that rose up against me.
⁴¹Thou hast also made mine enemies turn their backs unto me,
And I did cut off them that hate me.
⁴²They cried, but there was none to save;
Even unto the LORD, but He answered them not.
⁴³Then did I beat them small as the dust before the wind;
I did cast them out as the mire of the streets.
⁴⁴Thou hast delivered me from the contentions of the people;
Thou hast made me the head of the nations;
A people whom I have not known serve me.
⁴⁵As soon as they hear of me, they obey me;
The sons of the stranger dwindle away before me.
⁴⁶The sons of the stranger fade away,

And come trembling out of their close places.

47 The LORD liveth, and blessed be my Rock;
And exalted be the God of my salvation;
48 Even the God that executeth vengeance for me,
And subdueth peoples under me.
49 He delivereth me from mine enemies;

Yea, Thou liftest me up above them that rise up against me;
Thou deliverest me from the violent man.
50 Therefore I will give thanks unto Thee, O LORD, among the nations,
And will sing praises unto Thy name.
51 Great salvation giveth He to His king;
And showeth mercy to His anointed,
To David and to his seed, for evermore.

❧

God to the Rescue

When you already tend to believe in God, a single redemptive experience will clinch your faith. Psalm 18, ascribed to David, glows with ecstatic joy over a dramatic reversal in his circumstances: Suddenly, mortal danger vanishes. He feels as one saved from drowning: "He drew me out of the mighty waters and saved me from mine enemies" (v. 17–18). The God to whom he prayed in distress has become for him "my rock, my fortress and my deliverer" (v. 3).

If God is presumed to be just, it is not unreasonable to interpret a favorable change of fortune as a reward. In David's mind, God's deliverance and stunning victory over enemies becomes an endorsement of good character: "God rewarded me according to my righteousness . . . I was single-hearted with Him" (v. 21, 24).

He draws from his experience new insight into God's way with man. God responds to us on the level of our own conduct. As we do unto others, so are we being dealt with by God: "With the devout, You deal devotedly; with the honest, You act honestly; with the pure, You are pure and with the crooked, You are subtle" (v. 26–27).

God empowers the believer. David exclaims: "For by You I run upon a troop; and by my God do I scale a wall . . . He is a shield unto all them that take refuge in Him" (v. 30–31). Among the many memorable lines of this jubilant psalm is verse 29: "You light my lamp. God lights up my darkness."

❧

Reflection: "You Light My Lamp"

Do we feel closer to God when all goes well, or when we are in distress? This psalm tells of a crisis in which David desperately turns to God for help: "The cords of death compassed me. . . . In my distress I called upon God" (v. 5–7). He credits God with saving him: "He sent from on high; He took me; He drew me out of many waters" (v. 17). Are success and rescue from peril divine certification of our uprightness? David was sure of it: "God rewarded me according to my righteousness. . . . For I have kept the ways of God and have not wickedly departed from my God. . . . and I put not away His statutes from me. . . . And I was single-hearted with Him. . . . Therefore has God rewarded me according to my righteousness" (v. 21–25). When all is dark and we are groping for a way out, faith in God shines as a saving light and empowers the needy: "You light my lamp. God lights up my darkness. . . . For by You I run upon a troop and by my God I scale a wall" (v. 29–30).

❧ PSALM 19 ❧

For the Leader. A Psalm of David.

2 The heavens declare the glory of God,
And the firmament showeth His handiwork;
3 Day unto day uttereth speech,
And night unto night revealeth knowledge;
4 There is no speech, there are no words,
Neither is their voice heard.
5 Their line is gone out through all the earth,
And their words to the end of the world.
In them hath He set a tent for the sun,
6 Which is as a bridegroom coming out of his chamber,
And rejoiceth as a strong man to run his course.
7 His going forth is from the end of the heaven,
And his circuit unto the ends of it;
And there is nothing hid from the heat thereof.

8 The law of the LORD is perfect, restoring the soul;
The testimony of the LORD is sure, making wise the simple.

9 The precepts of the LORD are right, rejoicing the heart;
The commandment of the LORD is pure, enlightening the eyes.
10 The fear of the LORD is clean, enduring for ever;
The ordinances of the LORD are true, they are righteous altogether;
11 More to be desired are they than gold, yea, than much fine gold;
Sweeter also than honey and the honeycomb.
12 Moreover by them is Thy servant warned;
In keeping of them there is great reward.
13 Who can discern errors?
Clear Thou me from hidden faults.
14 Keep back Thy servant also from presumptuous sins,
That they may not have dominion over me; then shall I be faultless,
And I shall be clear from great transgression.
15 Let the words of my mouth and the meditation of my heart be acceptable before Thee,
O LORD, my Rock, and my Redeemer.

God Beyond Is Also Within

Do you ever wonder what might happen if you are no longer around? How will your dear ones cope without you? So you think you are indispensable to your family, to your place of work, to your organization? Step outside and look up at the sky. Try to get a sense of the immensity of the universe out there and be amazed at the trillions of worlds beyond our own. Everything is moving in a system of which you are a part but over which you have no control.

For the psalmist, the world is a revelation of God. Seeing it is believing: "The heavens declare the glory of God." (v. 2). There is no need for words, either spoken or written, to prove God's existence: "There is no speech, there are no words" (v. 4).

The psalmist is jubilant in his adoration of God, who rules by physical and spiritual laws. Through the gift of the spirit, God enables us to tell right from wrong and perceive His commandments: "The commandment of God is pure, enlightening the eye" (v. 9).

The God of the cosmos may seem infinitely far away, but there is a direct line of communication between God and man. Each of us has personal access to God. This is the psalm's conclusion: "May the words of my mouth and the meditation of my heart be acceptable before You, O Lord, my Rock and my Redeemer" (v. 15).

Reflection: The Law of God

Every human being lives in two worlds: the external environment and the strictly private, internal realm of thought and feeling. Psalm 19 reflects both the external and the internal world of our being, the world of nature (v. 1–7) and the world of the spirit (v. 8–14). Both realms are full of wonder. The philosopher Immanuel Kant may well have had Psalm 19 in mind when he wrote: "There are two things that fill my soul with holy reverence and ever-growing wonder: the starry sky above that virtually reduces us physical beings to the vanishing point, and the moral law within which raises us to infinite dignity as intelligent agents." Connecting these two worlds is God, the Creator of physical laws to govern the order of the universe and moral laws to govern our conduct. Rabbi Hirsch Rimanover (d. 1847) pondered the sentence "The law of God is perfect, restoring the soul" (v. 8) and saw in it a connection between the revealed law as recorded in Sacred

Scripture and our God-given, innate sense of justice that shapes our conscience. The Hebrew word for "restoring" should be understood in the sense of "settling, satisfying." The rabbi illustrated his idea with the case of a widow who came to him weeping and bitterly complaining about an unfavorable verdict in a court case. Nothing the rabbi said could calm the woman, whereupon the rabbi asked the court to review the case, and indeed the review revealed an error and the verdict was reversed in favor of the widow. Later the judge asked the rabbi: "What made you suspect that there was something wrong with the first judgment?" He replied by citing the verse "The law of God is perfect, restoring the soul" (v. 8). "A just decision should satisfy even the loser. But the woman could not be consoled. Hence I knew that the first verdict had to have a flaw." God's law of justice is not only revealed in Sacred Scripture, it is also inscribed in the human soul and conscience.

❧ PSALM 20 ❧

For the Leader. A Psalm of David.

2 The LORD answer thee in the day of trouble;
The name of the God of Jacob set thee up on high;
3 Send forth thy help from the sanctuary,
And support thee out of Zion;
4 Receive the memorial of all thy meal-offerings,
And accept the fat of thy burnt-sacrifice;   Selah
5 Grant thee according to thine own heart,
And fulfil all thy counsel.
6 We will shout for joy in thy victory,
And in the name of our God we will set up our standards;

The LORD fulfil all thy petitions.

7 Now know I that the LORD saveth His anointed;
He will answer him from His holy heaven
With the mighty acts of His saving right hand.
8 Some trust in chariots, and some in horses;
But we will make mention of the name of the LORD our God.
9 They are bowed down and fallen;
But we are risen, and stand upright.
10 Save, LORD;
Let the King answer us in the day that we call.

❧

The Power of Prayer

Is it demeaning to beg for God's help? Is it a surrender of self-reliance? Is worship an escape from personal responsibility, a flight into the world of illusions? Psalm 20 is a refutation of such charges. It tells of

David performing an act of worship immediately before leading his troops into battle. David and his warriors are in no way escaping from their duties; they are not looking away from deadly peril. They are ready to meet the task with all their strength. They are confronting reality.

However, they also know the limitations of physical and material resources. In their higher realism, gained from experience, they discover the power of the spirit, which magnifies the human potential through trust in God: "Some trust in chariots, and some in horses, but we will make mention of the name of the Lord our God. They are bowed down and fallen; but we are risen, and stand upright" (v. 8).

∞

Reflection: Dependence

Self-reliance is one of our most highly rated virtues. We consider it the essence of education to teach our young to fend for themselves, to solve their own problems, to become self-supporting and independent. There is much merit to this. But we must recognize the limits of self-reliance. The reality is that every human being, even the strongest, ablest, and most intelligent, is to a considerable degree dependent on conditions and resources other than his own. With every drink of water, you should recognize your dependence on vast numbers of people involved in maintaining and purifying our water system. Each time you turn on a light switch, know that you are enlisting the cooperation of entire industries in the energy business. Whenever you take medicine, remember that the pill you take is a benefit of various sciences developed by countless people over many generations. You could not live very long if limited to your own resources. David makes that point in Psalm 20: "Some trust in chariots and some in horses. But we will make mention of the name of God" (v. 8).

Our own material means cannot save us. God provides for us through the power and intelligence He has apportioned to the entire human race. The talents of many people and their cooperation for mutual benefits make possible our own achievements and survival. Self-reliance is great as far as it goes. But don't confuse it with self-sufficiency. Nobody is self-sufficient. Everybody is more or less dependent upon others. The idea of self-reliance must be matched by the knowledge of human interdependence and gratitude for what we receive from known and unknown hands, even the ever-giving hands of God.

❧ Psalm 21 ❧

For the Leader. A Psalm of David.

2 O Lord, in Thy strength the king
   rejoiceth;
And in Thy salvation how greatly
   doth he exult!
3 Thou hast given him his heart's
   desire,
And the request of his lips Thou hast
   not witholden.   Selah
4 For Thou meetest him with choicest
   blessings;
Thou settest a crown of fine gold on
   his head.
5 He asked life of Thee, Thou gavest it
   him;
Even length of days for ever and
   ever.
6 His glory is great through Thy
   salvation;
Honour and majesty dost Thou lay
   upon him.
7 For Thou makest him most blessed
   for ever;
Thou makest him glad with joy in
   Thy presence.
8 For the king trusteth in the Lord,

Yea, in the mercy of the Most High;
   he shall not be moved.

9 Thy hand shall be equal to all thine
   enemies;
Thy right hand shall overtake those
   that hate thee.
10 Thou shalt make them as a fiery
   furnace in the time of thine anger;
The Lord shall swallow them up in
   His wrath,
And the fire shall devour them.
11 Their fruit shalt thou destroy from
   the earth,
And their seed from among the
   children of men.
12 For they intended evil against thee,
They imagined a device, wherewith
   they shall not prevail.
13 For thou shalt make them turn their
   back,
Thou shalt make ready with thy bow-
   strings against the face of them.

14 Be Thou exalted, O Lord, in Thy
   strength;
So will we sing and praise Thy power.

❧

Hope Is Grounded in Past Experience

This psalm illustrates a point in the logic of prayer. The first part
(v. 1–8) refers to God's favor in the past. The second part (v. 9–13) is in
the future tense, expressing the hope for ongoing victories and benefits. It ends with words of praise for God "Who is exalted in strength"
(v. 14). The gifts granted to you by God in the past entitle you to count
on God's help in the future as well. So certain is the psalmist of God's
favor that he does not even ask for additional gifts. He takes it for
granted that more will be done by God for His people and their king.
This psalm has all the earmarks of a royal celebration. Was it a birthday or anniversary? Most likely the king headed a festive procession of
dignitaries to the temple, where he was greeted by the high priest and
a choir chanting this psalm of thanksgiving.

❧

Reflection: Joy-Sharing

This psalm of celebration and thanksgiving, composed for some special event in the life of the king, suggests to us not to miss opportunities for celebration and joy-sharing. Think of occasions in your life, besides birthdays and anniversaries, to celebrate in the company of family and friends. Why not arrange a party upon the completion of some major project? Or upon recovery from illness? Or on the safe return from a long trip and on other events that call for thanksgiving? Joy-sharing strengthens family relationships and bonds of friendship; it leads to thanksgiving, which, in turn, raises hopes, builds confidence, and makes for an optimistic outlook on life.

❧ PSALM 22 ❧

For the Leader; upon Aijeleth ha-Shahar. A Psalm of David.

2 My God, my God, why hast Thou forsaken me,
And art far from my help at the words of my cry?
3 O my God, I call by day, but Thou answerest not;
And at night, and there is no surcease for me.
4 Yet Thou art holy,
O Thou that art enthroned upon the praises of Israel.
5 In Thee did our fathers trust;
They trusted, and Thou didst deliver them.
6 Unto Thee they cried, and escaped;
In Thee did they trust, and were not ashamed.
7 But I am a worm, and no man;
A reproach of men, and despised of the people.
8 All they that see me laugh me to scorn;
They shoot out the lip, they shake the head:
9 "Let him commit himself unto the LORD! let Him rescue him;

Let Him deliver him, seeing He delighteth in him."

10 For Thou art He that took me out of the womb;
Thou madest me trust when I was upon my mother's breasts.
11 Upon Thee I have been cast from my birth;
Thou art my God from my mother's womb.
12 Be not far from me; for trouble is near;
For there is none to help.
13 Many bulls have encompassed me;
Strong bulls of Bashan have beset me round.
14 They open wide their mouth against me,
As a ravening and a roaring lion.
15 I am poured out like water,
And all my bones are out of joint;
My heart is become like wax;
It is melted in mine inmost parts.
16 My strength is dried up like a potsherd;
And my tongue cleaveth to my throat;
And Thou layest me in the dust of death.

¹⁷For dogs have encompassed me;
  A company of evil-doers have
    inclosed me;
  Like a lion, they are at my hands and
    my feet.
¹⁸I may count all my bones;
  They look and gloat over me.
¹⁹They part my garments among them,
  And for my vesture do they cast lots.
²⁰But Thou, O LORD, be not far off;
  O Thou my strength, hasten to help
    me.
²¹Deliver my soul from the sword;
  Mine only one from the power of the
    dog.
²²Save me from the lion's mouth;
  Yea, from the horns of the wild-oxen
    do Thou answer me.

²³I will declare Thy name unto my
    brethren;
  In the midst of the congregation will I
    praise Thee:
²⁴"Ye that fear the LORD, praise Him;
  All ye the seed of Jacob, glorify Him;
  And stand in awe of Him, all ye the
    seed of Israel.
²⁵For He hath not despised nor
    abhorred the lowliness of the poor;
  Neither hath He hid His face from
    him;

But when he cried unto Him, He
    heard."
²⁶From Thee cometh my praise in the
    great congregation;
  I will pay my vows before them that
    fear Him.
²⁷Let the humble eat and be satisfied;
  Let them praise the LORD that seek
    after Him;
  May your heart be quickened for
    ever!
²⁸All the ends of the earth shall remem-
    ber and turn unto the LORD;
  And all the kindreds of the nations
    shall worship before Thee.
²⁹For the kingdom is the LORD's;
  And He is the ruler over the nations.
³⁰All the fat ones of the earth shall eat
    and worship;
  All they that go down to the dust shall
    kneel before Him,
  Even he that cannot keep his soul
    alive.
³¹A seed shall serve him;
  It shall be told of the LORD unto the
    next generation.
³²They shall come and shall declare His
    righteousness
  Unto a people that shall be born, that
    He hath done it.

❦

An Experience of Salvation

This psalm will resonate with you if you have ever had moments of deliverance in your life. Think of a time when you were down and out and recovered as though reborn. Psalm 22 is the autobiography of someone who experienced salvation. Scholars theorize that it was the king, under siege by enemies, speaking on behalf of his starving people. It seemed as though the whole world was against him. He was despised, rejected, and ridiculed. He felt lost. The king likens his dire situation to one surrounded by ferocious animals: "Many bulls have surrounded me. . . . They open wide their mouths against me, as a raving and roaring lion" (v. 13–14).

 He was weakened by starvation: "My strength is dried up like a potsherd; and my tongue cleaves to my throat" (v. 16). Totally helpless, he turned to God, by whose will he had been brought into this world: "You are the One who took me out of the womb" (v. 10).

Amazingly, things turned around. He was pulled back from the brink of death and now wants his people to know what God did for him: "I will declare Your name unto my brethren and praise You in the midst of the congregation. For He has not despised nor abhorred the lowliness of the poor; neither has He hid His face from him. But when he cried unto Him, He heard" (v. 23, 25).

∞

Reflection: Hope

We must not despair too soon. The author of this psalm must have gone through a rough time. He felt godforsaken, abandoned, and cried out: "My God, my God, why have You forsaken me?" (v. 2). But as you read on to the end of the psalm (which may have been composed at a later time), it appears that things had turned around, which prompted the psalmist's prayer of thanksgiving: "I will declare Your name unto my brethren; in the midst of the congregation will I praise You" (v. 23). There is a lesson in this for all who suffer reverses in health or fortune. As suddenly as calamity strikes, so suddenly may deliverance come in the form of some unexpected remedy. The psalmist lived to see the error of his previous outburst: "There is none to help" (v. 12). He came to acknowledge God's answer to his prayers: "He has not despised nor abhorred the lowliness of the poor; neither has He hid His face from him; but when he cried unto Him, He heard" (v. 25). So when afflicted, hold on. Never say never—there is always hope.

∞ PSALM 23 ∞

A Psalm of David.

The LORD is my shepherd; I shall not want.
2 He maketh me to lie down in green pastures;
He leadeth me beside the still waters.
3 He restoreth my soul;
He guideth me in straight paths for His name's sake.
4 Yea, though I walk through the valley of the shadow of death,
I will fear no evil,
For Thou art with me;
Thy rod and Thy staff, they comfort me.
5 Thou preparest a table before me in the presence of mine enemies;
Thou hast anointed my head with oil; my cup runneth over.
6 Surely goodness and mercy shall follow me all the days of my life;
And I shall dwell in the house of the LORD for ever.

The Nightingale of
the Psalter

Though usually recited at funerals, Psalm 23 is one of the most cheerful and uplifting expressions of faith. Its imagery of a sunlit pasture alongside a gentle stream is the very symbol of peace and tranquillity. The phrase "valley of the shadow of death" (v. 4) does not only refer to death, but also to dangerous moments in one's life.

The ending, "I shall dwell in the house of the Lord forever" (v. 6), does not necessarily point to the hereafter but to the prolongation of life here on Earth in fellowship with God. You may be among those countless Jews and Christians who can recite the "Shepherd Psalm" from memory. It has been called "the nightingale of the Psalter." The author views God as guardian of the world, caring and guiding it like a good shepherd guides his flock. For the psalmist, God is not a theological concept. He speaks out of an intimate relationship with God: "The Lord is my shepherd" (v. 1).

It is a relationship of dependence. God is the protector and provider: "Your rod and your staff comfort me. . . . You prepare a table before me" (v. 4–5). With God as companion, watching out for him, the psalmist feels secure and trusts that goodness and kindness will abide with him throughout life.

Reflection: Intimacy with God

Do not overlook a revealing change in the psalmist's approach to God. At first he speaks of God in the third person ("*He* leads me . . ."). However, in the middle of the psalm there is a switch to the second person: "*You* are with me . . . *Your* rod . . ." This switch illustrates the intimacy one may gain in the process of prayer. The more you pray, the closer God will seem to you. Psalm 23 illustrates a progression of benefits from worship. First is the sense of tranquillity that comes over us as we walk with God "beside the still waters" of meditation. Then worship elevates the soul. You feel spiritually refreshed, "restored." You are now listening to God, Who may give you guidance through the still small voice within. Finally, God's presence may relieve you of fear: "Yea, though I walk through the valley of death, I will fear no evil, for You are with me" (v. 4).

❧ PSALM 24 ❧

A Psalm of David.

The earth is the LORD's, and the fulness thereof;
The world, and they that dwell
therein.
2 For He hath founded it upon the seas,
And established it upon the floods.
3 Who shall ascend into the mountain
of the LORD?
And who shall stand in His holy
place?
4 He that hath clean hands, and a pure
heart;
Who hath not taken My name in
vain,
And hath not sworn deceitfully.
5 He shall receive a blessing from the
LORD,
And righteousness from the God of his
salvation.

6 Such is the generation of them that
seek after Him,
That seek Thy face, even Jacob.
Selah

7 Lift up your heads, O ye gates,
And be ye lifted up, ye everlasting
doors;
That the King of glory may come in.
8 "Who is the King of glory?"
"The LORD strong and mighty,
The LORD mighty in battle."
9 Lift up your heads, O ye gates,
Yea, lift them up, ye everlasting doors;
That the King of glory may come in.
10 "Who then is the King of glory?"
"The LORD of hosts;
He is the King of glory."   Selah

❧

Who Is Nearest to God?

How can you, who are less than a speck of dust in the universe, ever get close to the Creator? Psalm 24 is the answer. After acknowledging God's awesome power over "the earth and its fullness, the world and all that dwell in it" (v. 1), the psalmist asks our question: "Who shall stand in His holy place?" (v. 3).

Are you any closer to God in the sanctuary than elsewhere? Psalm 24, much like Psalm 15, suggests that you approach God not by a change of place but by a change of heart. Nearest to God is one who "has clean hands and a pure heart" (v. 4). Reverence of God, together with moral decency, earn you God's blessings. Comparing Psalm 24 with Psalm 15, we note the similarity and the difference. Both psalms agree that the "entrance ticket" to God's presence is moral uprightness. The difference is that Psalm 15 defines specifically what some of these moral requirements are: righteous work, truthfulness, refraining from slander, not discrediting one's neighbor, doing no harm to a fellow man, despising the vile, honoring the God-fearing person, helping others with interest-free loans, and rejecting bribes. Psalm 24 abridges all these specific moral requirements into the general principle of keeping "clean hands and a pure heart," adding for emphasis the specific prohibition of perjury.

Clean hands and a pure heart are the marks of sincerity and integrity. We must bring our actions in harmony with our feelings. Each of us might well join in Thoreau's prayer-poem:

> That my weak hand may equal my firm faith,
> And my life practice more than my tongue saith.

❧

Reflection: Humility

An old legend comments on the dialogue of verses 7 and 8: "Lift up your heads, O ye gates, and be ye lifted up, ye everlasting doors, that the king of glory may come in. Who is the king of glory? The Lord strong and mighty." It was King Solomon who, according to the old legend, wishing to enter the Temple in Jerusalem, asked for the gates to be opened. When the gates heard Solomon's words, "that the king of glory may come," they thought that he referred to himself as "the king of glory." In punishment for his pride, the gates were about to fall and crush him to death. But in order to be sure, they asked: "Who then is the king of glory?" Solomon saved his life by answering: "The Lord of hosts; He is the king of glory." (v. 10) According to this legend, the characteristic of a "pure heart" is humility. It is also the mark of truly great persons. When Winston Churchill was honored on his eightieth birthday for his magnificent leadership role as statesman and orator in World War II, he received tributes from all over the world. Speaker after speaker referred to him as "the lion." Churchill modestly replied: "It was the nation that had the lion's heart. I had the luck to be called upon to give the roar." Abraham Lincoln introduced his Gettysburg Address, the most celebrated speech in America's history, with the humble statement: "The world will little note nor long remember what we say here."

❧ **PSALM 25** ❧

[A Psalm] of David.

Unto Thee, O LORD, do I lift up my soul.
2 O my God, in Thee have I trusted, let me not be ashamed;

Let not mine enemies triumph over me.
3 Yea, none that wait for Thee shall be ashamed;
They shall be ashamed that deal treacherously without cause.

⁴Show me Thy ways, O LORD;
Teach me Thy paths.
⁵Guide me in Thy truth, and teach me;
For Thou art the God of my salvation;
For Thee do I wait all the day.
⁶Remember, O LORD, Thy compassions and Thy mercies;
For they have been from of old.
⁷Remember not the sins of my youth, nor my transgressions;
According to Thy mercy remember Thou me,
For Thy goodness' sake, O LORD.
⁸Good and upright is the LORD;
Therefore doth He instruct sinners in the way.
⁹He guideth the humble in justice;
And He teacheth the humble His way.
¹⁰All the paths of the LORD are mercy and truth
Unto such as keep His covenant and His testimonies.
¹¹For Thy name's sake, O LORD,
Pardon mine iniquity, for it is great.
¹²What man is he that feareth the LORD?
Him will He instruct in the way that He should choose.
¹³His soul shall abide in prosperity;
And his seed shall inherit the land.
¹⁴The counsel of the LORD is with them that fear Him;
And His covenant, to make them know it.
¹⁵Mine eyes are ever toward the LORD;
For He will bring forth my feet out of the net.
¹⁶Turn Thee unto me, and be gracious unto me;
For I am solitary and afflicted.
¹⁷The troubles of my heart are enlarged;
O bring Thou me out of my distresses.
¹⁸See mine affliction and my travail;
And forgive all my sins.
¹⁹Consider how many are mine enemies,
And the cruel hatred wherewith they hate me.
²⁰O keep my soul, and deliver me;
Let me not be ashamed, for I have taken refuge in Thee.
²¹Let integrity and uprightness preserve me,
Because I wait for Thee.

²²Redeem Israel, O God,
Out of all his troubles.

❧

When Deep in Trouble

If you are facing trouble, embarrassment, and shame, Psalm 25 will express your feelings. A personal crisis triggered the writing of this psalm. Reaching out to God for help, the psalmist reexamines his life and is filled with remorse over wrongdoings earlier in life: "Remember not the sins of my youth, nor my transgressions" (v. 7). He begs forgiveness, not because of merit but counting on God's mercies: "According to Your mercy remember me, for Your goodness' sake, O God . . . For your name's sake, O God, pardon mine iniquity" (v. 11).

As for the future, he promises to be guided by God's teachings: "Teach me Your paths, guide me in your truth and teach me" (v. 5). Having already suffered much and being "solitary and afflicted"

(v. 16), he wants God to pull him out of trouble: "O bring me out of my distresses" (v. 17). However, he knows that in future his own integrity and uprightness will be crucial conditions for his preservation: "Let integrity and uprightness preserve me." (v. 21).

Having dealt so far only with personal needs, the author, as though ashamed of his self-centeredness, raises his sight to the needs of his people and concludes with the prayer: "Redeem Israel, O God, out of all their troubles" (v. 22).

※

Reflection: Prepare to Meet God

One of our national characteristics is being in a hurry. Friends abroad are amused if I stop by to see them and am about to leave in less than an hour. "We thought you'd come for a visit, have dinner with us, and stay overnight. You Americans are always in such a rush." It is true that we are always in a hurry. We want instant gratification. We are addicts to the quick fix. Nature teaches us that good fruit needs time to ripen. So it is with the things we value the most. Friendship is not the gift of a moment. It ripens in a prolonged relationship. Infatuation may happen quickly, but genuine love needs time to grow and must be tested again and again.

Time is also a factor in the religious life. God's presence and guidance are rarely gained all of a sudden. The prophet Amos said: "Prepare to meet your God" (Amos 4:12). The author of Psalm 25 is eager to connect with God: "Show me Your ways. Teach me Your paths" (v. 4). But he knows that we must first clear our mind of distractions, put ourselves in a listening mood, and approach God with prayer and meditation. It does take time, but the psalmist is willing to wait: "For You I wait all the day" (v. 5).

Madame Chiang Kai-Shek, wife of China's pre-Communist leader, once told of her mother's custom of spending hours every day in prayer. A certain room on the third floor of her house was set apart for her devotions. If any of the children asked her advice, she would answer: "I must first ask God." This was not a matter of a few minutes. She would stand asking for God's blessing upon her child and then wait for God until she felt certain that guidance had come to her.

≈ PSALM 26 ≈

[A Psalm] of David.

Judge me, O LORD, for I have walked
  in mine integrity,
And I have trusted in the LORD without wavering.
2 Examine me, O LORD, and try me;
  Test my reins and my heart.
3 For Thy mercy is before mine eyes;
  And I have walked in Thy truth.
4 I have not sat with men of falsehood;
  Neither will I go in with dissemblers.
5 I hate the gathering of evil-doers,
  And will not sit with the wicked.
6 I will wash my hands in innocency;
  So will I compass Thine altar, O
  LORD,
7 That I may make the voice of thanksgiving to be heard,

And tell of all Thy wondrous works.

8 LORD, I love the habitation of Thy
  house,
And the place where Thy glory
  dwelleth.
9 Gather not my soul with sinners,
  Nor my life with men of blood;
10 In whose hands is craftiness,
  And their right hand is full of bribes.
11 But as for me, I will walk in mine
  integrity;
  Redeem me, and be gracious unto me.
12 My foot standeth in an even place;
  In the congregations will I bless the
  LORD.

≈

Corruption Is Contagious

Must you avoid all contact with a corrupt person? Should you shun a friend who has committed a felony? The author of Psalm 26 evidently struggled hard to maintain his own integrity even when shady characters were all around him: "I hate the company of evildoers and will not sit with the wicked" (v. 5). He wants to have nothing to do with sinners, very much in line with the viewpoint of Psalm 1. You may wonder if such an attitude is not overly self-righteous. By avoiding all association with transgressors, are you not missing the opportunity, even the duty, of trying to improve them? Should not a morally superior person help others overcome their defects?

If you imagine that your good influence might help a person of low morals, consider the possibility that the person you aim to pull up to your level might also drag you down to his. Don't underestimate the seductive power of evil. Corruption is contagious. Contact with corrupt persons should be avoided, not because you are too good for them but because you may not be good enough. Only saints can be counted on to resist the seduction of evil. The psalmist goes to the sanctuary not only to pray, but to be in a safe environment: "God, I love Your temple, the place of Your glory. Do not sweep away my soul with sinners nor my life with men of blood" (v. 8–9). In a world full of slippery places, the sanctuary is a place of stability where a person will be morally strengthened and become more steadfast in his way of life. He is resolved to resist the temptations that corrupt so many: "But as for me, I will walk in mine integrity. . . . My foot stands in an even place, in the congregations I will bless the Lord" (v. 11–12).

❧

Reflection: Wonder

The philosopher Abraham Joshua Heschel once startled a congregation by beginning his sermon with the question: "Did you all see the great miracle that happened this morning?" After a pause, filled by the buzz of people asking each other what he was referring to, Heschel answered his own question: "This morning I stood at my hotel room window and watched the sun rise and light streaming upon the Earth, wondering how many other worlds were orbiting out there in infinite space. How wonderful that the eye can see and the mind fathom all that." Then Heschel talked about the dulling of our sense of wonder. Should we not marvel at the mystery of life at every pulse beat and with every breath we draw? Too many of us take our existence and the world for granted. Should we not ask questions about the origin and purpose of it all?

The psychologist Erich Fromm wrote, "One who has never been bewildered, who has never looked upon life and his own existence as phenomena which require answers and, yet, paradoxically, for which the only answers are new questions, can hardly understand what religious experience is." If curiosity is a mark of intelligence, wonder is the root of religious feeling. The author of Psalm 26 shows the close connection between prayer and the sense of wonder: "I will encircle Your altar, O God, that my thanksgiving be heard and I shall tell of Your wondrous works" (v. 6–7).

❧ PSALM 27 ❧

[A Psalm] of David.

The LORD is my light and my salvation; whom shall I fear?
The LORD is the stronghold of my life; of whom shall I be afraid?

2 When evil-doers came upon me to eat up my flesh,
Even mine adversaries and my foes, they stumbled and fell.
3 Though a host should encamp against me,

My heart shall not fear;
Though war should rise up against
me,
Even then will I be confident.

4One thing have I asked of the LORD,
that will I seek after:
That I may dwell in the house of the
LORD all the days of my life,
To behold the graciousness of the
LORD, and to visit early in His
temple.
5For He concealeth me in His pavilion
in the day of evil;
He hideth me in the covert of His
tent;
He lifteth me up upon a rock.
6And now shall my head be lifted up
above mine enemies round about
me;
And I will offer in His tabernacle sacrifices with trumpet-sound;
I will sing, yea, I will sing praises unto
the LORD.

7Hear, O LORD, when I call with my
voice,
And be gracious unto me, and answer
me.

8In Thy behalf my heart hath said:
"Seek ye My face";
Thy face, LORD, will I seek.
9Hide not Thy face from me;
Put not Thy servant away in anger;
Thou hast been my help;
Cast me not off, neither forsake me,
O God of my salvation.
10For though my father and my mother
have forsaken me,
The LORD will take me up.

11Teach me Thy way, O LORD;
And lead me in an even path,
Because of them that lie in wait for
me.
12Deliver me not over unto the will of
mine adversaries;
For false witnesses are risen up
against me, and such as breathe out
violence.
13If I had not believed to look upon the
goodness of the LORD
In the land of the living!—
14Wait for the LORD;
Be strong, and let thy heart take
courage;
Yea, wait thou for the LORD.

Don't Be Ashamed of Your Fears

You would not be human if you did not know fear. It is natural, even beneficial, to fear threatening conditions. Fear mobilizes your mental and physical resources for defense. Psalm 27, attributed to David, tells how this brave warrior faced up to the danger of capture by enemies. The opening verses of this psalm sound like whistling in the dark. Threatened by enemies, David reassures himself with the memory of past victories. He faced danger before and overcame it: "When evil-doers came upon me to eat up my flesh, even mine adversaries and my foes, they stumbled and fell" (v. 2).

With trust in God, he fights off fear: "God is my light and my salvation; whom shall I fear? God is the stronghold of my life; of whom shall I be afraid? . . . Though an army should encamp against me, my heart shall not fear; though war should rise up against me, even then will I be confident" (v. 1–3). As he is about to worship God, he has the feeling that God Himself is stirring his heart to pray: "In Your behalf my heart has said: 'Seek My face'; Your face, God, will I seek" (v. 8).

Then this brave warrior is facing up to his immediate peril, which is the possible capture by enemies. There is reason to fear, and so he prays: "Deliver me not unto the will of mine adversaries" (v. 12). A strong belief that he is not forsaken by God boosts his courage: "Though my father and mother leave me, God will take me in" (v. 10). Happy memories raise his hope that he might again worship in the sanctuary, as was his custom in earlier, carefree days (v. 4). Trusting in God, "the stronghold of my life" (v. 1), he is willing to "wait for God" (v. 14). Strengthened by faith, he masters his fears: "Though an army should encamp against me, my heart shall not fear" (v. 3).

∞

Reflection: Fear of Abandonment

One of our most persistent fears is the fear of abandonment. Walking on a crowded street, a small child will hold on tightly to the parent's hand, afraid of being left behind and lost. The very old live in fear of neglect by family and friends. Psalm 71 includes the memorable sentence: "Cast me not off in old age; forsake me not when my strength fails" (71:9).

The hero of anti-Communist resistance Natan Sharansky, who languished many years in Soviet prisons, after his liberation wrote in his autobiography that during his solitary confinement, a little booklet of the Psalms saved his sanity. Especially sustaining was a verse in Psalm 27: "When my father and my mother abandon me, then God will take me up" (v. 10). These words assured him that although he was cut off from all the people he cared most about, he was not alone. God was still with him. The nineteenth-century Bible scholar Rabbi Samson Raphael Hirsch suggested in his commentary that the psalmist did not mean actual abandonment of a child by parents, but rather giving up on the child who has turned out badly, in the belief that he would never straighten out. God never gives up on us. He waits for us to clean up our act and return to Him in repentance. The repentant sinner is always welcome back. Even when rejected by our own parents, we are still embraced by the fatherhood of God.

❧ Psalm 28 ❧

[A Psalm] of David.

Unto thee, O LORD, do I call;
My Rock, be not Thou deaf unto me;
Lest, if Thou be silent unto me,
I become like them that go down into
  the pit.
2 Hear the voice of my supplications,
  when I cry unto Thee,
When I lift up my hands toward Thy
  holy Sanctuary.

3 Draw me not away with the wicked,
  And with the workers of iniquity;
Who speak peace with their neighbours,
But evil is in their hearts.
4 Give them according to their deeds,
  and according to the evil of their
  endeavours;
Give them after the work of their
  hands;
Render to them their desert.

5 Because they give no heed to the
  works of the LORD,
  Nor to the operation of His hands;
  He will break them down and not
    build them up.

6 Blessed be the LORD,
  Because He hath heard the voice of
    my supplications.
7 The LORD is my strength and my
    shield,
  In Him hath my heart trusted,
  And I am helped;
  Therefore my heart greatly rejoiceth,
  And with my song will I praise Him.

8 The LORD is a strength unto them;
  And He is a stronghold of salvation to
    His anointed.
9 Save Thy people, and bless Thine
    inheritance;
  And tend them, and carry them for
    ever.

❧

Why Expect Help from God?

If you need help, who would you ask? Surely not a stranger, but someone who helped you before. This is the logic of prayers of petition to
God. When in need or trouble, it makes sense to turn to the One who
has kept you alive and of whose bounty you have partaken all along.
Trust in God is based on our belief that we survive by virtue of His
gifts: "God is my strength and my shield, in Him have I trusted" (v. 7).

There is another reason for expecting help from God: God is just.
The psalmist wants God to recognize that he is different from hypocrites: "Do not put me together with the wicked and the iniquitous
who speak peace with their neighbors but evil is in their hearts" (v. 3).
Without putting it into these words, the psalmist proceeds on the
assumption that a just God will take into account and reward his
integrity. In the end, the psalmist rises above personal needs and prays
for the welfare of all his people: "Save your people . . . and tend them
and carry them forever" (v. 9).

∞

Reflection: Unanswered Prayer

It is not uncommon for a worshipper to feel as though he were praying to a wall. That is how the psalmist felt, at least at one time: "Be not deaf unto me lest if You be silent I be like those who die" (v. 1). Is God deaf? If He can hear my prayer, why does He not answer? Maybe it is me, not God, who is deaf? Maybe God is trying to communicate a message or thought, but it won't get through to me because I am not attuned, because I have not sufficiently prepared myself to listen. When God seems distant, it is not because He is far away but because I have removed myself from Him. My mind is elsewhere, distracted by trivia. I have not yet surrendered myself to His will.

The psalmist cannot bear the loss of communication with God. Distance from God would be for him a form of death. For the medieval Jewish poet Judah Halevy, God's presence or distance were matters of life and death:

> When far from Thee, I die while yet alive.
> But if I cling to Thee, I live though I should die.

∞ PSALM 29 ∞

A Psalm of David.

Ascribe unto the LORD, O ye sons of might,
Ascribe unto the LORD glory and strength.

2 Ascribe unto the LORD the glory due unto His name;
Worship the LORD in the beauty of holiness.

3 The voice of the LORD is upon the waters;
The God of glory thundereth,
Even the LORD upon many waters.

4 The voice of the LORD is powerful;
The voice of the LORD is full of majesty.

5 The voice of the LORD breaketh the cedars;
Yea, the LORD breaketh in pieces the cedars of Lebanon.

6 He maketh them also to skip like a calf;
Lebanon and Sirion like a young wild-ox.

7 The voice of the LORD heweth out flames of fire.

8 The voice of the LORD shaketh the wilderness;
The LORD shaketh the wilderness of Kadesh.

9 The voice of the LORD maketh the hinds to calve,
And strippeth the forests bare;
And in His temple all say: "Glory."

10 The LORD sat enthroned at the flood;
Yea, the LORD sitteth as King for ever.

11 The LORD will give strength unto His people;
The LORD will bless His people with peace.

The God of Nature Shares Power with Man

What do you imagine God to be like? The pagans could not think of one God, but only of many gods. They depicted them as forces of nature or monsters, with animal or human features. The psalmist, true to the Hebrew idea of only One God whose likeness is unknowable, dares not describe the divine being. However, he may glorify the acts and the powers of God.

In issuing his call to the worship of God, "ascribe unto God glory and strength" (v. 1), the psalmist wants to make sure that we offer our prayers in a proper setting and the right frame of mind: "Worship God in the beauty of holiness" (v. 2). What is the beauty of holiness? Some think of it as grand architecture and artistic furnishings of the sanctuary. Others suggest that the impressive apparel of priests and ministers contributes beauty of holiness to the worship of God. The psalmist, however, points to the grandeur of nature, which instills in us something of the awe and beauty of holiness. We are inspired with a reverential mood as we behold the immeasurable force visible in storms at sea (v. 3), in lightning and volcanic eruptions that "hew out flames of fire" (v. 7), and in earthquakes that "shake the wilderness" (v. 8).

Reflection: God Empowers Man

After marveling at the gigantic forces of nature that convey to us the might of God, the psalmist realizes that God is more than the supreme power in the universe. God has personal aspects by which He relates to human beings, guiding and blessing them and even sharing some of His strength with them: "God will give strength to His people. God will bless His people with peace" (v. 11). What kind of strength do we receive from God? The strength for physical survival, and the mental power by which we gain superiority over all other creatures. Through the right exercise of this mental power that is our reasoning capacity, we have access to God's laws, which teach us how to live in peace with one another. Then, indeed, shall we enjoy God's blessing: "God will bless His people with peace" (v. 11).

❧ PSALM 30 ❧

A Psalm; a Song at the Dedication of the House; of David.

2 I will extol Thee, O LORD, for Thou hast raised me up,
And hast not suffered mine enemies to rejoice over me.
3 O LORD my God,
I cried unto Thee, and Thou didst heal me;
4 O LORD, Thou broughtest up my soul from the nether-world;
Thou didst keep me alive, that I should not go down to the pit.
5 Sing praise unto the LORD, O ye His godly ones,
And give thanks to His holy name.
6 For His anger is but for a moment,
His favour is for a life-time;
Weeping may tarry for the night,
But joy cometh in the morning.

7 Now I had said in my security:
"I shall never be moved."

8 Thou hadst established, O LORD, in Thy favour my mountain as a stronghold—
Thou didst hide Thy face; I was affrighted.
9 Unto Thee, O LORD, did I call,
And unto the LORD I made supplication:
10 "What profit is there in my blood, when I go down to the pit?
Shall the dust praise Thee? shall it declare Thy truth?
11 Hear, O LORD, and be gracious unto me;
LORD, be Thou my helper."

12 Thou didst turn for me my mourning into dancing;
Thou didst loose my sackcloth, and gird me with gladness;
13 So that my glory may sing praise to Thee, and not be silent;
O LORD my God, I will give thanks unto Thee for ever.

❧

God, Our Lifeline

If you have ever been saved from mortal danger or recovered from grave illness, you will appreciate this psalm. It acknowledges the insecurity of human existence. God is our lifeline. If He withdraws support, we turn to dust. The psalmist has lived through all kinds of problems and at least once looked into the very face of death. Experience taught him to acknowledge God as his Helper and Savior: "O my God, I cried unto You and You healed me; O God, You brought up my soul from the netherworld. You kept me alive that I should not go down to the pit" (v. 3–4).

We must not take our well-being for granted. If God withdraws support, we are done for: "I had said in my security: 'I shall never be

moved.' It was You, O God, that established, in Your favor, my mountain as a stronghold—But when You hid Your face, I was frightened"
(v. 7–8). The favors of God by far outweigh the afflictions that He may
impose on us: "His anger is but for a moment, His favor is for a lifetime" (v. 6).

The psalmist ends with words of thanksgiving for his life's dramatic
turn from sadness to gladness: "You turned my mourning into dancing" (v. 12). The optimistic outlook of this Psalm is expressed in the
memorable line: "Weeping may tarry for the night, but joy comes in
the morning" (v. 6).

Reflection: Optimism

Optimism permeates the Bible. God Himself is the first optimist.
Following each day of creation, the Bible tells, "God saw that it was
good" (Genesis 1). Without overlooking the reality of evil and suffering, the Bible assures us of God's care and help, referring to Him
again and again as "Savior." Seventy-two of the 150 Psalms strike an
optimistic note. Typical is the comforting line in Psalm 30: "Weeping
may tarry for the night, but joy comes in the morning" (v. 6). What
are some of the grounds for optimism? For one thing, nothing lasts
forever, including problems, crises, and calamities. Many go away
just as storm clouds are blown away and the sun shines again. Also,
setbacks are learning opportunities. We can learn from our mistakes.
Thomas Edison had an assistant who was very unhappy over his
inability to solve a mechanical problem. "How are you doing?" asked
Edison. "Terrible, I have done five hundred experiments and found
nothing. It's all been a waste." "You are wrong," said the great inven-
tor. "You have found five hundred wrong ways. Now go on until you
find the right way to a solution." The challenge of hardship teaches us
to put our abilities and resources to better use. Necessity is the
mother of invention. Our needs spur us on to greater efforts. For this
reason alone, tomorrow may be better than today. Optimism and
pessimism are not embedded in the facts but in our various ways of
looking at things: The optimist sees the glass half full, the pessimist
half empty. Different reactions to the same fact!

❧ PSALM 31 ❧

For the Leader. A Psalm of David.

2 In Thee, O Lord, have I taken
   refuge; let me never be ashamed;
   Deliver me in Thy righteousness.
3 Incline Thine ear unto me, deliver me
   speedily;
   Be Thou to me a rock of refuge, even
   a fortress of defence, to save me.
4 For Thou art my rock and my
   fortress;
   Therefore for Thy name's sake lead
   me and guide me.
5 Bring me forth out of the net that
   they have hidden for me;
   For Thou art my stronghold.
6 Into Thy hand I commit my spirit;
   Thou hast redeemed me, O Lord,
   Thou God of truth.
7 I hate them that regard lying vanities;
   But I trust in the Lord.
8 I will be glad and rejoice in Thy
   lovingkindness;
   For Thou hast seen mine affliction,
   Thou hast taken cognizance of the
   troubles of my soul,
9 And Thou hast not given me over
   into the hand of the enemy;
   Thou hast set my feet in a broad
   place.

10 Be gracious unto me, O Lord, for I
   am in distress;
   Mine eye wasteth away with vexation,
   yea, my soul and my body.
11 For my life is spent in sorrow, and my
   years in sighing;
   My strength faileth because of mine
   iniquity, and my bones are wasted
   away.
12 Because of all mine adversaries I am
   become a reproach,
   Yea, unto my neighbours exceedingly,
   and a dread to mine acquaintance;
   They that see me without flee from
   me.
13 I am forgotten as a dead man out of
   mind;

I am like a useless vessel.
14 For I have heard the whispering of
   many,
   Terror on every side;
   While they took counsel together
   against me,
   They devised to take away my life.

15 But as for me, I have trusted in Thee,
   O Lord;
   I have said: "Thou art my God."
16 My times are in Thy hand;
   Deliver me from the hand of mine
   enemies, and from them that persecute me.
17 Make Thy face to shine upon Thy
   servant;
   Save me in Thy lovingkindness.
18 O Lord, let me not be ashamed, for I
   have called upon Thee;
   Let the wicked be ashamed, let them
   be put to silence in the nether-
   world.
19 Let the lying lips be dumb,
   Which speak arrogantly against the
   righteous,
   With pride and contempt.

20 Oh how abundant is Thy goodness,
   which Thou hast laid up for them
   that fear Thee;
   Which Thou hast wrought for them
   that take their refuge in Thee, in
   the sight of the sons of men!
21 Thou hidest them in the covert of
   Thy presence from the plottings of
   man;
   Thou concealest them in a pavilion
   from the strife of tongues.
22 Blessed be the Lord;
   For He hath shown me His wondrous
   lovingkindness in an entrenched
   city.
23 As for me, I said in my haste: "I am
   cut off from before Thine eyes";
   Nevertheless Thou heardest the voice
   of my supplications when I cried
   unto Thee.

24 O love the LORD, all ye His godly
    ones;
  The LORD preserveth the faithful,
  And plentifully repayeth him that
    acteth haughtily.

25 Be strong, and let your heart take
    courage,
  All ye that wait for the LORD.

❧

The War of Words

If you have ever been the victim of malicious gossip or the target of schemes designed to hurt you, Psalm 31 will have a very personal relevance for you. Snubbed by neighbors (see v. 12) and aware of whispering behind his back (see v. 14), the psalmist knows that enemies are out to get him. He begs God for protection against "the intrigues of man . . . and the war of words" (v. 21).

For a time, he mistakenly thinks that God is paying no attention to his plight: "I said in my haste, I am cut off from before Your eyes" (v. 23). Yet he lives to see deliverance: "You have taken cognizance of my troubles and have not surrendered me to the enemy" (v. 8–9). Now he commits his spirit into God's hands (see v. 6) and wants others to learn from his experience that "God preserves the faithful and punishes the arrogant sinner" (v. 24). Those who must face similar problems should patiently trust God: "Take courage and wait for God" (v. 25).

❧

Reflection: Self-Esteem

Is there anyone who has not, at one time or the other, suffered the hurt of neglect and disrespect? You feel it every time the other does not return your telephone call or fails to answer your letter. First you wonder, What's the matter with the other person? Then you question yourself, What is the matter with me? Why am I not getting attention? Am I so unimportant or socially undesirable? The hurt cuts more deeply when you are left out of an event or party to which others of your acquaintance are invited.

The psalmist tells of his anguish at being snubbed by people he cares about: "I am forgotten as a dead man out of mind" (v. 13). The disrespect he experiences has a devastating effect on his self-esteem: "I am like a useless vessel" (v. 13). The sociologist Thorstein Veblen recognized the psychological process by which, with rare exceptions, the opinion or attitude of others toward you shapes your self-image: "Only individuals with an aberrant temperament can in the long run retain their self-esteem in the face of the disrespect of their fellows." How does the psalmist cope with his loss of self-esteem? He looks elsewhere for acceptance. He turns to God: "In You I have taken refuge. . . . Into Your hand I commit my spirit" (v. 2, 6). Knowing himself to be loved by God, he feels better about himself: "I will be glad and rejoice in Your loving-kindness. For You have seen mine anguish. You know the troubles of my heart" (v. 8).

❧ PSALM 32 ❧

[A Psalm] of David. Maschil.

Happy is he whose transgression is
 forgiven, whose sin is pardoned.
2 Happy is the man unto whom the
 LORD counteth not iniquity,
And in whose spirit there is no guile.

3 When I kept silence, my bones wore
 away
Through my groaning all the day
 long.
4 For day and night Thy hand was
 heavy upon me;
My sap was turned as in the droughts
 of summer.   Selah
5 I acknowledged my sin unto Thee,
 and mine iniquity have I not hid;
I said: "I will make confession concerning my transgressions unto the
 LORD"—
And Thou, Thou forgavest the
 iniquity of my sin.   Selah

6 For this let every one that is godly
pray unto Thee in a time when
 Thou mayest be found;
Surely, when the great waters over-
 flow, they will not reach unto him.
7 Thou art my hiding-place; Thou wilt
 preserve me from the adversary;
With songs of deliverance Thou wilt
 compass me about.   Selah
8 "I will instruct thee and teach thee in
 the way which thou shalt go;
I will give counsel, Mine eye being
 upon thee."
9 Be ye not as the horse, or as the mule,
 which have no understanding;
Whose mouth must be held in with
 bit and bridle,
That they come not near unto thee.

10 Many are the sorrows of the wicked;
But he that trusteth in the LORD,
 mercy compasseth him about.
11 Be glad in the LORD, and rejoice, ye
 righteous;
And shout for joy, all ye that are
 upright in heart.

❧

Confession Brings Relief

What is worse, being tormented by others or tormenting yourself? The author of the previous psalm, Psalm 31, complains bitterly about harm done to him by others. In Psalm 32, the author is embittered by what he himself has done. He is oppressed by a guilty conscience. It makes him ill: "When I kept silent, my bones wore away through my groaning all day long. For day and night Your hand was heavy upon me" (v. 3–4).

Relief comes only when he breaks his silence and confesses his wrongdoing before God: "I acknowledge my sin to You" (v. 5). Now he would advise everyone of faith to do likewise and share the joy of setting himself right with God: "Shout for joy all who are upright in heart" (v. 11).

❧

Reflection: Confession

The burden of guilt is a heavy burden to carry. It can make you physically ill. How can one be relieved of guilt feelings? The psalmist points to the first step of guilt relief: "When I kept silence, my bones wore away through my groaning all day long. For day and night Your hand was heavy upon me; I felt dried up as in the droughts of summer" (v. 3–4). The acknowledgment and expression of guilt is the first step of the remedy. It need not be a public declaration, unless the offense has done great public damage. However, one must start with a conscious recognition of the wrong one has done. The second step, if we are to follow the psalmist's example, is to confess it all before God: "I acknowledge my sin unto You and mine iniquity have I not hid; I said: 'I will make confession concerning my transgressions unto God'" (v. 5). Many will make their confession privately in prayer to God. Others may want to do it in the hearing of a trusted spiritual leader. In either case, we shall find relief by expressing remorse silently or aloud. The psalmist reports what he perceived as God's answer to his confession: "I will instruct you and teach you in the way which you shall go" (v. 8).

The message implies action on the part of the repentant sinner. It is not enough that he feel badly about the wrong he committed. Remorse must be followed by restitution to the injured party to undo the wrong that was done.

❧ PSALM 33 ❧

Rejoice in the LORD, O ye righteous,
Praise is comely for the upright.
2 Give thanks unto the LORD with
  harp,
  Sing praises unto Him with the
  psaltery of ten strings.
3 Sing unto Him a new song;
  Play skilfully amid shouts of joy.

4 For the word of the LORD is upright;
  And all His work is done in
  faithfulness.
5 He loveth righteousness and justice;
  The earth is full of the lovingkindness
  of the LORD.
6 By the word of the LORD were the
  heavens made;

And all the host of them by the breath
of His mouth.
⁷He gathereth the waters of the sea
together as a heap;
He layeth up the deeps in storehouses.
⁸Let all the earth fear the LORD;
Let all the inhabitants of the world
stand in awe of Him.
⁹For He spoke, and it was;
He commanded, and it stood.
¹⁰The LORD bringeth the counsel of
the nations to nought;
He maketh the thoughts of the
peoples to be of no effect.
¹¹The counsel of the LORD standeth for
ever,
The thoughts of His heart to all
generations.

¹²Happy is the nation whose God is the
LORD;
The people whom He hath chosen
for His own inheritance.
¹³The LORD looketh from heaven;
He beholdeth all the sons of men;
¹⁴From the place of His habitation He
looketh intently

Upon all the inhabitants of the earth;
¹⁵He that fashioneth the hearts of them
all,
That considereth all their doings.
¹⁶A king is not saved by the multitude
of a host;
A mighty man is not delivered by
great strength.
¹⁷A horse is a vain thing for safety;
Neither doth it afford escape by its
great strength.
¹⁸Behold, the eye of the LORD is toward
them that fear Him,
Toward them that wait for His mercy;
¹⁹To deliver their soul from death,
And to keep them alive in famine.

²⁰Our soul hath waited for the LORD;
He is our help and our shield.
²¹For in Him doth our heart rejoice,
Because we have trusted in His holy
name.
²²Let Thy mercy, O LORD, be upon
us,
According as we have waited for
Thee.

God Is in Charge

This psalm will cheer you up. If you think that the world is turning into chaos, that things are happening by pure chance, without rhyme or reason, think again. Psalm 33 sees the hand of God in the physical universe as well as in human history. God, the Creator ("He spoke and it was," v. 9), also has designs for all mankind: "God's plans endure forever, His designs for all generations" (v. 11).

God the Creator knows all about His creatures and what they are doing: "God looks from heaven and beholds all human beings. . . . He that fashions the hearts of them all, that considers all their doings" (v. 13–15). Neither physical strength nor the powerful resources of a king are guarantees for survival: "A king is not saved by the multitude of a host; a mighty man is not delivered by great strength" (v. 16). The issues of life and death are in God's hands, "to deliver their souls from death and to keep them alive in famine. . . . He is our help and shield" (v. 19–20).

❦

Reflection: God's Omniscience

The psalmist asserts with firm conviction what many of us find difficult to imagine: "God looks down from heaven; He beholds all human beings. . . . He oversees all the inhabitants of the earth, He who fashions the hearts of them all, Who considers all their doings" (v. 13–15). Can it be that God knows everything that is happening in the universe and everything done by every human being? It is not given to human beings to understand God, how He knows and what He knows. However, if we believe God to be our Creator, it makes sense to say that He cares for His creatures and, through His unbreakable connection with us, is aware of our doings. It is inconceivable to the human mind that anyone could be in communication with countless beings. But as Horatio was told in Shakespeare's *Hamlet*, "There are more things in heaven and earth, Horatio, than are dreamed of in your philosophy."

❦ PSALM 34 ❦

[A Psalm] of David; when he
changed his demeanour before
Abimelech, who drove him away,
and he departed.

2 I will bless the LORD at all times;
His praise shall continually be in my
mouth.
3 My soul shall glory in the LORD;
The humble shall hear thereof, and
be glad.
4 O magnify the LORD with me,
And let us exalt His name together.
5 I sought the LORD, and He answered
me,
And delivered me from all my fears.
6 They looked unto Him, and were
radiant;
And their faces shall never be
abashed.
7 This poor man cried, and the LORD
heard,
And saved him out of all his troubles.

8 The angel of the LORD encampeth
round about them that fear Him,
And delivereth them.
9 O consider and see that the LORD is
good;
Happy is the man that taketh refuge
in Him.
10 O fear the LORD, ye His holy ones;
For there is no want to them that fear
Him.
11 The young lions do lack, and suffer
hunger;
But they that seek the LORD want not
any good thing.
12 Come, ye children, hearken unto me;
I will teach you the fear of the LORD.
13 Who is the man that desireth life,
And loveth days, that he may see good
therein?
14 Keep thy tongue from evil,
And thy lips from speaking guile.
15 Depart from evil, and do good;
Seek peace, and pursue it.

16 The eyes of the LORD are toward the
     righteous,
   And His ears are open unto their cry.
17 The face of the LORD is against them
     that do evil,
   To cut off the remembrance of them
     from the earth.
18 They cried, and the LORD heard,
   And delivered them out of all their
     troubles.
19 The LORD is nigh unto them that are
     of a broken heart,
   And saveth such as are of a contrite
     spirit.

20 Many are the ills of the righteous,
   But the LORD delivereth him out of
     them all.
21 He keepeth all his bones;
   Not one of them is broken.
22 Evil shall kill the wicked;
   And they that hate the righteous shall
     be held guilty.

23 The LORD redeemeth the soul of His
     servants;
   And none of them that take refuge in
     Him shall be desolate.

❧

Does Personal Experience Confirm Your Faith?

Does your experience in life bear out your beliefs about God? Does God measure up to your expectations? Some psalmists are exasperated by God's nonperformance. Psalm 10, for example, opens with the complaint: "Why, O God, are you aloof, heedless in time of trouble?" However, most psalms, especially Psalm 34, point to experiences that confirm trust in God. The author repeatedly testifies to God's response to the needs of the faithful: "I turned to God and He answered me, He saved me from all my fears" (v. 5). Similar testimony to God's attentiveness to the prayers of the righteous is given in verses 7, 16, and 18.

The psalmist's belief in God is not derived from theory, but from personal experience: "Taste and see how good God is" (v. 9). You may find God nearest precisely in times of suffering and humiliation: "The Lord is close to the brokenhearted and saves those of a contrite spirit" (v. 19). The psalmist admits, in all candor, that the righteous, like so many others, may suffer misfortunes, but in the end "God will save him from them all" (v. 20).

Some of the wisest words of the Bible are found in this psalm: "If you want the good life and enjoy many years, keep your tongue from evil and your lips from deceitful speech" (v. 13–14). This is followed immediately by a sentence that summarizes all of biblical ethics: "Depart from evil and do good; seek peace and pursue it" (v. 15).

The psalmist does not explain why there is evil in God's world, but *one* thing he knows, wrongdoers will themselves be destroyed by the evil they generate: "Evil shall kill the wicked" (v. 22).

❧

Reflection: Be Positive

The question of why we find so much evil and suffering in this life is unanswerable. However, we have been given the power to overcome evil. Psalm 34 assumes that we have the ability to recognize evil and stay away from it, if we have the will to avoid it. But this negative approach, the rejection of evil, must be matched by a positive response, which is the embrace of the good: "Depart from evil and do good" (v. 15). The nineteenth-century Hassidic leader Rabbi Yitzhak Meir of Ger (d. 1866) was no friend of the fire-and-brimstone style of preaching. Instead of raging against sin and intensifying feelings of guilt, he would try to inspire his listeners to do good. On a certain Day of Atonement he preached the following message:

> He who has done ill and talks about it and thinks about it all the time does not cast the evil thing out of his thoughts and wherever your thoughts are, that's where you are. . . . What is the point of morbid reflection upon one's own sinfulness? Rake the dirt this way, rake it that way—it will always remain dirt. Have I sinned, have I not sinned? What does Heaven get out of that? In the time I waste brooding over it I could be stringing pearls for the delight of Heaven. That is why the Psalmist warns us: "*Depart* from evil and do good." Turn mentally away from evil, do not dwell upon it, and do good. . . . You have sinned? Offset it by doing good!

❧ PSALM 35 ❧

[A Psalm] of David.

Strive, O LORD, with them that strive
  with me;
Fight against them that fight against
  me.
2 Take hold of shield and buckler,
  And rise up to my help.
3 Draw out also the spear, and the
  battle-axe, against them that pursue
  me;
Say unto my soul: "I am thy salvation."
4 Let them be ashamed and brought to
  confusion that seek after my soul;

Let them be turned back and be
  abashed that devise my hurt.
5 Let them be as chaff before the wind,
  The angel of the LORD thrusting
  them.
6 Let their way be dark and slippery,
  The angel of the LORD pursuing
  them.
7 For without cause have they hid for
  me the pit, even their net,
Without cause have they digged for
  my soul.
8 Let destruction come upon him
  unawares;

And let his net that he hath hid catch
  himself;
With destruction let him fall therein.
⁹And my soul shall be joyful in the
  LORD;
It shall rejoice in His salvation.
¹⁰All my bones shall say: "LORD, who is
  like unto Thee,
Who deliverest the poor from him
  that is too strong for him,
Yea, the poor and the needy from him
  that spoileth him?"

¹¹Unrighteous witnesses rise up;
  They ask me of things that I know
  not.
¹²They repay me evil for good;
  Bereavement is come to my soul.
¹³But as for me, when they were sick,
  my clothing was sackcloth,
I afflicted my soul with fasting;
And my prayer, may it return into
  mine own bosom.
¹⁴I went about as though it had been
  my friend or my brother;
I bowed down mournful, as one that
  mourneth for his mother.
¹⁵But when I halt they rejoice, and
  gather themselves together;
The abjects gather themselves
  together against me, and those
  whom I know not;
They tear me, and cease not;
¹⁶With the profanest mockeries of
  backbiting
They gnash at me with their teeth.

¹⁷LORD, how long wilt Thou look on?
  Rescue my soul from their destruc-
  tions,
Mine only one from the lions.
¹⁸I will give Thee thanks in the great
  congregation;

I will praise Thee among a numerous
  people.
¹⁹Let not them that are wrongfully
  mine enemies rejoice over me;
Neither let them wink with the eye
  that hate me without a cause.
²⁰For they speak not peace;
But they devise deceitful matters
  against them that are quiet in the
  land.
²¹Yea, they open their mouth wide
  against me;
They say: "Aha, aha, our eye hath
  seen it."
²²Thou hast seen, O LORD; keep not
  silence;
O LORD, be not far from me.
²³Rouse Thee, and awake to my judgment,
Even unto my cause, my God and my
  LORD.
²⁴Judge me, O LORD my God, according to Thy righteousness;
And let them not rejoice over me.
²⁵Let them not say in their heart: "Aha,
  we have our desire";
Let them not say: "We have swallowed him up."
²⁶Let them be ashamed and abashed
  together that rejoice at my hurt;
Let them be clothed with shame and
  confusion that magnify themselves
  against me.
²⁷Let them shout for joy, and be glad,
  that delight in my righteousness;
Yea, let them say continually: "Magnified be the LORD,
Who delighteth in the peace of His
  servant."
²⁸And my tongue shall speak of Thy
  righteousness,
And of Thy praise all the day.

❧

When Former Friends Repay Good with Evil

Can you imagine the hurt when former friends become your enemies?
The psalmist is trying to cope with such a shocking blow. He remembers how he cared and even prayed for some of those friends in time of

their illness and now cannot understand why they have turned against him: "They repay me evil for good" (v. 12). Without cause, they try to do him harm (see v. 7). He has become the target of their malice and ridicule: "They laugh when I stumble" (v. 15).

He begs God to pass fair judgment upon him (see v. 24) so that he and his true friends might "always say, 'magnified be God who delights in the well-being of His servant'" (v. 27).

∾

Reflection: Words

Words are weapons. If aimed with malice, words can wound, even kill. Among the cruel abuses a person may suffer is being taunted with bigoted expletives or unflattering nicknames. Who could count the tears shed by children whose physical defects inspired such nicknames as "Fatso," "Shorty," and so forth? William Hazlitt had it right when he wrote: "A nickname is the heaviest stone that the devil can throw at a man." Much of Psalm 35 is an outcry against the verbal beating the psalmist received from people of ill will: "With profane mockeries of backbiting they gnash at me with their teeth" (v. 16). The Talmud states: "Shaming another in public is like shedding blood." This is no exaggeration in the light of innumerable cases of murder triggered by insults. Among these are some of the shocking incidents of schoolyard shooting rampages of students enraged by the jibes of classmates or teachers. How well the Bible said it: "Death and life are in the power of the tongue" (Proverbs 18:21).

∾ PSALM 36 ∾

For the Leader. [A Psalm] of David the servant of the LORD.

2 Transgression speaketh to the wicked, methinks—
There is no fear of God before his eyes.
3 For it flattereth him in his eyes,
Until his iniquity be found, and he be hated.
4 The words of his mouth are iniquity and deceit;
He hath left off to be wise, to do good.

5 He deviseth iniquity upon his bed;
He setteth himself in a way that is not good;
He abhorreth not evil.
6 Thy lovingkindness, O LORD, is in the heavens;
Thy faithfulness reacheth unto the skies.
7 Thy righteousness is like the mighty mountains;
Thy judgments are like the great deep;
Man and beast Thou preservest, O LORD.

8 How precious is Thy lovingkindness,
  O God!
  And the children of men take refuge
  in the shadow of Thy wings.
9 They are abundantly satisfied with
  the fatness of Thy house;
  And Thou makest them drink of the
  river of Thy pleasures.
10 For with Thee is the fountain of life;
  In Thy light do we see light.

11 O continue Thy lovingkindness unto
  them that know Thee;

And Thy righteousness to the upright
  in heart.
12 Let not the foot of pride overtake me,
  And let not the hand of the wicked
  drive me away.
13 There are the workers of iniquity
  fallen;
  They are thrust down, and are not
  able to rise.

❧

In God's Light We See Light

How do you connect with God? What kind of relationship can you have with the Almighty? Psalm 36 refers to God as the Protector of life: "Man and beast You deliver, O God . . . mankind finds shelter under Your wings" (v. 7, 8).

God is also the Provider: "They are satisfied with the abundance of Your house" (v. 9). Then the psalmist says something memorable about our connection with God. God is not only the source of life, but also of our powers of perception: "With You is the fountain of life and in Your light we see light" (v. 10). As impassioned as the psalmist is in his adoration of God, so is he in his anger with the wicked who do not recognize God's majesty and plot mischief day and night (see v. 2–5). The God of love is also the God of justice who will bring down the evildoers, never to rise again: "There are the workers of iniquity fallen; they are thrown down and unable to rise" (v. 13).

❧

Reflection: God, Our Preserver

This psalm radiates positive thinking, the joy of life and thanksgiving. The psalmist is overwhelmed by the immensity of the visible and invisible world. What we can see is only an infinitesimal fraction of the universe. Nearly all of it is unknowable and invisible. If we perceive any part of it at all, it is because of God's gracious gifts of perception. Light created by God illuminates the things we see through eyes divinely created as part of the human body and mind: "In Your light we see light" (v. 10).

The psalmist thanks God for the preservation of life: "Man and beast You preserve, O God" (v. 7). Physical and spiritual laws stand out like mountains, symbols of permanence: "Your righteousness is like the mighty mountains" (v. 7). But much of God's work and purpose is hidden in the depth of the unknown: "Your judgments are like the great deeps" (v. 7).

The psalmist acknowledges God's love for humankind: "How precious is Your loving-kindness, O God" (v. 8). Only a loving God would enable us to find joy in life. While others are obsessed with suffering and evil, this psalm brims with appreciation for all the good we human beings may enjoy in this life: "They are abundantly satisfied . . . You make them drink of the river of Your pleasures" (v. 9).

❧ PSALM 37 ❧

[A Psalm] of David.

Fret not thyself because of evildoers,
Neither be thou envious against them
that work unrighteousness.
2 For they shall soon wither like the
grass,
And fade as the green herb.

3 Trust in the LORD, and do good;
Dwell in the land, and cherish
faithfulness.
4 So shalt thou delight thyself in the
LORD;
And He shall give thee the petitions
of thy heart.

5 Commit thy way unto the LORD;
Trust also in Him, and He will bring
it to pass.
6 And He will make thy righteousness
to go forth as the light,
And thy right as the noonday.

7 Resign thyself unto the LORD, and
wait patiently for Him;
Fret not thyself because of him who
prospereth in his way,
Because of the man who bringeth
wicked devices to pass.

8 Cease from anger, and forsake wrath;

Fret not thyself, it tendeth only to
evil-doing.
9 For evil-doers shall be cut off;
But those that wait for the LORD, they
shall inherit the land.

10 And yet a little while, and the wicked
is no more;
Yea, thou shalt look well at his place,
and he is not.
11 But the humble shall inherit the land,
And delight themselves in the abundance of peace.

12 The wicked plotteth against the
righteous,
And gnasheth at him with his teeth.
13 The LORD doth laugh at him;
For He seeth that his day is coming.

14 The wicked have drawn out the
sword, and have bent their bow;
To cast down the poor and needy,
To slay such as are upright in the way;
15 Their sword shall enter into their
own heart,
And their bows shall be broken.

16 Better is a little that the righteous
hath
Than the abundance of many wicked.

17 For the arms of the wicked shall be
    broken;
  But the LORD upholdeth the
    righteous.

18 The LORD knoweth the days of them
    that are wholehearted;
  And their inheritance shall be for
    ever.
19 They shall not be ashamed in the
    time of evil;
  And in the days of famine they shall
    be satisfied.

20 For the wicked shall perish,
  And the enemies of the LORD shall be
    as the fat of lambs—
  They shall pass away in smoke, they
    shall pass away.

21 The wicked borroweth, and payeth
    not;
  But the righteous dealeth graciously,
    and giveth.
22 For such as are blessed of Him shall
    inherit the land;
  And they that are cursed of Him shall
    be cut off.

23 It is of the LORD that a man's goings
    are established;
  And He delighted in his way.
24 Though he fall, he shall not be utterly
    cast down;
  For the LORD upholdeth his hand.

25 I have been young, and now am old;
  Yet have I not seen the righteous
    forsaken,
  Nor his seed begging bread.
26 All the day long he dealeth graciously,
    and lendeth;
  And his seed is blessed.

27 Depart from evil, and do good;
  And dwell for evermore.
28 For the LORD loveth justice,
  And forsaketh not His saints;
  They are preserved for ever;
  But the seed of the wicked shall be
    cut off.

29 The righteous shall inherit the land,
  And dwell therein for ever.

30 The mouth of the righteous uttereth
    wisdom,
  And his tongue speaketh justice.
31 The law of his God is in his heart;
  None of his steps slide.

32 The wicked watcheth the righteous,
  And seeketh to slay him.
33 The LORD will not leave him in his
    hand,
  Nor suffer him to be condemned
    when he is judged.

34 Wait for the LORD, and keep His way,
  And He will exalt thee to inherit the
    land;
  When the wicked are cut off, thou
    shalt see it.

35 I have seen the wicked in great power,
  And spreading himself like a leafy tree
    in its native soil.
36 But one passed by, and, lo, he was not;
  Yea, I sought him, but he could not be
    found.

37 Mark the man of integrity, and behold
    the upright;
  For there is a future for the man of
    peace.
38 But transgressors shall be destroyed
    together;
  The future of the wicked shall be cut
    off.

39 But the salvation of the righteous is of
    the LORD;
  He is their stronghold in the time of
    trouble.
40 And the LORD helpeth them, and
    delivereth them;
  He delivereth them from the wicked,
    and saveth them,
  Because they have taken refuge in
    Him.

Don't Fight Fire with Fire

Can you refrain from resenting someone who hates you and wants to do you harm? It would seem unnatural not to strike back at an adversary who threatens you. The authors of the previous two psalms (35 and 36) have harsh words for personal enemies. One begs God to fight his battle: "Fight against them that fight against me. . . . let them be as chaff in the wind" (Psalm 35:4–5). The other, exasperated by the arrogance of adversaries, wants God to strike them down: "There are the evildoers fallen, thrust down and unable to rise" (Psalm 36:13).

Psalm 37 sounds like the opposite side in the debate. This psalmist, too, has had his problems with despicable persons, but instead of anger, he suggests patience and trust in God's judgments: "Fret not because of evildoers" (v. 1). Make sure that you keep yourself clean and turn your burden of anxiety over to God: "Trust in God and do good. . . . turn your way over to God; Trust in Him and He will act" (v. 3, 5).

The psalmist wisely argues that anger will only make matters worse: "Let go of anger and abandon wrath; fret not, it can only do harm" (v. 8). In due time, "the arms of the wicked shall be broken, whereas the Lord upholds the righteous" (v. 17).

Stressing the positive, he repeats the words of Psalm 34:5: "Depart from evil and do good," to which he adds: "and you will endure" (v. 27). The righteous will remain steady under trial as long as "the law of his God is in his heart; his feet do not slip" (v. 31).

The psalmist reaffirms belief in the rule of justice in human affairs. The righteous may suffer for a time, but will outlast the wicked: "Mark the blameless and note the upright, for the future belongs to the man of peace" (v. 37). The opposite fate awaits the wicked: "Transgressors shall be utterly destroyed; the future of the wicked shall be cut off" (v. 38).

Reflection: Anger and Resentment

A major theme of this psalm is the management of anger: "Fret not because of evildoers, neither be incensed against those who work unrighteousness" (v. 1). Fretting is an explosive cocktail of irritation and anger. Anger rapidly inflates itself and drives a person to lash out against the source of annoyance. Angry words lead to violent acts, which makes the control of anger all the more important. But that is easier said than done.

The Bible pays high tribute to a person who can keep his anger under control: "He that is slow to anger is superior to the mighty; and he that controls his spirit to one who conquers a city" (Proverbs 16:32). What guidance does Psalm 37 offer for the control of anger?

The best first aid against the vehemence of anger is delay: "Be patient and wait for God" (v. 7). Take time out to cool off. Thomas Jefferson advised: "When angry, count 10 before you speak; if very angry, 100." But suppressed anger does not disappear. The fire of anger may have been subdued, but its embers continue to glow as resentment. For the long run, to put an end to it altogether, the psalmist urges us to "wait for God" (v. 7).

The wrong that aroused your anger is also of concern to God. "Turn your way over to God. Trust in Him and He will act" (v. 5). God is not neutral in the struggle between good and evil. You are not alone. God "will make your righteousness shine as the light and your justice as the noonday" (v. 6). God's moral law will in time bring down the wrongdoer and vindicate the upright. The psalm ends with supreme confidence: "Mark the person of integrity and behold the upright; for there is a future for the person of peace. But transgressors shall be destroyed; the future of the wicked shall be cut off" (v. 37).

❧ PSALM 38 ❧

A Psalm of David, to make memorial.

2 O LORD, rebuke me not in Thine anger;
Neither chasten me in Thy wrath.

3 For Thine arrows are gone deep into me,
And Thy hand is come down upon me.

4 There is no soundness in my flesh because of Thine indignation;
Neither is there any health in my bones because of my sin.

5 For mine iniquities are gone over my head;
As a heavy burden they are too heavy for me.

6 My wounds are noisome, they fester,
Because of my foolishness.

7 I am bent and bowed down greatly;
I go mourning all the day.

8 For my loins are filled with burning;
And there is no soundness in my flesh.

9 I am benumbed and sore crushed;
I groan by reason of the moaning of my heart.

10 LORD, all my desire is before Thee;
And my sighing is not hid from Thee.

11 My heart fluttereth, my strength faileth me;
As for the light of mine eyes, it also is gone from me.

12 My friends and my companions stand aloof from my plague;
And my kinsmen stand afar off.

13 They also that seek after my life lay
    snares for me;
And they that seek my hurt speak
    crafty devices,
And utter deceits all the day.
14 But I am as a deaf man, I hear not;
And I am as a dumb man that openeth
    not his mouth.
15 Yea, I am become as a man that
    heareth not,
And in whose mouth are no
    arguments.

16 For in Thee, O LORD, do I hope;
Thou wilt answer, O LORD my God.
17 For I said: "Lest they rejoice over me;
When my foot slippeth, they magnify
    themselves against me."

18 For I am ready to halt,
And my pain is continually before me.
19 For I do declare mine iniquity;
I am full of care because of my sin.
20 But mine enemies are strong in
    health;
And they that hate me wrongfully are
    multiplied.
21 They also that repay evil for good
Are adversaries unto me, because I
    follow the thing that is good.
22 Forsake me not, O LORD;
O my God, be not far from me.
23 Make haste to help me,
O LORD, my salvation.

The Trial of Illness

Illness may change your whole view of life, your attitude toward others, and your self-image. The author of Psalm 38 is afflicted by grave illness and like all persons so stricken wonders, Why is this happening to me? What did I do wrong? This is a question that torments many sufferers. Is illness really punishment for wrongdoing? You may not think so, but the psalmist is sure that he is paying the penalty for his sins. His suffering prompts him to a critical review of his conduct. He has mixed feelings about himself. Conscious of guilt, he seeks relief by way of confession: "I confess my guilt" (v. 19). On the other hand, he regards himself superior to his enemies who hate him because he follows "the thing that is good" (v. 21).

The psalmist displays some of the hypersensitivity typical of the sick. He feels neglected and avoided: "My friends and companions stay away . . . and my relatives keep far from me" (v. 12). He feels cut off from people. Words fail him: "I am like one who does not hear and has nothing to say" (v. 15). However, there is a ray of light that dispels the darkness of his gloomy mood. He is not alone. God is with him and God knows of his misery: "O Lord, You know what I need and my pain is not hidden from You" (v. 10).

The crisis has brought him closer to God: "I wait for You, O God, You will answer, my God . . . Hasten to help me, O God, my deliverer" (v. 16, 23).

❧

Reflection: Guilt

The psalmist comes through as a thoroughly honest and sincere person without a shred of self-righteousness. He is ill and in pain and believes that his suffering is punishment for his sins. Deserted by friends and family and maligned by enemies, he makes no defense for himself. He is too worn out to argue. He acts as though deaf and keeps silent (v. 13–15). Among his detractors are persons for whom he once did favors, and now they "repay evil for good" (v. 21). Rather than trying to restore his former reputation and status in the community, he wants, above all, to be right with God: "God, all my desire is before You" (v. 10). For this purpose he makes full confession of his failings, sins, and foolishness, counting on God for relief from his burden of guilt: "For in You, O God, I hope; You will answer" (v. 16).

Not many have tolerance for criticism. They don't want to hear about their faults. They resent so-called guilt trips. But how can we hope to correct and reform our ways unless we confront what's wrong with us? Benjamin Franklin said we should be grateful to our enemies for telling us our faults.

The psalmist shows courage in coping with guilt. He recognizes all the wrong within him and shows remorse for his misdeeds. Finally, somewhat relieved by his confession, he throws himself upon the mercy of God: "Forsake me not, O God . . . be not far from me. Hasten to help me, O God, my deliverer" (v. 22–23).

❧ PSALM 39 ❧

For the Leader, for Jeduthun. A Psalm of David.

2I said: "I will take heed to my ways, That I sin not with my tongue; I will keep a curb upon my mouth, While the wicked is before me."
3I was dumb with silence; I held my peace, had no comfort; And my pain was held in check.
4My heart waxed hot within me; While I was musing, the fire kindled; Then spoke I with my tongue:

5"LORD, make me to know mine end, And the measure of my days, what it is; Let me know how short-lived I am.
6Behold, Thou hast made my days as hand-breadths; And mine age is as nothing before Thee; Surely every man at his best estate is altogether vanity. Selah
7Surely man walketh as a mere semblance; Surely for vanity they are in turmoil;

He heapeth up riches, and knoweth not who shall gather them.

8And now, LORD, what wait I for?
My hope, it is in Thee.
9Deliver me from all my transgressions;
Make me not the reproach of the base.
10I am dumb, I open not my mouth;
Because Thou hast done it.
11Remove Thy stroke from off me;
I am consumed by the blow of Thy hand.

12With rebukes dost Thou chasten man for iniquity,
And like a moth Thou makest his beauty to consume away;
Surely every man is vanity.   Selah

13Hear my prayer, O LORD, and give ear unto my cry;
Keep not silence at my tears;
For I am a stranger with Thee,
A sojourner, as all my fathers were.
14Look away from me, that I may take comfort,
Before I go hence, and be no more."

Is Life Worth Living?

How do you face death—not somebody else's, but your own? Do you remember when you first came to grips with the thought of your death? While young, the idea of dying scarcely occurs to us, and if it does, we quickly put it out of our mind. But later in life, events force us to reckon seriously with our mortality. It dawns upon us how much of an endangered species we are. We realize that our life hangs on a thin thread.

We do not know what triggered the psalmist's shocked recognition of the brevity of life. Was it a narrow escape from danger? A health crisis? The loss of a dear one? Whatever the cause, he first reacted with stunned silence: "I was dumb with silence. . . . My heart was in turmoil" (v. 3, 4). He did not dare say aloud what was on his mind, lest his words encourage the godless in their cynicism: "I will hold my tongue in the presence of the wicked" (v. 2).

However, his sense of despair could not be repressed much longer. What troubled him was not just the brevity of life, as short as "handbreadths" (v. 6), nor was it the fear of death, but a paralyzing sense of the worthlessness and vanity of human existence. What is the use of all this hustle and bustle? "Man is a mere futility, . . . he gains wealth, not knowing who will use it. . . . Everything dear to him vanishes like a moth" (v. 7, 12). Stripped of hope and meaning in this life, he turns to God: "What may I expect, O God? In You lies my hope" (v. 8).

The psalmist was left to wonder about the brevity of life. Is it a waste and futility? Believing, however, that he may have dialogue with God, he hoped God would pay attention to his prayer and tears even though he was of small account, a mere "stranger and sojourner":

"Hear my prayer, O God, and give ear to my cry; keep not silent at my tears; for I am a stranger with You and a sojourner, as all my ancestors were" (v. 13). Having scaled down his expectations, he would settle for very little: "Spare me and let me have some comfort before I go and be no more" (v. 14).

∞

Reflection: Death

From the human point of view, death is an incomprehensible scandal. It drives home not only the brevity of life but the indignity of being reduced, in the end, to a condition no better than that of insects. Franz Kafka, in one of his parables, tells of the transformation of a human being into a cockroach. The psalmist compares man to a moth: "Like a moth You make his beauty to be consumed. Surely every person is vanity" (v. 12). Other psalmists affirm the presence of God at the very heights of enthusiasm. The author of Psalm 8, for example, is enthralled by God's majesty, reflected in the heavens and in the order of nature on Earth. However small the human creature appears to be in the cosmic context, man still is God's crowning creation, destined to rule over all other creatures on Earth. The author of Psalm 19 is jubilant at the sight of the heavenly bodies that run their orbits, under God's laws and God's spiritual gifts to man. On the other hand, the author of Psalm 39 speaks to us out of the depths of futility as he contemplates the prospect of annihilation in death. In his condition of helplessness, he feels driven into the arms of God: "And now, God, what do I wait for? My hope, it is in You" (v. 8). He believes in his abiding connection with God through prayer: "Hear my prayer, O God, and give ear unto my cry. Keep not silence at my tears . . ." (v. 13). Evidently, the human being, even if reduced to a moth, is significant enough to have a relationship with God.

∞ PSALM 40 ∞

For the Leader. A Psalm of David.

2 I waited patiently for the LORD;
And He inclined unto me, and heard my cry.
3 He brought me up also out of the tumultuous pit, out of the miry clay;
And He set my feet upon a rock, He established my goings.
4 And He hath put a new song in my mouth, even praise unto our God;
Many shall see, and fear,
And shall trust in the LORD.

5 Happy is the man that hath made the
LORD his trust,
And hath not turned unto the
arrogant, nor unto such as fall away
treacherously.
6 Many things hast Thou done, O
LORD my God,
Even Thy wondrous works, and Thy
thoughts toward us;
There is none to be compared unto
Thee!
If I would declare and speak of them,
They are more than can be told.
7 Sacrifice and meal-offering Thou hast
no delight in;
Mine ears hast Thou opened;
Burnt-offering and sin-offering hast
Thou not required.
8 Then said I: "Lo, I am come
With the roll of a book which is
prescribed for me;
9 I delight to do Thy will, O my God;
Yea, Thy law is in my inmost parts."
10 I have preached righteousness in the
great congregation,
Lo, I did not refrain my lips;
O LORD, Thou knowest.
11 I have not hid Thy righteousness
within my heart;
I have declared Thy faithfulness and
Thy salvation;
I have not concealed Thy mercy
and Thy truth from the great
congregation.

12 Thou, O LORD, wilt not withhold
Thy compassions from me;
Let Thy mercy and Thy truth contin-
ually preserve me.

13 For innumerable evils have compassed me about,
Mine iniquities have overtaken me, so
that I am not able to look up;
They are more than the hairs of my
head, and my heart hath failed me.
14 Be pleased, O LORD, to deliver me;
O LORD, make haste to help me.
15 Let them be ashamed and abashed
together
That seek after my soul to sweep it
away;
Let them be turned backward and
brought to confusion
That delight in my hurt.
16 Let them be appalled by reason of
their shame
That say unto me: "Aha, aha."
17 Let all those that seek Thee rejoice
and be glad in Thee;
Let such as love Thy salvation say
continually:
"The LORD be magnified."
18 But, as for me, that am poor and
needy,
The LORD will account it unto me;
Thou art my help and my deliverer;
O my God, tarry not.

Back to God for More Help

If you were in need of help, it would make sense to turn first to someone who had helped before. For this very reason, the psalmist, overwhelmed by a host of new troubles, reaches out to God, his helper in
the past: "He pulled me out of the dreadful pit, the slippery clay, and
firmly set my feet on a rock" (v. 3).

But does he deserve God's help? How can he be sure of God's
favor? The psalmist makes three points. First, he offers fervent praise
to God: "Many things You have done, O God. . . . more than I can put
into words" (v. 6). Then he declares obedience to God's commands: "I

delight to do your will, O my God. Your teaching is deep in my heart" (v. 9). Finally, he refers to his public propagation of the faith: "I have spoken publicly of your righteousness in a great assembly . . . I did not hold back my words nor did I keep to myself Your beneficence" (v. 10–11).

Now he hopes that God will respond with the help he so desperately needs: "You are my helper and deliverer, O my God; do not delay" (v. 18).

Note that Psalm 40:14–18 duplicates, with some minor changes, Psalm 70.

∞

Reflection: Indecision

Change is the law of life. You can also say that about personal problems. They are subject to constant change, for better or worse. One of the problems likely to grow progressively worse is that of indecision. If you can't choose between two options, postponement of the decision will take its toll. A proverb says: "Between two stools, one falls to the ground."

Something like that may have happened to the psalmist, who found himself sinking ever more deeply into a swamp of indecision until he was brought up again on firm footing: "I waited patiently for God. . . . He brought me up out of the miry clay; and He set my foot upon a rock. He established my goings" (v. 2–3). The psychologist William James said, "There is no more miserable human being than one in whom nothing is habitual but indecision." When you can't make up your mind about something, you get that sinking feeling. Indecision is enfeebling. What hinders your ability to act decisively? There are any number of causes: fear of losing what you have; fear of the risk in a new situation; unwillingness to pay the price of adjustment; self-doubt as to whether you will be equal to the new challenge; and so on. What a relief it is to take a stand and act. For this the psalmist thanked God: "He set my foot upon a rock. He established my goings." Somehow, in the course of his prayers and reflections, he received God's guidance and from it the power to act: "I delight to do Your will, O my God" (v. 9).

❧ PSALM 41 ❧

For the Leader. A Psalm of David.

2 Happy is he that considereth the poor;
  The LORD will deliver him in the day of evil.
3 The LORD preserve him, and keep him alive, let him be called happy in the land;
  And deliver not Thou him unto the greed of his enemies.
4 The LORD support him upon the bed of illness;
  Mayest Thou turn all his lying down in his sickness.
5 As for me, I said: "O LORD, be gracious unto me;
  Heal my soul; for I have sinned against Thee."
6 Mine enemies speak evil of me:
  "When shall he die, and his name perish?"
7 And if one come to see me, he speaketh falsehood;
  His heart gathereth iniquity to itself;
  When he goeth abroad, he speaketh of it.

8 All that hate me whisper together against me,
  Against me do they devise my hurt:
9 "An evil thing cleaveth fast unto him;
  And now that he lieth, he shall rise up no more."
10 Yea, mine own familiar friend, in whom I trusted, who did eat of my bread,
  Hath lifted up his heel against me.

11 But Thou, O LORD, be gracious unto me, and raise me up,
  That I may requite them.
12 By this I know that Thou delightest in me,
  That mine enemy doth not triumph over me.
13 And as for me, Thou upholdest me because of mine integrity,
  And settest me before Thy face for ever.

14 Blessed be the LORD, the God of Israel,
  From everlasting and to everlasting.
  Amen, and Amen.

❧

The Test of Friendship

If someone befriends you when you are riding high, you can't be sure whether he is a true friend, or an opportunist who looks for an advantage by associating with you. A real test of your friend's sincerity is his behavior when you are brought low. Will he stand by you? Will he offer help?

The author of Psalm 41 laments a double blow. First he is stricken with grave illness; then he is betrayed by his friend: "My trusted friend, who ate my bread, has kicked me" (v. 10). This bitter disappointment prompts him to offer a special prayer for those who act kindly toward the weak: "Happy is he who is thoughtful of the lowly . . . May the Lord keep him happy and alive" (v. 2–3).

What about those false friends who, visiting him on his sickbed, pretend concern but in their hearts wish him dead (v. 6–7)? He hopes that his recovery will frustrate those enemies and prove that God has not forsaken him: "O God, have mercy and raise me up . . . When mine enemies can do me no harm, I shall know that you are pleased with me" (v. 11–12). The treachery of his former friends turns him all the more to God, on whom one can rely come what may: "As for me, You will maintain me . . . and keep me forever in Your presence" (v. 13).

∞

Reflection: Illness

Illness is a trial in every sense of the word as affliction and test. The loss of health is surely the most common of all afflictions. Who can count the number of diseases that could befall us? And who can escape them all? Illness affects us not only physically but also emotionally and mentally. Most often, the ill person is plagued by intensified feelings of insecurity, suspicion, and guilt. Without naming a specific transgression, the psalmist calls himself a sinner: "Heal me, for I have sinned." (v. 5).

Many a person smitten with illness convinces himself, "I must have done something wrong to bring on this tribulation." He suspects that others want to do him harm. He imagines that they are gossiping about him: "Mine enemies speak evil of me" (v. 6). They look forward to his death, asking, "When shall he die?" (v. 6). He even distrusts visitors. They only come to see how he is deteriorating: "If one comes to see me, his words are false" (v. 7). He is afraid others are taking advantage of his weakened condition: "All who hate me whisper together against me, planning to do me harm" (v. 8). Most painful is the thought that an old friend has also turned against him. In his despondency, the only comfort he can find is the faith that when all else fails and people prove to be false and untrustworthy, the door to God's love remains open: "You will maintain me . . . and keep me forever in Your presence" (v. 13).

∞ PSALM 42 ∞

For the Leader; Maschil of the sons of Korah.

2 As the hart panteth after the water brooks,
So panteth my soul after Thee, O God.
3 My soul thirsteth for God, for the living God:

"When shall I come and appear before God?"
4 My tears have been my food day and night,
While they say unto me all the day: "Where is thy God?"
5 These things I remember, and pour out my soul within me,

How I passed on with the throng, and
  led them to the house of God,
With the voice of joy and praise, a
  multitude keeping holyday.
6Why art thou cast down, O my soul?
  And why moanest thou within me?
Hope thou in God; for I shall yet
  praise Him
For the salvation of His countenance.

7O my God, my soul is cast down
  within me;
Therefore do I remember Thee from
  the land of Jordan,
And the Hermons, from the hill
  Mizar.
8Deep calleth unto deep at the voice of
  Thy cataracts;
All Thy waves and Thy billows are
  gone over me.

9By day the LORD will command His
  lovingkindness,
And in the night His song shall be
  with me,
Even a prayer unto the God of my
  life.
10I will say unto God my Rock: "Why
  hast Thou forgotten me?
Why go I mourning under the
  oppression of the enemy?"
11As with a crushing in my bones, mine
  adversaries taunt me;
While they say unto me all the day:
  "Where is thy God?"
12Why art thou cast down, O my soul?
  And why moanest thou within me?
Hope thou in God; for I shall yet
  praise Him,
The salvation of my countenance, and
  my God.

The Dark Night of the Soul

What is worse, not getting what you want, or losing what you had?
The author of Psalm 42 is among those who mourn for happier times.
Most of all, he misses the celebrations he shared with friends: "These
things I remember . . . How I walked with the crowd in procession to
the Temple, singing and feasting" (v. 5). Now, far away from the people with whom he used to celebrate, he is taunted by his pagan neighbors: "Where is your God?" (v. 4). The question hurts all the more
because he feels out of touch with God and yearns for His presence:
"As the hind pants after the water brooks, so pants my soul after You,
O God. My soul thirsts for God, for the living God" (v. 2–3).

What kind of thirst is this? Is it a craving for something like a "God
experience"? Or does the psalmist want to hear God calling him?
There is no response to his cry. Nothing is happening. Yet somehow
the mere expression of his yearning raises his hope to feel God's presence again. He keeps repeating to himself: "Hope in God. I will yet
praise Him, my very present help, my God" (v. 12).

Reflection: God Experience

Many believers in God wonder if the God in Whose existence they
believe can ever be encountered in a personal experience. For some it

is a matter of curiosity. Others imagine that the very presence of God must be terrifying. The psalmist, a most devout person, speaks of his yearning for God, for the living presence of God, as something like a thirst that must be quenched. How can such yearning be satisfied? People choose different ways to gain a sense of God's presence. Many think that a God experience requires special preparations: clearing the mind of all other concerns and preoccupations; a quiet, isolated place for meditation; reading the Bible and other inspirational writings; gazing at the starry sky or some awesome landscape. Most people turn to prayer as the most direct channel of communication with God. The psalmist remembers the happiness he felt at worship in the sanctuary: "How I passed on with the crowd and led them to the house of God, with song and praise, a multitude of celebrants" (v. 5). He also practices daily prayer privately at home: "By day may God extend His faithful care so that by night I might have a song for Him, a prayer to the God of my life" (v. 9). Jewish mystics of the Hasidic movement stress the point that God is neither absent nor hidden but present at all times, wherever our thoughts reach out to Him. The psalmist comes to a similar conclusion. The God he yearns for is close at hand: "Hope in God. I shall yet praise Him, my *ever present* help, my God" (v. 12).

❧ PSALM 43 ❧

Be Thou my judge, O God, and plead my cause against an ungodly nation;
O deliver me from the deceitful and unjust man.
2 For Thou art the God of my strength; why hast Thou cast me off?
Why go I mourning under the oppression of the enemy?
3 O send out Thy light and Thy truth; let them lead me;
Let them bring me unto Thy holy mountain, and to Thy dwelling-places;

4 Then will I go unto the altar of God, unto God, my exceeding joy;
And praise Thee upon the harp, O God, my God.
5 Why art thou cast down, O my soul? And why moanest thou within me?
Hope thou in God; for I shall yet praise Him,
The salvation of my countenance, and my God.

❧

Turn to the Future

When remembrance of your losses in the past deepens your gloom, thoughts about the future may change your mood and cheer you up.

The author of Psalm 42 bemoans the lost happiness he had known in past years. However, in Psalm 43, generally believed to be a continuation of the previous psalm, the author is in a much better mood as he imagines the joys that are in store for him, if only God will lead him by His light in the right way: "O let Your light and truth lead me. Then will I go to the altar of God and be with God, my great delight" (v. 3–4). No longer worrying about his enemies and about being abandoned by God, he sees no reason for being depressed. He says to himself: "Why be despondent? Hope in God; I will yet praise Him, my very present help and my God" (v. 5).

❧

Reflection: Overcoming Gloom

What remedy is there for depression other than psychotherapy and medication? The French pharmacist and hypnotist Emile Coue advocated a formula of autosuggestion or self-hypnosis. Look into the mirror every morning and say aloud, "Every day, in every way, I'm getting better and better." Coueism was wildly popular for a few years in the early part of the last century, but then faded. One reason for its ineffectiveness is that Coue's formula keeps the mind fixed on the problematic present day, which is the very source of gloom. Psalm 43 suggests another kind of self-help: Look beyond today with its troubles. Right now all seems dark and gloomy. But there is light at the end of the tunnel. If today is dismal, pin your hopes on tomorrow. The future may hold better prospects. The psalmist is trying to shake off his gloom. His problem—conflict with a "deceitful and unjust man" (v. 1)—won't go away. But neither will it last forever. Turning his mind to the future, he asks for God's guidance: "O send Your light and Your truth; let them lead me" (v. 3). Once again, he dares to hope for better days: "Hope in God . . . I will yet praise Him, my very present help, my God" (v. 5).

❧ PSALM 44 ❧

For the Leader; [a Psalm] of the sons of Korah. Maschil.

2 O God, we have heard with our ears, our fathers have told us;
A work Thou didst in their days, in the days of old.

3 Thou with Thy hand didst drive out the nations, and didst plant them in;
Thou didst break the peoples, and didst spread them abroad.

4 For not by their own sword did they get the land in possession,

Neither did their own arm save them;
But Thy right hand, and Thine arm,
  and the light of Thy countenance,
Because Thou wast favourable unto
  them.

5 Thou art my King, O God;
  Command the salvation of Jacob.
6 Through Thee do we push down our
    adversaries;
  Through Thy name do we tread them
    under that rise up against us.
7 For I trust not in my bow,
  Neither can my sword save me.
8 But Thou hast saved us from our
    adversaries,
  And hast put them to shame that hate
    us.
9 In God have we gloried all the day,
  And we will give thanks unto Thy
    name for ever.   Selah

10 Yet Thou hast cast off, and brought us
    to confusion;
  And goest not forth with our hosts.
11 Thou makest us to turn back from the
    adversary;
  And they that hate us spoil at their
    will.
12 Thou hast given us like sheep to be
    eaten;
  And hast scattered us among the
    nations.
13 Thou sellest Thy people for small
    gain,
  And hast not set their prices high.
14 Thou makest us a taunt to our
    neighbours,
  A scorn and a derision to them that
    are round about us.
15 Thou makest us a byword among the
    nations,
  A shaking of the head among the
    peoples.

16 All the day is my confusion before
    me,
  And the shame of my face hath
    covered me,
17 For the voice of him that taunteth and
    blasphemeth;
  By reason of the enemy and the
    revengeful.

18 All this is come upon us; yet have we
    not forgotten Thee,
  Neither have we been false to Thy
    covenant.
19 Our heart is not turned back,
  Neither have our steps declined from
    Thy path;
20 Though Thou hast crushed us into a
    place of jackals,
  And covered us with the shadow of
    death.
21 If we had forgotten the name of our
    God,
  Or spread forth our hands to a
    strange god;
22 Would not God search this out?
  For He knoweth the secrets of the
    heart.
23 Nay, but for Thy sake are we killed all
    the day;
  We are accounted as sheep for the
    slaughter.

24 Awake, why sleepest Thou, O LORD?
  Arouse Thyself, cast not off for ever.
25 Wherefore hidest Thou Thy face,
  And forgettest our affliction and our
    oppression?
26 For our soul is bowed down to the
    dust;
  Our belly cleaveth unto the earth.
27 Arise for our help,
  And redeem us for Thy mercy's sake.

Keeping the Faith Despite God's Silence

God's involvement in human affairs and the effect of prayer are among
the mysteries of religious faith. Does God take note of our prayers?

Even if we get what we pray for, how do we know that it was God's doing? Reading Psalm 44, you encounter a Hebrew patriot who implores God's help for his defeated people. He is puzzled by the turn of events. He gives God credit for his nation's victories, but also attributes to God the misery into which his people have fallen: "Through You we have driven off our enemies. . . . You have turned us over to be consumed like sheep and scattered among the nations" (v. 6, 12).

The psalmist has no proof of God's involvement in the battles Israel has won or lost. It is not a matter of knowledge, but belief. But that belief is now badly shaken in the crisis that gives birth to this psalm. Israel, God's partner in the covenant, has suffered a crushing defeat. Why is there no help from God? The psalmist rings the alarm: "Awake, why do You sleep? Why do you hide Yourself, paying no attention to our plight and oppression?" (v. 24–25).

This psalm does not explain the workings of prayer, nor does it solve the riddle of God's involvement in human affairs. Though confused and disheartened, the psalmist holds on to his faith: "All this has happened to us, yet we have not forgotten You, neither have we been false to Your covenant. Our heart has not turned, neither have we swerved from Your pathway" (v. 18–19). It is this same passionate loyalty to God that inspired an unknown Jew, hiding from the Nazis in a secret underground shelter in Cologne, to scribble on the wall:

> I believe in the sun though it is not shining
> I believe in love even when feeling it not
> I believe in God even when He is silent.

※

Reflection: God in Hiding

As you read to the end of this psalm, you may be somewhat shocked by the way the psalmist talks to God: "Awake, why do You sleep, O God? Arouse Yourself. . . . Why do You hide Yourself . . . ?" (v. 24–25). Is this a proper way to address God? Isn't the psalmist impudent, even insulting to God? Consider the situation: The psalmist has just returned from the battlefield where his people suffered a disastrous defeat. Horrible scenes of slaughter are fresh in his mind. Where was God when Israel, God's partner in covenant, most needed help? The psalmist, speaking for his people, feels terribly let down by God. He is bursting with anger and despair. He can no longer contain his feelings. A person who tells you exactly how he feels must trust you and feel close to you. The psalmist's bluntness is not meant as an insult, but as proof of his intimacy with God. He is free to show God his hurt. This attitude of frankness toward God is well documented in various passages of the Bible and later became characteristic of the Jewish approach to God. A person may question God's ways, express doubts, even argue and protest before God. Abraham dared criticize God's intention of destroying the city of Sodom: What if there were some righteous persons among its population? "Will You indeed sweep away the righteous with the wicked? . . . Shall not the Judge of all the earth do justly?" (Genesis 18:23, 25).

While protesting God's failure to save his people from defeat, the psalmist has no intention of renouncing his faith. In the end, he turns to God again: "Arise for our help and redeem us for Your mercy's sake" (v. 27). The American poet Edmund Clarence Stedman commented on the candor of the Bible: "In the narrative books of the Bible, the good and the bad appear without disguise. All is set forth with a frankness that made the heart of the Hebrew tent-dweller the heart of the world thereafter."

❧ Psalm 45 ❧

For the Leader; upon Shoshannim;
　　[a Psalm] of the sons of Korah.
　　Maschil. A Song of loves.

2 My heart overfloweth with a goodly
　　matter;
　I say: "My work is concerning a king";
　My tongue is the pen of a ready
　　writer.

3 Thou art fairer than the children of
　　men;
　Grace is poured upon thy lips;
　Therefore God hath blessed thee for
　　ever.
4 Gird thy sword upon thy thigh, O
　　mighty one,
　Thy glory and thy majesty.
5 And in thy majesty prosper, ride on,
　In behalf of truth and meekness and
　　righteousness;
　And let thy right hand teach thee
　　tremendous things.
6 Thine arrows are sharp—

The peoples fall under thee—
　[They sink] into the heart of the
　　king's enemies.
7 Thy throne given of God is for ever
　　and ever;
　A sceptre of equity is the sceptre of
　　thy kingdom.
8 Thou hast loved righteousness, and
　　hated wickedness;
　Therefore God, thy God, hath
　　anointed thee
　With the oil of gladness above thy
　　fellows.
9 Myrrh, and aloes, and cassia are all
　　thy garments;
　Out of ivory palaces stringed
　　instruments have made thee glad.
10 Kings' daughters are among thy
　　favourites;
　At thy right hand doth stand the
　　queen in gold of Ophir.
11 "Hearken, O daughter, and consider,
　　and incline thine ear;

Forget also thine own people, and thy father's house;

12 So shall the king desire thy beauty;
For he is thy lord; and do homage unto him.

13 And, O daughter of Tyre, the richest of the people
Shall entreat thy favour with a gift."

14 All glorious is the king's daughter within the palace;
Her raiment is of chequer work inwrought with gold.

15 She shall be led unto the king on richly woven stuff;

The virgins her companions in her train being brought unto thee.

16 They shall be led with gladness and rejoicing;
They shall enter into the king's palace.

17 Instead of thy fathers shall be thy sons,
Whom thou shalt make princes in all the land.

18 I will make thy name to be remembered in all generations;
Therefore shall the peoples praise thee for ever and ever.

❧

Family Values in a Royal Wedding Song

This psalm sparkles with gladness and celebration. Composed for a royal wedding, it describes first the groom (v. 1–9) and then the bride (v. 10–16). The author extols the handsome appearance of the king waiting for his bride to make her entrance: "You are fairer than all men" (v. 3). But true to the biblical scale of moral values, he also expands on the king's inner qualities of courage and character. He is an admirable leader in war, but most of all a champion of righteousness: "The scepter of your kingdom is a scepter of justice; You love righteousness and hate iniquity" (v. 7–8).

Turning to the bride, the psalmist speaks of her beauty and magnificent dress, "embroidered with golden weaving" (v. 14), surrounded by her maiden friends. She receives a poignant reminder that her marriage must have priority over all other family bonds, including the parent-child relationship: "Listen, O daughter, forget your folk and family, for the king desires your beauty; he is your lord" (v. 11–12).

The subordination of the wife to her husband gradually became unacceptable. Postbiblical Jewish law largely equalized the obligations of the spouses. Both husband and wife owe highest allegiance to each other. Marriage must not take second place to any other relationship.

❧

Reflection: Enjoy Life

Every major religion knows of ascetics who believe that one reaches a higher level of spirituality by suppressing one's physical needs. They subject the body to mortification through fasting and sleepless vigils, wear rough clothes, live on alms, or vegetate as hermits in total isolation. This aberration is based on the notion that the body is the abode of evil, and the spirit the source of good. There is no biblical basis for the treatment of body and spirit as opposites. On the contrary, the Hebrew Bible condemns any form of deprivation and self-inflicted mutilation, including tattooing. It regards food, health, strength, sexual gratification, and childbearing within marriage as God's blessings. Religious festivals are to be enjoyed with feasting and song. It is in the light of this positive attitude toward physical pleasure that we should appreciate Psalm 45. It overflows with praise of the splendor and beauty of a royal wedding. The groom is said to be "the most handsome of men" (v. 3). The bride is beautiful in her stunning dress of gold (v. 12, 14). The psalmist revels in the luxurious beauty of the ivory palace, its fragrance and enchanting music. In his unashamed glorification of opulence and material splendor, the psalmist does not ignore moral concerns and spiritual values. He urges the royal groom to "ride on in behalf of truth and meekness and righteousness" (v. 5) and praises him for "loving the good and hating evil" (v. 8). The psalm sees no conflict between physical enjoyment and moral values. Both can and should be in harmony.

❧ PSALM 46 ❧

For the Leader; [a Psalm] of the sons of Korah; upon Alamoth. A Song.

2 God is our refuge and strength,
A very present help in trouble.
3 Therefore will we not fear, though the earth do change,
And though the mountains be moved into the heart of the seas;
4 Though the waters thereof roar and foam,
Though the mountains shake at the swelling thereof.   Selah

5 There is a river, the streams whereof make glad the city of God,
The holiest dwelling-place of the Most High.
6 God is in the midst of her, she shall not be moved;
God shall help her, at the approach of morning.

7 Nations were in tumult, kingdoms were moved;
He uttered His voice, the earth melted.
8 The LORD of hosts is with us;
The God of Jacob is our high tower.   Selah

9 Come, behold the works of the LORD, Who hath made desolations in the earth.
10 He maketh wars to cease unto the end of the earth;
He breaketh the bow, and cutteth the spear in sunder;
He burneth the chariots in the fire.
11 "Let be, and know that I am God;
I will be exalted among the nations, I will be exalted in the earth."
12 The LORD of hosts is with us;
The God of Jacob is our high tower.   Selah

God, Our Refuge and Fortress

Put yourself in the place of a defender of Jerusalem whose city is under siege. Looking down from his post on the wall, he sees a huge army spread out all around, preparing to storm the city by daybreak. The situation seems hopeless. The people are terror-stricken. Will they live to see another day?

Scholars take this psalm as an eyewitness account of the campaign against Jerusalem by the Assyrian conqueror Sennacherib, reported elsewhere in the Bible (see Isaiah, chapters 34 to 37). Anxiously waiting for the expected assault, the people of Jerusalem strain their eyes at dawn to watch the expected attack. But to their utter amazement, the surrounding camps are empty except for thousands of corpses. The Assyrian army has vanished overnight. To this day, the reason for Sennacherib's hasty retreat is something of a mystery. But to the psalmist, the matter is clear: God saved the city: "God is our refuge and fortress, a ready help in trouble. Therefore, we are not afraid" (v. 2).

History is full of sudden breaks that turn despair into jubilation. So is our personal life experience. As suddenly as disaster strikes, so suddenly does salvation come to our rescue. The psalmist repeats: "The Lord of hosts is with us" (v. 8, 12). You are never alone. God is with you. Powers other than yourself have a part in shaping your destiny, and the greatest of these is the One Who is always with us.

Reflection: Crisis-Born Vision

Crises have often been the cradle of great hopes and visions of a more perfect world. Both world wars, which pitted many nations against each other in horrendous bloodshed, empowered the demand for disarmament under the supervision of a more unified world. The result was, at first, the short-lived League of Nations, and later the more successful United Nations.

In the United States, the Great Depression of the 1930s gave rise to a new concept of government with more responsibility for public welfare. Psalm 46, composed amidst the turmoil of war that threatened to destroy the people of Israel, brings us the vision of the destruction of all weapons and the coming of universal peace "unto the ends of the earth" (v. 10). What inspired this vision? The psalmist does not refer to any powerful national leader, statesman, or military hero capable of putting an end to all wars. He has faith that God will act. Man is not the only player in history. God has the leading role in the destiny of mankind. The psalmist calls on the nations to stop their futile activities and let God do His thing: "Let go, and know that I am God" (v. 11). This psalm has been called by biblical scholars "the song of songs of faith." Its opening words, "God is our refuge and strength, a very present help in trouble" (v. 2), inspired Martin Luther to write the most popular Protestant hymn, "A Mighty Fortress Is Our God."

❧ PSALM 47 ❧

For the Leader; a Psalm of the sons of Korah.

2 O clap your hands, all ye peoples;
Shout unto God with the voice of triumph.
3 For the LORD is most high, awful;
A great King over all the earth.
4 He subdueth peoples under us,
And nations under our feet.
5 He chooseth our inheritance for us,
The pride of Jacob whom He loveth.
                                    Selah

6 God is gone up amidst shouting,
The LORD amidst the sound of the horn.

7 Sing praises to God, sing praises;
Sing praises unto our King, sing praises.

8 For God is the King of all the earth;
Sing ye praises in a skilful song.
9 God reigneth over the nations;
God sitteth upon His holy throne.

10 The princes of the peoples are gathered together,
The people of the God of Abraham;
For unto God belong the shields of the earth;
He is greatly exalted.

❧

God Rules

What do we mean when we say God is king? Does God run a government? Does He have an administration? Does He maintain a bureaucracy with department heads and officials, like our government? The answer is, nobody knows. The Bible does not tell us anything about God's management system. There is a suggestion here and there of ministering angels carrying out God's will, but what angels are made of is likewise a mystery. It is all left to our imagination.

The author of Psalm 47 knows no more than any of us *how* God rules, but this does not lessen his belief that God is in charge. The world does not run itself; neither is it subject to sheer chance: "The Lord is most high, awesome, a great king over all the earth" (v. 3). The psalmist believes that God has a hand in history. He may not want to mix in every one of our problems and control every happening, but in the long run things lead to the fulfillment of His will: "God reigns over the nations" (v. 9).

❧

Reflection: God and Reverence for Life

This psalm glorifies God as a "great king over all the earth" (v. 3). God's kingship is fundamental doctrine in Judaism, Islam, and Christianity. What are the moral and spiritual implications for the individual believer in God as king? If God is king of all humanity, then all human beings share in some relationship with God. All of us are recipients of His care and subject to His will and law. Is there anything in the human condition that confirms the rule of a higher power over our lives? We all share the "creature feeling," that is, we know that we did not make ourselves; we were created, brought into life, not by our own will or decision. We came into being by a will other than our own, under laws not of our making. We are aware of life-sustaining powers that keep us alive. We also know that our life may be cut short at any moment. All this imbues us with a sense of total dependence on that higher power that determines our life and death.

Instinctively, we respond to that power with a mixture of fear, love, and reverence. Reverence for God goes hand in hand with reverence for what is godly in the human being. The poet Samuel Taylor Coleridge recognized this connection after learning of the custom among pious Jews never to step upon the smallest piece of paper because possibly the name of God may be on it. Wrote Coleridge in his essay *Aids to Reflection*: "There is nothing but good religion in it, if we apply it to men, trample not on any; there may be some work of grace there, that thou knowest not of. The name of God may be written upon that soul thou treadest on; it may be a soul that Christ thought so much of, as to give His precious blood for it; therefore despise it not."

❧ PSALM 48 ❧

A Song; a Psalm of the sons of Korah.

2 Great is the LORD, and highly to be praised,
In the city of our God, His holy mountain,

3 Fair in situation, the joy of the whole earth;
Even mount Zion, the uttermost parts of the north,
The city of the great King.
4 God in her palaces

Hath made Himself known for a
stronghold.

5 For, lo, the kings assembled
themselves,
They came onward together.
6 They saw, straightway they were
amazed;
They were affrighted, they hasted
away.
7 Trembling took hold of them there,
Pangs, as of a woman in travail.
8 With the east wind
Thou breakest the ships of Tarshish.
9 As we have heard, so have we seen
In the city of the LORD of hosts, in
the city of our God—
God establish it for ever.   Selah

10 We have thought on Thy lovingkindness, O God,

In the midst of Thy temple.
11 As is Thy name, O God,
So is Thy praise unto the ends of the
earth;
Thy right hand is full of
righteousness.
12 Let mount Zion be glad,
Let the daughters of Judah rejoice,
Because of Thy judgments.
13 Walk about Zion, and go round about
her;
Count the towers thereof.
14 Mark ye well her ramparts,
Traverse her palaces;
That ye may tell it to the generation
following.
15 For such is God, our God, for ever
and ever;
He will guide us eternally.

∞

Thank God, It Didn't Happen!

As a well-mannered person, you will give thanks for any gift you receive. Have you ever thought of giving thanks for things that did *not* happen? Stop to think how much could go wrong in your life. Think of the many diseases you have escaped. Are you self-supporting and materially comfortable? Imagine the sudden loss of all your possessions, which did not happen; or worse, the loss of those dearest to you, who are still with you.

The truth is that we take too much for granted. Unbeknownst to you, you have been shielded against many dangers; therefore, you survived. If you believe that thanks are due to God for His daily gifts, should you not also give thanks for the things that did *not* happen?

Psalm 48 appears to have been composed immediately after Jerusalem survived a ferocious attack by enemies set to destroy the city: "The kings joined forces; they attacked together" (v. 5). But Jerusalem withstood the assault, and the attackers "panicked and ran away" (v. 6). Now the jubilant psalmist calls on his people to see for themselves that their beloved Jerusalem suffered no damage: "Walk about Zion and go around her; count her towers, check her ramparts; go through her palaces, that you may tell it to future generations" (v. 13–14).

Looking back on what happened as well as on what did not happen, the author opens Psalm 48 with thankful praise of God: "Great is God, and highly to be praised" (v. 2), and closes with confidence in God's ongoing care: "He is our God forever; He will lead us always" (v. 15).

❧

Reflection: Appreciation

William James, one of the founders of modern psychology, received an azalea plant from his class of young ladies at Radcliffe College. In his letter of thanks he told his students how much their appreciation meant to him, and then acknowledged somewhat ashamedly that he had entirely overlooked the importance of appreciation in his own book on psychology: "I now perceive one immense omission in my Psychology—the deepest principle of Human Nature is the craving to be appreciated, and I left it out altogether from the book."

It stands to reason that appreciation must go both ways. We who so much want to be appreciated must also show appreciation for what we receive. We are quick to complain about the things we are missing or the things that go wrong, but fail to express gratitude for what we get and the things that go well for us. Psalm 48 can teach us a lesson in appreciation. After Jerusalem escaped destruction by a formidable enemy, much of the population must have celebrated with singing, dancing, and feasting. Others, the psalmist among them, went to the sanctuary in appreciation of the happy turn of events: "We have thought about Your loving-kindness, O God, in the midst of Your Temple" (v. 10). We, too, should be thinking of all the good we receive. Daily prayer, in the sanctuary or at home, at mealtime, before retiring to sleep, and upon awakening in the morning, will keep us focused on things to be grateful for. The more we appreciate what has been given us, the healthier will be our frame of mind.

❧ PSALM 49 ❧

For the Leader; a Psalm of the sons of Korah.

2 Hear this, all ye peoples;
  Give ear, all ye inhabitants of the world,
3 Both low and high,
  Rich and poor together.
4 My mouth shall speak wisdom,
And the meditation of my heart shall be understanding.
5 I will incline mine ear to a parable;
  I will open my dark saying upon the harp.

6 Wherefore should I fear in the days of evil,

When the iniquity of my supplanters compasseth me about,

7 Of them that trust in their wealth, And boast themselves in the multitude of their riches?

8 No man can by any means redeem his brother, Nor give to God a ransom for him—

9 For too costly is the redemption of their soul, And must be let alone for ever—

10 That he should still live alway, That he should not see the pit.

11 For he seeth that wise men die, The fool and the brutish together perish, And leave their wealth to others.

12 Their inward thought is, that their houses shall continue for ever, And their dwelling-places to all generations; They call their lands after their own names.

13 But man abideth not in honour; He is like the beasts that perish.

14 This is the way of them that are foolish, And of those who after them approve their sayings.   Selah

15 Like sheep they are appointed for the nether-world; Death shall be their shepherd; And the upright shall have dominion over them in the morning; And their form shall be for the nether-world to wear away, That there be no habitation for it.

16 But God will redeem my soul from the power of the netherworld; For He shall receive me.   Selah

17 Be not thou afraid when one waxeth rich, When the wealth of his house is increased;

18 For when he dieth he shall carry nothing away; His wealth shall not descend after him.

19 Though while he lived he blessed his soul: "Men will praise thee, when thou shalt do well to thyself";

20 It shall go to the generation of his fathers; They shall never see the light.

21 Man that is in honour understandeth not; He is like the beasts that perish.

He Shall Take Nothing with Him

There is not much to cheer about in Psalm 49, but it's the truth, like it or not. The psalmist tells us right at the beginning that what he has to say concerns all human beings. "Hear this, all you peoples, listen, all you dwellers on earth, both low and high, rich and poor together" (v. 2). His message is that we all share the same destiny. Death comes to all: *Wise men die, the fool and the brute perish together and leave their wealth to others*" (v. 11). Don't be bothered by the prosperity of the wealthy man who goes on amassing a fortune, for "when he dies, he shall take nothing with him" (v. 18).

The psalmist, who evidently does not count himself among the rich, is consoled by the faith that when his time comes, he will be with God: "God will redeem me from Sheol. He will take me" (v. 16). Sheol is the place where, according to biblical thinking, the dead are gathered. Everything about it is vague and shadowy. Are the dead, who are hovering in Sheol, conscious? Do they suffer pain? Are they purely spiritual? The Bible offers no answer. The psalmist, however, is satisfied in his confidence that he will be with God in life and death: "God will redeem me from the power of Sheol. He will receive me" (v. 16).

While enjoying health and wealth, you avoid thinking about death. But it is the inescapable truth. You must face the humbling fact of man's mortality: "He is like the beasts that perish" (v. 21).

※

Reflection: Death

This psalm, a somber contemplation of death, conveys serene acceptance rather than despair and fright at our inescapable demise. The psalmist tells us what enables him to face death with calm confidence: "God will redeem my soul from the clutches of the netherworld; For He shall receive me" (v. 16). Death of the body does not mean the end of existence. Alive or dead, one remains part of the world. Death marks a change, a transition. It is not total annihilation. There is continuity of some kind.

This idea of continuity was beautifully expressed in Mitch Albom's luminous account of conversations with a dying man, *Tuesdays with Morrie*. Morrie tells his young friend by way of a parable how he views death: The story is about a little wave, bobbing along in the ocean, having a grand old time. He's enjoying the wind and the fresh air until he notices the other waves in front of him, crashing against the shore. "My God, this is terrible," the wave says. "Look what's going to happen to me!" Then along comes another wave. Seeing the first wave looking grim, it says, "Why do you look so sad?" The wave answers, "You don't understand. We're all going to crash! All of us waves are going to be nothing! Isn't it terrible?" To which the other wave replies: "No, *you* don't understand. You're not a wave, you're part of the ocean." We should say to ourselves: "I am not just a single human being, but part of all being. Dead or alive, I remain connected with the infinite ocean of existence, under God's care. He will receive me."

❧ Psalm 50 ❧

A Psalm of Asaph.

God, God, the LORD, hath spoken,
   and called the earth
From the rising of the sun unto the
   going down thereof.
2 Out of Zion, the perfection of beauty,
   God hath shined forth.
3 Our God cometh, and doth not keep
   silence;
   A fire devoureth before Him,
   And round about Him it stormeth
   mightily.
4 He calleth to the heavens above,
   And to the earth, that He may judge
   His people:
5 "Gather My saints together unto Me;
   Those that have made a covenant
   with Me by sacrifice."
6 And the heavens declare His
   righteousness;
   For God, He is judge.   Selah
7 "Hear, O My people, and I will speak;
   O Israel, and I will testify against
   thee:
   God, thy God, am I.
8 I will not reprove thee for thy
   sacrifices;
   And thy burnt-offerings are continually before Me.
9 I will take no bullock out of thy
   house,
   Nor he-goats out of thy folds.
10 For every beast of the forest is Mine,
   And the cattle upon a thousand hills.
11 I know all the fowls of the mountains;
   And the wild beasts of the field are
   Mine.
12 If I were hungry, I would not tell
   thee;
   For the world is Mine, and the fulness
   thereof.
13 Do I eat the flesh of bulls,
   Or drink the blood of goats?

14 Offer unto God the sacrifice of
   thanksgiving;
   And pay thy vows unto the Most
   High;
15 And call upon Me in the day of
   trouble;
   I will deliver thee, and thou shalt
   honour Me."

16 But unto the wicked God saith:
   "What hast thou to do to declare My
   statutes,
   And that thou hast taken My
   covenant in thy mouth?
17 Seeing thou hatest instruction,
   And castest My words behind thee.
18 When thou sawest a thief, thou hadst
   company with him,
   And with adulterers was thy portion.
19 Thou hast let loose thy mouth for
   evil,
   And thy tongue frameth deceit.
20 Thou sittest and speakest against thy
   brother;
   Thou slanderest thine own mother's
   son.
21 These things hast thou done, and
   should I have kept silence?
   Thou hadst thought that I was
   altogether such a one as thyself;
   But I will reprove thee, and set the
   cause before thine eyes.

22 Now consider this, ye that forget
   God,
   Lest I tear in pieces, and there be
   none to deliver.
23 Whoso offereth the sacrifice of
   thanksgiving honoureth Me;
   And to him that ordereth his way
   aright
   Will I show the salvation of God."

〰

What God Wants from You

Does God care about any of your rituals? Is God pleased if you recite certain prayers? Light candles? Sing a hymn? Handle the rosary or prayer beads? Does God want any of that? The psalmist suggests that there is nothing wrong with ritual, but God is not in need of it. He has God tell the people of Israel that the sacrificial cult, though part of their covenant, is not something God cares about: "Do I eat the flesh of bulls or drink the blood of goats?" (v. 13).

Reading your prayer book or the Bible is worthless if you merely mouth those words but fail to live up to the moral standards required of you by these sacred texts: "What is the point of reciting My laws and mouthing My Covenant when you reject the moral discipline and turn your back on My commandments?" (v. 16–17). What is important to God is that you shun evildoers and stay away from thieves, adulterers, and liars (see v. 17–19). The offering God wants is thanksgiving and the right way of life: "Whoever makes an offering of thanksgiving honors Me and whoever corrects his way will be shown the salvation of God" (v. 23).

〰

Reflection: Intimacy with God

Every public opinion survey shows that an overwhelming proportion of the people say they believe in God. However, the quality of this belief is not clear. Is yours a general belief in the existence of a cosmic deity, a God "out there" Who minds the universe? Or is your God personal, a God Who knows you by name and cares for you? How does your belief in God affect your feelings and conduct? Psalm 50 has God say of Himself: "I am God, *your* God" (v. 7). This brief statement seems to distinguish between the God of the universe and *your* God, that is, the God with Whom you have a personal relationship. One can feel reverence and awe toward the God of the universe, but it would be pointless to pray to such a God unless you believe that God pays attention to every individual. The psalmist makes the assumption that there is a direct line of connection and communication between God and the human being. How do we reach a "personal" God consciousness? Books and preachers can teach us something about God, but the personal connection is something we have to work out by and for ourselves. Vital religion is more than a philosophic worldview. It is predominantly a matter of relationship. A little girl, after learning Psalm 23 in Sunday school, tried to include it in her night prayer. She began to pray: "The Lord is my Shepherd"—and not exactly remembering the next sentence, she continued: "that's all I want." What we most want from our religion is the assurance that the God of the universe is truly *my* God and *my* Shepherd.

❧ PSALM 51 ❧

For the Leader. A Psalm of David;
²when Nathan the prophet came unto
    him, after he had gone in to Bath-
    sheba.

³Be gracious unto me, O God, accord-
    ing to Thy mercy;
According to the multitude of Thy
    compassions blot out my
    transgressions.
⁴Wash me thoroughly from mine
    iniquity,
And cleanse me from my sin.
⁵For I know my transgressions;
And my sin is ever before me.
⁶Against Thee, Thee only, have I
    sinned,
And done that which is evil in Thy
    sight;
That Thou mayest be justified when
    Thou speakest,
And be in the right when Thou
    judgest.

⁷Behold, I was brought forth in
    iniquity,
And in sin did my mother conceive
    me.
⁸Behold, Thou desirest truth in the
    inward parts;
Make me, therefore, to know wisdom
    in mine inmost heart.
⁹Purge me with hyssop, and I shall be
    clean;
Wash me, and I shall be whiter than
    snow.
¹⁰Make me to hear joy and gladness;

That the bones which Thou hast
    crushed may rejoice.
¹¹Hide Thy face from my sins,
And blot out all mine iniquities.
¹²Create me a clean heart, O God;
And renew a stedfast spirit within me.
¹³Cast me not away from Thy presence;
And take not Thy holy spirit from me.
¹⁴Restore unto me the joy of Thy
    salvation;
And let a willing spirit uphold me.
¹⁵Then will I teach transgressors Thy
    ways;
And sinners shall return unto Thee.
¹⁶Deliver me from bloodguiltiness, O
    God, Thou God of my salvation;
So shall my tongue sing aloud of Thy
    righteousness.
¹⁷O LORD, open Thou my lips;
And my mouth shall declare Thy
    praise.
¹⁸For Thou delightest not in sacrifice,
    else would I give it;
Thou hast no pleasure in burnt-
    offering.
¹⁹The sacrifices of God are a broken
    spirit;
A broken and a contrite heart, O
    God, Thou wilt not despise.

²⁰Do good in Thy favour unto Zion;
Build Thou the walls of Jerusalem.
²¹Then wilt Thou delight in the sacri-
    fices of righteousness, in burnt-
    offering and whole offering;
Then will they offer bullocks upon
    Thine altar.

Coping with Guilt

If you are tormented by memories of wrongdoing and a gnawing sense of guilt, Psalm 51 shows you how to cope with it. First, you must unburden yourself by acknowledging the transgression, without minimizing it or trying to shift blame onto someone else. It should be a full confession, with no cover-up: "I know my transgression and my sin is ever before me" (v. 5). Because of the gravity of his sin, the psalmist feels that he cannot regain purity by his own efforts alone. He begs for God's help: "Wash me thoroughly from mine iniquity and cleanse me from my sin" (v. 4).

Remorse leads him to profound self-abasement and revulsion at the depth of evil within himself: "I was brought forth in iniquity and in sin did my mother conceive me" (v. 7). This should not be understood as a universal doctrine of original sin. The psalmist is not arguing that *all* human beings are congenital sinners. He is talking strictly about himself as a person rotten to the core from the very beginning of his existence. In his condition, he can see only one possible way to wipe the slate of his sins clean, and that would be a total change, a spiritual rebirth: "Create me a clean heart, O God, and renew a steadfast spirit within me" (v. 12).

The psalmist closes with an ingenious proposition. If given a chance, he suggests, he might yet put his sinful past to some good use. His own experience might enable him to help rehabilitate other sinners and bring them back to God in repentance: "Then will I teach transgressors Your ways; and sinners shall return to You" (v. 15).

Reflection: Guilt

"Guilt" has become an unpopular, somewhat distasteful word. "Don't guilt-trip me!" is the often angry response to rebuke. Most people take criticism badly. The most common reaction is defensiveness, denial, and cover-up. When King Frederick the Great of Prussia inspected a Potsdam prison, every prisoner he interviewed protested innocence. Finally, one man lowered his eyes and said: "Your Majesty, I am guilty and deserve punishment." The king turned to the warden and said: "Get this rascal out of prison before he corrupts all the good innocent men around here."

Contrary to the common pattern of guilt denial, the author of Psalm 51 stands out by determined confrontation of his sinfulness:

"I know my transgression and my sin is ever before me" (v. 5). Unlike most others, who become quickly defensive when told of their offense, the psalmist makes no excuses. Admitting his sin, he rejects his former self and begs God for help to change himself: "Create me a clean heart and renew a steadfast spirit within me" (v. 12). Psalm 51 should make us see the value of guilt. It is the driving force in the psalmist's will for moral purification and rehabilitation. We should thank God for having the sensitivity of guilt. It is the stamp of human nobility, as Archibald MacLeish pointed out: "Without guilt, what is man? An animal, isn't he?"

∾ PSALM 52 ∾

For the Leader. Maschil of David;
2 when Doeg the Edomite came and
   told Saul, and said unto him: "David
   is come to the house of Ahimelech."

3 Why boastest thou thyself of evil, O
   mighty man?
   The mercy of God endureth
   continually.
4 Thy tongue deviseth destruction;
   Like a sharp razor, working
   deceitfully.

5 Thou lovest evil more than good;
   Falsehood rather than speaking
   righteousness.   Selah
6 Thou lovest all devouring words,
   The deceitful tongue.
7 God will likewise break thee for ever,
   He will take thee up, and pluck thee
   out of thy tent,

And root thee out of the land of the
   living.   Selah

8 The righteous also shall see, and fear,
   And shall laugh at him:
9 "Lo, this is the man that made not
   God his stronghold;
   But trusted in the abundance of his
   riches,
   And strengthened himself in his
   wickedness."
10 But as for me, I am like a leafy olive-
   tree in the house of God;
   I trust in the mercy of God for ever
   and ever.
11 I will give Thee thanks for ever,
   because Thou hast done it;
   And I will wait for Thy name, for it is
   good, in the presence of Thy saints.

∾

When Words Are Weapons

In childhood, name-calling is a form of teasing, perhaps painful but not meant to destroy the victim. The damage is limited. But it is altogether different when adults use words as a weapon. Slander can destroy the reputation of another person, his livelihood, and his family life. The psalmist calls it "devouring words" (v. 6). Such wrongdoing, the psalmist is certain, will not go unpunished. Turning to the liar, the psalmist predicts: "God will finally ruin you" (v. 7). He feels secure in his integrity, "like an olive tree growing in the house of God forever trusting in God's love" (v. 10).

Reflection: Words and Silence

Special moral codes apply to different areas of life: business ethics, medical ethics, ethics of sexuality, ethics of sportsmanship, and so forth. Psalm 52 has something to say about the ethics of speech. Words are weapons: "Your tongue is like a sharp razor" (v. 4). Evil persons spread falsehood; they speak words that "devour and deceive" (v. 5, 6). The power of speech, for good or evil, is a recurrent topic in the Bible. Most often quoted is: "Death and life are in the power of the tongue" (Proverbs 18:21). Because of the fateful consequences of words, we are urged to use them with caution—and the fewer, the better: "He that spares his words has knowledge" (Proverbs 17:27). Words can also help and heal. The virtuous woman, we are told, "opens her mouth with wisdom and has kindness on her tongue" (Proverbs 31:26). In a bitter argument or quarrel, "a soft answer turns away wrath. . . . and a soothing tongue is a tree of life" (Proverbs 15:1, 4). The wise preacher Kohelet (Ecclesiastes) reminds us that neither speech nor silence is appropriate at all times: "There is a time to keep silence and a time to speak" (Ecclesiastes 3:7).

Silence in the presence of suffering shows indifference. Silence at vile and bigoted talk is either consent or cowardice. If falsehood or slander is spoken, it is a moral duty to speak up for truth.

❧ PSALM 53 ❧

For the Leader; upon Mahalath. Maschil of David.

2 The fool hath said in his heart: "There is no God";
They have dealt corruptly, and have done abominable iniquity;
There is none that doeth good.
3 God looked forth from heaven upon the children of men,
To see if there were any man of under-standing, that did seek after God.

4 Every one of them is unclean, they are together become impure;
There is none that doeth good, no, not one.

5 "Shall not the workers of iniquity know it,
Who eat up My people as they eat bread,
And call not upon God?"
6 There are they in great fear, where no fear was;

For God hath scattered the bones of
   him that encampeth against thee;
Thou hast put them to shame, because
   God hath rejected them.

7 Oh that the salvation of Israel were
   come out of Zion!

When God turneth the captivity of
   His people,
Let Jacob rejoice, let Israel be glad.

See the commentary and reflection to Psalm 14, which is virtually identical to Psalm 53.

❧ Psalm 54 ❧

For the Leader; with string-music.
   Maschil of David:
2 when the Ziphites came and said to
   Saul: "Doth not David hide himself
   with us?"

3 O God, save me by Thy name,
   And right me by Thy might.
4 O God, hear my prayer;
   Give ear to the words of my mouth.
5 For strangers are risen up against me,
   And violent men have sought after my
   soul;
   They have not set God before them.
                                    Selah

6 Behold, God is my helper;
   The Lord is for me as the upholder of
   my soul.
7 He will requite the evil unto them that
   lie in wait for me;
   Destroy Thou them in Thy truth.
8 With a freewill-offering will I sacrifice
   unto Thee;
   I will give thanks unto Thy name, O
   Lord, for it is good.
9 For He hath delivered me out of all
   trouble;
   And mine eye hath gazed upon mine
   enemies.

Let God Be Your Judge

Do you feel threatened by enemies? Are there people who want to hurt you and even now plan mischief against you? What if there is nothing you can do about it? In such a predicament, you may find relief by invoking, like the psalmist, God as your judge: "O God, let me have justice by Your power" (v. 3). He counts on God's help, "behold, God is my helper" (v. 6), and is confident that the time will come when he will be able to exclaim: "He has saved me from all trouble" (v. 9).

Reflection: Wonder

When we say a person is on life support, we refer to a gravely ill person who is receiving intravenous feeding and oxygen for breathing.

The author of Psalm 54 acknowledges the life support he is receiving every day, in health or in illness: "Behold, God is my helper; God is for me the upholder of my life" (v. 6). Many of us have a lopsided view of God's involvement in our lives. If something exceptional happens, we call it an "act of God." If a critically ill person suddenly pulls back from the brink of death, we say, "It's a miracle." Far more amazing is the normal course of nature and the normal functioning of our body, with the regeneration of countless cells and nearly 100,000 heartbeats day after day. The miracle of the human body moved another psalmist to exclaim: "I am fearfully and wonderfully made" (Psalm 139:14). Truly, each of us is constantly upheld by God's life support system.

❧ PSALM 55 ❧

For the Leader; with string-music. Maschil of David.

2 Give ear, O God, to my prayer;
And hide not Thyself from my supplication.
3 Attend unto me, and answer me;
I am distraught in my complaint, and will moan;
4 Because of the voice of the enemy,
Because of the oppression of the wicked;
For they cast mischief upon me,
And in anger they persecute me.
5 My heart doth writhe within me;
And the terrors of death are fallen upon me.
6 Fear and trembling come upon me,
And horror hath overwhelmed me.
7 And I said: "Oh that I had wings like a dove!
Then would I fly away, and be at rest.
8 Lo, then would I wander far off,
I would lodge in the wilderness.
                            Selah
9 I would haste me to a shelter
From the stormy wind and tempest."
10 Destroy, O LORD, and divide their tongue;
For I have seen violence and strife in the city.

11 Day and night they go about it upon the walls thereof;
Iniquity also and mischief are in the midst of it.
12 Wickedness is in the midst thereof;
Oppression and guile depart not from her broad place.
13 For it was not an enemy that taunted me,
Then I could have borne it;
Neither was it mine adversary that did magnify himself against me,
Then I would have hid myself from him.
14 But it was thou, a man mine equal,
My companion, and my familiar friend;
15 We took sweet counsel together,
In the house of God we walked with the throng.
16 May He incite death against them,
Let them go down alive into the nether-world;
For evil is in their dwelling, and within them.

17 As for me, I will call upon God;
And the LORD will save me.
18 Evening, and morning, and at noon-day, will I complain, and moan;
And He hath heard my voice.

19He hath redeemed my soul in peace
   so that none came nigh me;
For they were many that strove with
   me.
20God shall hear, and humble them,
   Even He that is enthroned of old,
                              Selah
Such as have no changes,
And fear not God.
21He hath put forth his hands against
   them that were at peace with him;
He hath profaned his covenant.
22Smoother than cream were the
   speeches of his mouth,

But his heart was war;
His words were softer than oil,
Yet were they keen-edged swords.

23Cast thy burden upon the LORD, and
   He will sustain thee;
He will never suffer the righteous to
   be moved.
24But Thou, O God, wilt bring them
   down into the nethermost pit;
Men of blood and deceit shall not live
   out half their days;
But as for me, I will trust in Thee.

❧

Cast Your Burden upon God

Have you been in a situation from which you desperately wanted to escape? You see no solution for the problems that beset you and fantasize an escape from it all, as did the psalmist: "If only I had wings like a bird, I would fly away and be at rest" (v. 7).

The feeling that everybody has turned against him shakes the psalmist. He can put up with abuse by enemies, but the treachery of his best friend is too much. Remembering the happy times when they used to talk in confidence as they walked with the crowd to the temple (v. 15), he cries out in pain: "You, my equal, my companion, my intimate friend!" (v. 14). Since no human being can remedy his situation, he reaches out to God: "As for me, I will call upon God and He will save me" (v. 17). The psalmist finds relief and lives to tell of the happy turn of events: "He has redeemed my embattled soul" (v. 19). In the end, the psalmist thinks of others who must cope with similar problems and offers advice based on his own experience: "Cast your burden upon God and He will sustain you" (v. 23).

❧

Reflection: Escapism

If mounting problems at work or at home are more than you can handle, you will have the urge to escape. You will daydream about all sorts of changes, with one common conclusion: getting out of your present situation. You will fantasize about a new job, career change, relocation, even a new marriage or no marriage at all. The psalmist, under pressure by enemies, dreamed of escape: "Oh that I had wings like a dove!

Then would I fly away, and be at rest. Then would I wander far off, I would lodge in the wilderness. I would hasten to a shelter from the stormy wind and tempest" (v. 7–9). If you indulge such fantasies of escape, consider Eric Hoffer's warning: "We feel free when we escape—even if it but be from the frying pan into the fire." Running away from your old problems might only get you into new ones, and those might be worse.

What else can you do? The psalmist did not carry out his fantasy of flying away. He stayed put, trying to come to terms with reality. In his struggle, he turned to God and was helped: "Cast your burden upon God; He will sustain you" (v. 23). What does this mean? Is it conceivable that God would step in and do your job for you? Don't expect God to finish your long-overdue project, pay your debts, or solve your family crisis.

You must deal with these matters yourself. But you *can* unburden yourself by sharing with God in prayer the things that trouble you. As prayer leads to reflection and self-examination, you will sort out and define your problems. You will gain new insight into yourself, your strength, and your weakness. You will recognize your errors and faults. Different ways of coping with your problems may occur to you. You will think of reordering your relationships and way of life. The words "cast your burden upon God" mean no more and no less than reaching out to God in prayer and reflection. No one knows how God, in response, will reach out to you, but at the very least you will, in the process, clear your mind and be better prepared for new decisions.

❧ PSALM 56 ❧

For the Leader; upon Jonath-elem-rehokim. [A Psalm] of David; Michtam; when the Philistines took him in Gath.

2 Be gracious unto me, O God, for man would swallow me up;
All the day he fighting oppresseth me.
3 They that lie in wait for me would swallow me up all the day;
For they are many that fight against me, O Most High,
4 In the day that I am afraid,
I will put my trust in Thee.
5 In God—I will praise His word—
In God do I trust, I will not be afraid;
What can flesh do unto me?

6 All the day they trouble mine affairs;
All their thoughts are against me for evil.
7 They gather themselves together, they hide themselves,
They mark my steps;
According as they have waited for my soul.

8Because of iniquity cast them out;
In anger bring down the peoples, O
God.
9Thou hast counted my wanderings;
Put Thou my tears into Thy bottle;
Are they not in Thy book?
10Then shall mine enemies turn back in
the day that I call;
This I know, that God is for me.
11In God—I will praise His word—
In the LORD—I will praise His
word—

12In God do I trust, I will not be afraid;
What can man do unto me?

13Thy vows are upon me, O God;
I will render thank-offerings unto
Thee.
14For Thou hast delivered my soul
from death;
Hast Thou not delivered my feet
from stumbling?
That I may walk before God in the
light of the living.

❧

God Knows Your Pain

Have you ever had a narrow escape from death? You might have been killed in a car crash, or hit by a stray bullet, or died of illness, yet you survived. Were you saved by luck? Or was it some mysterious power that took control of your life? The psalmist is certain that it was God Who came to his rescue in time of danger. God not only keeps track of our every move, but takes note of our pain: "You keep a count of my wanderings; You save my tears in Your bottle" (v. 9).

Thrice the psalmist avows that trusting God, he has no fear (v. 4, 5, 12). In the believer's mind things don't happen by chance, but by God's design. Survival prompts thanksgiving: "I will render thanks unto You, for You have rescued me from death and kept me from stumbling" (v. 13–14).

❧

Reflection: Trust

This psalm may well be the source for the inscription on American coins "In God We trust." Atheists sneer at the believer's trust in God. They argue: "Your trust is another word for ignorance. The more knowledge, the less need for trust. Trust in God simply fills the believer's vacuum of knowledge."

My answer is, I trust God because what little I do know about the world, about life, and about myself convinces me that there is a higher power—God. The world is not a rudderless boat floating down an endless stream from nowhere to nowhere. I see signs of order, plan, purpose, and awesome mystery in the totality of life, which, I believe, must originate with God. Our Creator remains connected with all there is. There is love in this connection. It assures me that I am not alone, as Ignazio Silone acknowledged: "He who has faith is never alone. But the atheist is always alone, even if from morning to night he lives in crowded streets." Twice the psalmist says: "In God do I trust; I will not be afraid" (v. 5, 12). Then he continues, "What can man do unto me?" Despite our trust in God, we can suffer plenty of harm at the hands of fellow men. But trust in God keeps us from being consumed by fear. Trust in God means believing that the world was not made for destruction and that for every evil there is some good to overcome it. Even in dire need, illness, or adversity, trust in God gives me hope for a good turn. By the same measure, as my trust in God grows, my fear diminishes. This, I believe, is what the psalmist meant when he said: "In God do I trust; I will not be afraid" (v. 5, 12).

❧ PSALM 57 ❧

For the Leader; Al-tashheth. [A Psalm] of David; Michtam; when he fled from Saul, in the cave.

2 Be gracious unto me, O God, be gracious unto me,
For in Thee hath my soul taken refuge;
Yea, in the shadow of Thy wings will I take refuge,
Until calamities be overpast.
3 I will cry unto God Most High;
Unto God that accomplisheth it for me.
4 He will send from heaven, and save me,
When he that would swallow me up taunteth;   Selah
God shall send forth His mercy and His truth.
5 My soul is among lions, I do lie down among them that are aflame;
Even the sons of men, whose teeth are spears and arrows,
And their tongue a sharp sword.

6 Be Thou exalted, O God, above the heavens;
Thy glory be above all the earth.
7 They have prepared a net for my steps,
My soul is bowed down;
They have digged a pit before me,
They are fallen into the midst thereof themselves.   Selah
8 My heart is stedfast, O God, my heart is stedfast;
I will sing, yea, I will sing praises.
9 Awake, my glory; awake, psaltery and harp;
I will awake the dawn.
10 I will give thanks unto Thee, O LORD, among the peoples;
I will sing praises unto Thee among the nations.
11 For Thy mercy is great unto the heavens,
And Thy truth unto the skies.
12 Be Thou exalted, O God, above the heavens;
Thy glory be above all the earth.

∞

Steadfastness Comes with Faith

A crisis such as the collapse of health, a major loss, or threat to your security casts the spell of anxiety upon your life. You are afraid of the future. The author of Psalm 57 found himself in great danger: "My soul is among lions . . . men whose teeth are spears and whose tongues are sharp swords" (v. 5). Evidently he got entangled in bitter conflict with people who were out to destroy him by words or deeds. Emerging from the crisis unharmed, he credits God for saving him: "In You has my soul taken refuge" (v. 2). Trust in God restores his stability. He can face the storms of life: "My heart is steadfast, O God; my heart is steadfast" (v. 8). A sense of security and stability comes with faith.

Note that Psalm 57:8–12 is duplicated in Psalm 108:2–6.

∞

Reflection: Appreciation

The enthusiasm of the psalmist is amazing. He turns to God with praise and song and is full of joy despite heaps of calamities (v. 2); he feels swallowed up (v. 4) and threatened as though surrounded by lions (v. 5). He is attacked by people whose tongue is "a sharp razor" (v. 7). He fears being caught in the net of enemies (v. 7). Nevertheless, he exclaims: "My heart is steadfast, O God, my heart is steadfast; I will sing, I will sing praises. Awake, my glory, awake, psaltery and harp, I will awake the dawn. I will give thanks unto You, O God, among the peoples. I will sing praises unto You among the nations" (v. 8–10). These words seem to dance for joy. How could he, with so little to cheer about in his circumstances, be so full of praise for God? There is only one possible answer: Instead of moaning over what is missing or going wrong in his life, he is mindful of his benefits. He is grateful for the security he finds in trusting God: "In You have I taken refuge; in the shadow of Your wings will I take refuge" (v. 2). He recognizes, in whatever he has, the gift of a merciful God: "For Your mercy extends unto the heaven" (v. 11). We can all share in the enthusiasm of the psalmist if we have his appreciation of the gift of life and all that sustains us and are conscious, as he is, of the presence of God in our lives.

❧ Psalm 58 ❧

For the Leader; Al-tashheth. [A Psalm] of David; Michtam.

2 Do ye indeed speak as a righteous company?
Do ye judge with equity the sons of men?
3 Yea, in heart ye work wickedness;
Ye weigh out in the earth the violence of your hands.
4 The wicked are estranged from the womb;
The speakers of lies go astray as soon as they are born.
5 Their venom is like the venom of a serpent;
They are like the deaf asp that stoppeth her ear;
6 Which hearkeneth not to the voice of charmers,
Or of the most cunning binder of spells.

7 Break their teeth, O God, in their mouth;

Break out the cheek-teeth of the young lions, O Lord.
8 Let them melt away as water that runneth apace;
When he aimeth his arrows, let them be as though they were cut off.
9 Let them be as a snail which melteth and passeth away;
Like the untimely births of a woman, that have not seen the sun.
10 Before your pots can feel the thorns,
He will sweep it away with a whirlwind, the raw and the burning alike.

11 The righteous shall rejoice when he seeth the vengeance;
He shall wash his feet in the blood of the wicked.
12 And men shall say: "Verily there is a reward for the righteous;
Verily there is a God that judgeth in the earth."

❧

Leave Vengeance to God

You are outraged by crimes that go unpunished, especially when you are one of the victims. Your anger almost overpowers you. Suppressing it is risky because long-suppressed anger may explode in uncontrollable acts of violence. The author of Psalm 58 is enraged by gross corruption among the leaders and judges of his community. He cannot contain his feelings of disgust. He shouts curses but soon realizes that his ranting and raving will not change their ways. Those scoundrels are beyond reform. They are congenital liars, "speakers of falsehood, they go astray from birth" (v. 4).

He recovers peace of mind by putting his trust in God's justice. Villains will get punished: "The righteous shall rejoice when he sees vengeance. . . . and men shall say, there is yet a reward for the righteous. Indeed, God judges the earth" (v. 11–12).

❧

Reflection: Retribution

Divine retribution—God's judgment by rewards and punishments—is one of the basic doctrines of the Bible. It thunders in Psalm 58. The psalmist is full of wrath as he points to the corruption of justice in the land. Falsehood is in the saddle. While the company of evildoers pursues their nefarious work, the psalmist hopes that "God will break their teeth" (v. 7) and hasten the day of reckoning: "Then all shall say, 'Verily, there is a reward for the righteous; verily, there is a God that judges the earth'" (v. 12).

Throughout the centuries, Jews and Christians have clung to the belief in retribution despite its many lapses. The immense bloodshed of the Civil War, regarded by many as punishment for America's sin of slavery, gave the doctrine of retribution a grim boost. Early on in the war, Julia Ward Howe's "Battle Hymn of the Republic" envisaged God passing terrible judgment on the nation:

> Mine eyes have seen the glory of the coming of the
>   Lord;
> He is trampling out the vintage where the grapes of
>   wrath are stored;
> He hath loosed the fateful lightning of His terrible,
>   swift sword
> His truth is marching on.

Toward the end of the war, Abraham Lincoln reinforced belief that the nation's suffering was America's just punishment by God. In his address to an Indiana regiment, he said:

> Fondly do we hope, fervently do we pray, that this mighty scourge of war may speedily pass away. Yet, if God wills that it continue until all the wealth piled by the bondsman's two hundred and fifty years of unrequited toil shall be sunk, and until every drop of blood drawn with the lash shall be paid by another drawn with sword, as was said three thousand years ago, so still it must be said: "The judgments of the Lord are true and righteous altogether" [Psalm 19:10].

❧ PSALM 59 ❧

For the Leader; Al-tashheth. [A Psalm] of David; Michtam; when Saul sent, and they watched the house to kill him.

2 Deliver me from mine enemies, O my God;
  Set me on high from them that rise up against me.
3 Deliver me from the workers of iniquity,
  And save me from the men of blood.
4 For, lo, they lie in wait for my soul;
  The impudent gather themselves together against me;
  Not for my transgression, nor for my sin, O LORD.
5 Without my fault, they run and prepare themselves;
  Awake Thou to help me, and behold.
6 Thou therefore, O LORD God of hosts, the God of Israel,
  Arouse Thyself to punish all the nations;
  Show no mercy to any iniquitous traitors.   Selah

7 They return at evening, they howl like a dog,
  And go round about the city.
8 Behold, they belch out with their mouth;
  Swords are in their lips:
  "For who doth hear?"
9 But Thou, O LORD, shalt laugh at them;
  Thou shalt have all the nations in derision.

10 Because of his strength, I will wait for Thee;
  For God is my high tower.
11 The God of my mercy will come to meet me;
  God will let me gaze upon mine adversaries.
12 Slay them not, lest my people forget,
  Make them wander to and fro by Thy power, and bring them down,
  O LORD our shield.
13 For the sin of their mouth, and the words of their lips,
  Let them even be taken in their pride,
  And for cursing and lying which they speak.
14 Consume them in wrath, consume them, that they be no more;
  And let them know that God ruleth in Jacob,
  Unto the ends of the earth.   Selah

15 And they return at evening, they howl like a dog,
  And go round about the city;
16 They wander up and down to devour,
  And tarry all night if they have not their fill.
17 But as for me, I will sing of Thy strength;
  Yea, I will sing aloud of Thy mercy in the morning;
  For Thou hast been my high tower,
  And a refuge in the day of my distress.
18 O my strength, unto Thee will I sing praises;
  For God is my high tower, the God of my mercy.

❧

God Will Justify the Innocent

Have you ever been the target of groundless hate? Have ruthless rivals plotted to destroy you? If you have ever been the victim of harassment and persecution, you will understand the outpouring of bitterness from the psalmist's heart. Protesting his own innocence, he begs God to help him against enemies: "Without my fault, they hasten their preparations. Bestir Yourself to help me" (v. 5). His trust in God enables him to resist the threatening words and actions of his enemies: "The God who loves me will hurry toward me; God will let me look down on mine adversaries" (v. 11). The crisis passes, and the psalmist gives thanks to God: "As for me, I will sing of Your power. Yes, I will sing of Your mercy in the morning because You have been my high tower and a refuge in the day of my distress" (v. 17).

∽

Reflection: Morning Prayer

After barely escaping death or injury, with enemies lurking all night to attack him, the psalmist credits God for his survival. What shall he do now? Before preparing new ways of defending himself, he resolves to offer morning prayers: "I will sing of Your mercy in the morning" (v. 17).

Prayer is always appropriate, but our mood and mind-set differ at various times. The night prayer, with the events of the day on your mind, is often said in the mood of thanksgiving for all that went well but also regret for mistakes, failures, or wrongdoing. What was done is done. The morning prayer, on the other hand, looks to the future. It is accompanied by hope.

The new day is the time for a fresh start, for turning over a new leaf. God has renewed your life—what will you do with it today? It is usually in the morning that you make plans for the day. If you take time out for prayer, you might very well think about your goals not only for this new day, but for your life. Don't let defeatism tempt you to give up before you have even tried. Set your sights high, whether or not you achieve what you set out to do. Remember James Russel Lowell's challenge:

> Greatly begin! though thou have time
> But for a line, be that sublime,
> Not failure, but low aim, is crime.

Morning is the best time to pray for God's guidance. Ask that your first steps in this new day be in the right direction, as the old saying goes: "Well begun, is half done."

❧ Psalm 60 ❧

For the Leader; upon Shushan Eduth; Michtam of David, to teach; ²when he strove with Aram-naharaim and with Aram-zobah, and Joab returned, and smote of Edom in the Valley of Salt twelve thousand.

³O God, Thou hast cast us off, Thou hast broken us down;
Thou hast been angry; O restore us.
⁴Thou hast made the land to shake, Thou hast cleft it;
Heal the breaches thereof; for it tottereth.
⁵Thou hast made Thy people to see hard things;
Thou hast made us to drink the wine of staggering.
⁶Thou hast given a banner to them that fear Thee,
That it may be displayed because of the truth.   Selah
⁷That Thy beloved may be delivered,
Save with Thy right hand, and answer me.

⁸God spoke in His holiness, that I would exult;
That I would divide Shechem, and mete out the valley of Succoth.
⁹Gilead is mine, and Manasseh is mine;
Ephraim also is the defence of my head;
Judah is my sceptre.
¹⁰Moab is my washpot;
Upon Edom do I cast my shoe;
Philistia, cry aloud because of me!

¹¹Who will bring me into the fortified city?
Who will lead me unto Edom?
¹²Hast not Thou, O God, cast us off?
And Thou goest not forth, O God, with our hosts.
¹³Give us help against the adversary;
For vain is the help of man.
¹⁴Through God we shall do valiantly;
For He it is that will tread down our adversaries.

❧

"Vain Is the Help of Man"

Setbacks, defeats, and losses are part of everyone's life. Even King David, one of history's greatest heroes, suffered calamitous reverses. Attacks by enemies have cut up the land in ribbons (v. 4). The people face tough times: "You have made Your people see hard things" (v. 5). The psalm lists the different tribes and nations in the region, which God disposes of at will (v. 8–11). In this hour of national crisis, David, the mighty warrior, humbly recognizes the limits of human power and realizes that he can prevail only with God's help: "Vain is the help of man. Through God we shall do valiantly" (v. 13–14).

Note that Psalm 60:7–14 is duplicated in Psalm 108:7–14.

❦

Reflection: Rejection

You cannot go through life without suffering rejection. It may be rejection by the college of your choice, by the exclusive club whose membership you crave, by the company for which you want to work, or, most painfully, by the person you love and hope to marry. Like so many aspiring writers who collect rejection slips, all of us at various times in life must swallow the bitter pill of rejection. This psalm is a woeful recital of rejection: "O God, You have cast us off. . . . You have made Your people to see hard things. . . . Have You not, O God, cast us off?" (v. 3, 5, 12).

Is there a good way of coping with rejection? The psalmist, in the fewest possible words, suggests the first step: "O restore us" (v. 3). Think of restoration. Don't quit your effort. Nothing is final in life. As the Roman sage Seneca said, "Even after a bad harvest, there must be sowing." So try again, and try to do better next time. The precondition of any self-improvement is an honest self-assessment. Can you acknowledge your shortcomings, faults, and defects?

❦ # PSALM 61 ❧

For the Leader; with string-music.
[A Psalm] of David.

2 Hear my cry, O God;
Attend unto my prayer.
3 From the end of the earth will I call
unto Thee, when my heart fainteth;
Lead me to a rock that is too high for
me.
4 For Thou hast been a refuge for me,
A tower of strength in the face of the
enemy.

5 I will dwell in Thy Tent for ever;
I will take refuge in the covert of Thy
wings.   Selah

6 For Thou, O God, hast heard my
vows;
Thou hast granted the heritage of
those that fear Thy name.

7 Mayest Thou add days unto the king's
days!
May his years be as many generations!
8 May he be enthroned before God for
ever!
Appoint mercy and truth, that they
may preserve him.

9 So will I sing praise unto Thy name
for ever,
That I may daily perform my vows.

❦

God, Our Refuge

This psalm, attributed to David, tells of his return to power after almost losing his throne and being forced to live away from Jerusalem. To him, that was like living "at the end of the earth" (v. 3). He remembers God's help in desperate times: "You have been a refuge for me, a tower of strength in the presence of the enemy" (v. 4). Now he asks for long life: "May You extend the king's life and may his years go on for generations" (v. 7).

❧

Reflection: To Pray and to Pray For

Twice the psalmist refers to God as his refuge: "You have been a refuge for me . . . I will take refuge in the covert of Your wings" (v. 4, 5). In what sense is God a refuge? There are two kinds of people who seek God. First are those who turn to God trying to escape from an immediate threat. Like a ship caught in a storm, they seek safe haven under God. To this group also belong persons in illness or pain who turn to God primarily for help in their need or for relief from suffering. Then are those who seek God purely for the joy of being in His presence. They want the serenity that comes over them in the nearness of God. They feel empowered and raised to a higher level of human dignity when connected with God Who made us in His image. In either case, whether you turn to God as a refuge from trouble or for the sense of blessedness in His presence, "God is near to all who call upon Him, who call upon Him in truth" (Psalm 145:18).

❧ PSALM 62 ❧

For the Leader; for Jeduthun. A Psalm of David.

2 Only for God doth my soul wait in stillness;
From Him cometh my salvation.
3 He only is my rock and my salvation,
My high tower, I shall not be greatly moved.
4 How long will ye set upon a man,
That ye may slay him, all of you,
As a leaning wall, a tottering fence?
5 They only devise to thrust him down from his height, delighting in lies;
They bless with their mouth, but they curse inwardly.   Selah

6 Only for God wait thou in stillness, my soul;
For from Him cometh my hope.
7 He only is my rock and my salvation,
My high tower, I shall not be moved.
8 Upon God resteth my salvation and my glory;
The rock of my strength, and my refuge, is in God.
9 Trust in Him at all times, ye people;
Pour out your heart before Him;
God is a refuge for us.   Selah

10 Men of low degree are vanity, and men of high degree are a lie;
If they be laid in the balances, they are together lighter than vanity.
11 Trust not in oppression,
And put not vain hope in robbery;

If riches increase, set not your heart
  thereon.
12 God hath spoken once,
  Twice have I heard this:
  That strength belongeth unto God;

13 Also unto Thee, O LORD, belongeth
  mercy;
  For Thou renderest to every man
  according to his work.

❧

The Reward Is According
to Your Deeds

In times of distress, you will find this psalm comforting. You are not alone. God is with you: "Only for God do I quietly wait. From Him comes my salvation" (v. 2). You will feel secure as you entrust yourself to God's care and protection: "He is my rock and my salvation, my high tower, I shall not be moved" (v. 3, 7).

If you feel threatened, remember: "Strength belongs to God, also mercy" (v. 12–13). Don't bottle up your feelings; cry out and ask for help: "Pour out your heart before Him; God is a refuge for us" (v. 9). You may be sure justice will prevail: "You reward everyone according to his deeds" (v. 13).

❧

Reflection: Patience

In a time of political or financial collapse one hears a variety of advice, even conflicting advice: "Do this, do that, act now, wait." The psalmist, a person of faith, is not bowled over by all the turmoil. Despite rampant violence and corruption, he puts his trust in God: "He only is my rock and my salvation, my high tower. I shall not be greatly moved" (v. 3, 7). Curbing the impulse to frantic action, he prefers to wait out the crisis, trusting that God may turn things around: "Only for God do I quietly wait; from Him comes my salvation" (v. 2). What kind of salvation does he look for? Verse 6 gives us a clue. It repeats verse 2, changing the word "salvation" to "hope." The verse reads: "Only for God do I quietly wait; from Him comes my *hope*."

The eighteenth-century soldier and moralist the Marquis de Vauvenargues likewise connected patience with hope. He said: "Patience is the art of hoping." The argument in favor of waiting is that many problems, if only we give them time to unwind, move to a solution without the need to intervene. We may misread the present situation, seeing only a limited phase of a development that is heading toward a favorable ending. The seventeenth-century poet Francis Quarles argued for the wisdom of quietly waiting in these lines:

> My soul, sit thou a patient looker-on;
> Judge not the Play before the Play is done;
> Her plot has many changes; every day
> Speaks a new scene; the last act crowns the Play

People of faith will make allowance for God to determine the outcome of all things.

∞ PSALM 63 ∞

A Psalm of David, when he was in the wilderness of Judah.

2 O God, Thou art my God, earnestly will I seek Thee;
My soul thirsteth for Thee, my flesh longeth for Thee,
In a dry and weary land, where no water is.
3 So have I looked for Thee in the sanctuary,
To see Thy power and Thy glory.

4 For Thy lovingkindness is better than life;
My lips shall praise Thee.
5 So will I bless Thee as long as I live;
In Thy name will I lift up my hands.

6 My soul is satisfied as with marrow and fatness;
And my mouth doth praise Thee with joyful lips;

7 When I remember Thee upon my couch,
And meditate on Thee in the night-watches.

8 For Thou hast been my help,
And in the shadow of Thy wings do I rejoice.
9 My soul cleaveth unto Thee;
Thy right hand holdeth me fast.

10 But those that seek my soul, to destroy it,
Shall go into the nethermost parts of the earth.
11 They shall be hurled to the power of the sword;
They shall be a portion for foxes.
12 But the king shall rejoice in God;
Every one that sweareth by Him shall glory;
For the mouth of them that speak lies shall be stopped.

∞

Absence Makes the Heart Grow Fonder

For full appreciation of the good things we enjoy, we need to be deprived of them, at least for a while. Health will be more precious after a time of illness; a beloved spouse will be dearer when you are temporarily separated; a warm room and soft bed will feel like heaven after trudging home through heavy snow in a freezing storm; a day without food will make a simple crust of bread taste like a gourmet meal. In this light we understand the psalmist's exuberant praise of God. He has just survived a time of extreme stress: "Sheltered under Your wings, I rejoice because You have been my help" (v. 8).

During his time of struggle, he had to miss the quiet hours of meditation and prayer "when I looked for You in the sanctuary to contemplate Your power and glory" (v. 3). It has been well said that "absence makes the heart grow fonder." Now, out of danger, the psalmist yearns for the comforting sense of God's presence: "Early will I seek You; my soul thirsts for You" (v. 2). He connects again with God at bedtime: "When I remember You upon my bed and meditate on You during the night" (v. 7). He feels again close to God: "My soul cleaves unto You; Your right hand upholds me"(v. 9).

✎

Reflection: Organized Worship

Among visitors to churches and synagogues are occasionally those who profess antagonism toward organized religion. One such person told the minister of the church he had visited, "I really don't care much for organized religion," to which the minister replied, "Then you'll love our church. It's completely disorganized." Once after services I greeted an unfamiliar-looking gentleman as he came through the receiving line. I asked, "Are you, by chance, a member of our congregation?" He said, "I wouldn't join your congregation. It's full of hypocrites." I reassured him: "Sir, we always have room for one more."

The psalmist was a true devotee of organized religion. He loved the temple services. He describes himself as serious in the search for God (v. 2), coming to the temple looking for God "in the sanctuary" (v. 3). Much can be said in favor of communal or congregational worship. The sanctuary is usually a place of architectural beauty. Choral and instrumental music uplift the spirit. The mood for prayer is enhanced by the fellowship of others who join in worship and song. The worship experience in the temple leaves the psalmist spiritually satisfied: "My soul is satisfied" (v. 6). He is ecstatic as he senses the presence of God: "Your loving-kindness is better than life. So will I bless You as long as I live" (v. 5). Having said all that, we recognize that we may also seek and find God's presence outside the sanctuary, any place, any time. One can feel close to God resting on a meadow "beside the still waters," watching a sunrise in the mountains or at the seashore, or looking at the starry sky at night.

❧ PSALM 64 ❧

For the Leader. A Psalm of David.

2 Hear my voice, O God, in my complaint;
Preserve my life from the terror of the enemy.
3 Hide me from the council of evil-doers;
From the tumult of the workers of iniquity;
4 Who have whet their tongue like a sword,
And have aimed their arrow, a poisoned word;
5 That they may shoot in secret places at the blameless;
Suddenly do they shoot at him, and fear not.
6 They encourage one another in an evil matter;
They converse of laying snares secretly;
They ask, who would see them.
7 They search out iniquities, they have accomplished a diligent search;
Even in the inward thought of every one, and the deep heart.

8 But God doth shoot at them with an arrow suddenly;
Thence are their wounds.
9 So they make their own tongue a stumbling unto themselves;
All that see them shake the head.
10 And all men fear;
And they declare the work of God,
And understand His doing.
11 The righteous shall be glad in the LORD, and shall take refuge in Him;
And all the upright in heart shall glory.

❧

"They Will Stumble over Their Own Tongues"

How do you deal with people who bad-mouth you? What is your best defense against those who, in the words of the psalmist, "have sharpened their tongues like a sword and aimed poisoned speech like an arrow" (v. 4)? Deny their lies? Retaliate by spreading gossip about them? Or turn a deaf ear to all their talking and ignore them? The psalmist, badly hurt by gossip and slander, asks for God's intervention: "In my anxiety, hear my voice, O God; guard my life against the frightening enemy" (v. 2). He counts on the self-destructive nature of mischief: "They will stumble over their own tongues" (v. 9).

God's justice guarantees the vindication of the upright: "The righteous shall be glad with God and take refuge in Him" (v. 11).

❧

Reflection: Joy in Worship

There are plants that grow only in dark places. Similarly, there are people whose religious feelings develop not in the sunshine of joy but in the shadow of a somber mood and sullen solemnity. They frown on smiles and consider it obscene to laugh in the sanctuary. Such an attitude perversely contradicts the spirit of the Bible. The Psalms especially sparkle with joy. Psalmist after psalmist calls on the faithful to rejoice before God: "Make a joyful sound" (Psalm 66:1); "sing a new song" (Psalm 33:3); "praise God in dance" (Psalm 149:3); "clap your hands all you peoples, shout unto God with singing" (Psalm 47:1). Musical instruments accompanying the singing include the harp, cymbals, and tambourines. The author of Psalm 64 forgets the terrors of his time as he calls on all to be happy in God's presence: "The righteous shall be glad with God" (v. 11). Robert Louis Stevenson believed that our moral and spiritual life should generate a sense of gladness: "If your morals make you dreary, depend upon it, they are wrong." The English writer John Lubbock Avebury, once also a banker and parliamentarian, stressed the mutuality of happiness and moral duty: "Dwell on the duty of happiness as well as on the happiness of duty." The psalms teach us to live with joy in the presence of God and be thankful for His many gifts.

∽ PSALM 65 ∽

For the Leader. A Psalm. A Song of David.

2 Praise waiteth for Thee, O God, in Zion;
And unto Thee the vow is performed.
3 O Thou that hearest prayer,
Unto Thee doth all flesh come.
4 The tale of iniquities is too heavy for me;
As for our transgressions, Thou wilt pardon them.
5 Happy is the man whom Thou choosest, and bringest near,
That he may dwell in Thy courts;
May we be satisfied with the goodness of Thy house,
The holy place of Thy temple!

6 With wondrous works dost Thou answer us in righteousness,
O God of our salvation;
Thou the confidence of all the ends of the earth,
And of the far distant seas;

7 Who by Thy strength settest fast the mountains,
Who art girded about with might;
8 Who stillest the roaring of the seas, the roaring of their waves,
And the tumult of the peoples;
9 So that they that dwell in the uttermost parts stand in awe of Thy signs;
Thou makest the outgoings of the morning and evening to rejoice.

10 Thou hast remembered the earth, and watered her, greatly enriching her,
With the river of God that is full of water;
Thou preparest them corn, for so preparest Thou her.
11 Watering her ridges abundantly,
Settling down the furrows thereof,
Thou makest her soft with showers;
Thou blessest the growth thereof.
12 Thou crownest the year with Thy goodness;

And Thy paths drop fatness.
13 The pastures of the wilderness do
    drop;
   And the hills are girded with joy.

14 The meadows are clothed with flocks;
   The valleys also are covered over with
    corn;
   They shout for joy, yea, they sing.

❦

The More Grateful You Are, the Happier You Will Be

If you are enjoying good health and prosperity, remember, things don't have to stay that way. The psalmist recognizes well-being as a gift for which one must give thanks. Being in the habit of worship, he thinks of God as one "Who hears prayer" (v. 3). He praises God for keeping the forces of nature under control. It is God "Who subdues the roaring sea" (v. 8) and Who "waters the earth, greatly enriching it" (v. 10). The psalmist thinks of God as the source of all good things: "You crown the year with Your goodness. . . . the hills are girded with joy. The meadows are clothed with flocks; the valleys are covered with corn" (v. 12–14).

Appreciation, thanksgiving, and joy go together. The more things you can name for which you are grateful, the more cheerful will be your mood. So count your blessings at all times.

❦

Reflection: The Purpose of Prayer

The psalmist calls God "You who hears prayer" (v. 3). What is he praying for? Nothing at all; he approaches God without complaints and without petitions, only to offer praise and thanksgiving. He only wants to be in God's presence. Of all the purposes, none is higher than the wish to be with God. Rabbi Leo Baeck, who miraculously survived the Holocaust in one of Hitler's concentration camps, said: "The purpose of prayer is to be alone with God." To be alone with God is not easy. You may be physically alone, but not mentally if your mind is preoccupied with other interests, concerns, and desires. Can you divest yourself of all that keeps you busy and focus your thoughts on meeting with God? Are you conscious of the audacity of asking the Supreme Being of the Universe to pay attention to your words? Angelus Silesius expressed amazement at the possibility of communication between God and man: "How marvelous that I, a filthy clod,/May yet hold friendly converse with my God?"

This is what prayer is all about: a daring outreach to connect with

God. We can never know what effect our prayer has on God. We only know our side of it, our longing, our need for God's presence, our feeling of relief and renewed confidence after unburdening ourselves before God. We dare hope, however, that prayer is not wasted breath, that it accomplishes some good, as Tennyson suggested in his lines: "More things are wrought in prayer/Than this world dreams of."

∾ Psalm 66 ∾

For the Leader. A Song, a Psalm.

Shout unto God, all the earth;
2 Sing praises unto the glory of His
  name;
  Make His praise glorious.
3 Say unto God: "How tremendous is
  Thy work!
  Through the greatness of Thy power
    shall Thine enemies dwindle away
    before Thee.
4 All the earth shall worship Thee,
  And shall sing praises unto Thee;
  They shall sing praises to Thy name."
                                    Selah

5 Come, and see the works of God;
  He is terrible in His doing toward the
    children of men.
6 He turned the sea into dry land;
  They went through the river on foot;
  There let us rejoice in Him!
7 Who ruleth by His might for ever;
  His eyes keep watch upon the nations;
  Let not the rebellious exalt them-
    selves.   Selah

8 Bless our God, ye peoples,
  And make the voice of His praise to
    be heard;
9 Who hath set our soul in life,
  And suffered not our foot to be
    moved,
10 For Thou, O God, hast tried us;
  Thou hast refined us, as silver is
    refined.
11 Thou didst bring us into the hold;

Thou didst lay constraint upon our
  loins.
12 Thou hast caused men to ride over
  our heads;
  We went through fire and through
    water;
  But Thou didst bring us out unto
    abundance.

13 I will come into Thy house with
  burnt-offerings,
  I will perform unto Thee my vows,
14 Which my lips have uttered,
  And my mouth hath spoken, when I
    was in distress.
15 I will offer unto Thee burnt-offerings
  of fatlings,
  With the sweet smoke of rams;
  I will offer bullocks with goats.
                                    Selah

16 Come, and hearken, all ye that fear
  God,
  And I will declare what He hath done
    for my soul.
17 I cried unto Him with my mouth,
  And He was extolled with my tongue.
18 If I had regarded iniquity in my heart,
  The LORD would not hear;
19 But verily God hath heard;
  He hath attended to the voice of my
    prayer.
20 Blessed be God,
  Who hath not turned away my prayer,
    nor His mercy from me.

Thanksgiving Is Due at All Times

A mishap, disturbance, or pain will get your immediate attention. How aware are you of your good fortune when nothing happens to upset your normal way of life? Do you realize the many perils from which you are escaping each day without ever knowing it? The author of Psalm 66 does not take his well-being for granted. He invites us to consider God's work for our benefit: "Come and see the works of God" (v. 5).

God keeps order in the world: "He rules the world with might; He watches the nations" (v. 7). God may at times test us with afflictions, but also keeps us safe: "He has granted us life and kept our feet from stumbling" (v. 9).

The psalmist remembers when his people were sorely tried but, in the end, delivered: "We went through fire and water, but You brought us out into abundance" (v. 12). The experience of many deliverances in his own life and in his people's history convinces him that God hears our prayers: "God does listen. He gives attention to my prayer" (v. 19).

Reflection: Our Interdependence

The psalmist went to the Sanctuary to "perform my vows which my lips have uttered . . . when I was in distress" (v. 13–14). No doubt he felt good after paying off his debt, as would any orderly person when discharging an obligation. But does a human being ever repay all he owes? Think of all the persons who helped you, from birth on, become what you are now: your parents, doctors, nurses, teachers. Could you repay all those who taught you skills, who helped you get your first job, gave you advice, introduced you to people you needed to meet and helped advance your career? Add to your list of helpers those countless other people, unknown to you by name, whose inventions, products, and labor keep you safe and well supplied.

No person is, or ever was, self-sufficient. As the world keeps shrinking in communication, trade, and interaction, we become even more interdependent than we were when William Blake wrote: "No man is an island, entire of itself; every man is a piece of the continent, a part of the main." Our indebtedness goes beyond contemporary mankind. It extends to all the generations before you whose accumulated knowledge, including the language you speak, was passed on to you as a gift. You may well be proud of what you have accomplished, but do not exaggerate your own part in the making of yourself or underrate what others, alive and dead, have done for you.

PSALM 67

For the Leader; with string-music. A
   Psalm, a Song.

2God be gracious unto us, and bless us;
May He cause His face to shine
   toward us;   Selah
3That Thy way may be known upon
   earth,
Thy salvation among all nations.

4Let the peoples give thanks unto
   Thee, O God;
Let the peoples give thanks unto
   Thee, all of them.
5O let the nations be glad and sing for
   joy;

For Thou wilt judge the peoples with
   equity,
And lead the nations upon earth.
                              Selah
6Let the peoples give thanks unto
   Thee, O God;
Let the peoples give thanks unto
   Thee, all of them.
7The earth hath yielded her increase;
May God, our own God, bless us.
8May God bless us;
   And let all the ends of the earth fear
   Him.

Our God Cares for All Nations

If you love someone, it will seem to you that others must also love and
admire the person so dear to you. Thus the psalmist, in his great love
for God, thinks that all peoples share his feelings: "Let all peoples give
thanks to You, all of them; let the nations be glad and sing for joy"
(v. 4–5). If all nations thank and worship God, it is plausible, according
to the psalmist, that God in turn cares for all nations: "You rule the
peoples with equity and guide the nations of the earth" (v. 5).

Although the psalmist speaks out of a personal relationship with
the God of his people, Israel ("May God, *our own* God, bless us"—v. 7),
he wants to share his belief in God with all humanity: "May Your way
be known to all the earth, Your salvation among all nations" (v. 3).

Reflection: Retribution

This happy psalm, exuberant in praise and thanksgiving for God's
blessings, includes a jubilant endorsement of God's justice: "Let the
nations be glad and sing for joy, for You will judge the peoples with
equity" (v. 5). Why would God's judgment make the psalmist so happy?
Try to imagine the world and mankind going their way without any
order, rules, or laws. It would be a chaotic world in which no one could
be trusted and nothing could ever be predicted. But this is not reality.

Nature and human beings seem to be regulated in such a way that much that happens day by day is predictable. There is evidence of order in the world of physics as well as in the world of morality, in human relations. The psalmist's faith in God's judgment has persisted through the generations, although the rule of retribution—reward for good and penalty for evil—does not operate with the unfailing regularity we would expect. There are righteous people who live their lives in misery, apparently unrewarded for the good they have done, and there are transgressors who escape the penalty they so richly deserve. What supports belief in God's judgment despite so much contradictory evidence? Experience teaches us that everything we do has consequences. Despite seeming irregularities, a moral law of causality is operative in human relations. Kindness and love beget a loving response; an honest person is trusted. A helpful neighbor will be helped in need. On the other hand, a known liar is not believed even when he speaks the truth; a thief is watched; a man of violence is beaten in return. As the African-American cult leader, Father Divine, used to say, "Things don't just happen; they happen just." As you treat others, so will you be treated. But being human, with a short life span, we are impatient. We must take the long view and give justice time to run its course, as Longfellow reminds us:

> Though the mills of God grind slowly,
> Yet they grind exceeding small;
> Though with patience he stands waiting,
> With exactness grinds he all.

❧ PSALM 68 ❧

For the Leader. A Psalm of David, a Song.

2 Let God arise, let His enemies be scattered;
And let them that hate Him flee before Him.

3 As smoke is driven away, so drive them away;
As wax melteth before the fire,
So let the wicked perish at the presence of God.

4 But let the righteous be glad, let them exult before God;
Yea, let them rejoice with gladness.

5 Sing unto God, sing praises to His name;
Extol Him that rideth upon the skies, whose name is the LORD;
And exult ye before Him.

6 A father of the fatherless, and a judge of the widows,
Is God in His holy habitation.

7 God maketh the solitary to dwell in a house;
He bringeth out the prisoners into prosperity;

The rebellious dwell but in a parched land.

8 O God, when Thou wentest forth before Thy people,
When Thou didst march through the wilderness;   Selah

9 The earth trembled, the heavens also dropped at the presence of God;
Even yon Sinai trembled at the presence of God, the God of Israel.

10 A bounteous rain didst Thou pour down, O God;
When Thine inheritance was weary, Thou didst confirm it.

11 Thy flock settled therein;
Thou didst prepare in Thy goodness for the poor, O God.

12 The LORD giveth the word;
The women that proclaim the tidings are a great host.

13 Kings of armies flee, they flee;
And she that tarrieth at home divideth the spoil.

14 When ye lie among the sheepfolds,
The wings of the dove are covered with silver,
And her pinions with the shimmer of gold.

15 When the Almighty scattereth kings therein,
It snoweth in Zalmon.

16 A mountain of God is the mountain of Bashan;
A mountain of peaks is the mountain of Bashan.

17 Why look ye askance, ye mountains of peaks,
At the mountain which God hath desired for His abode?
Yea, the LORD will dwell therein for ever.

18 The chariots of God are myriads, even thousands upon thousands;
The LORD is among them, as in Sinai, in holiness.

19 Thou hast ascended on high, Thou hast led captivity captive;
Thou hast received gifts among men,
Yea, among the rebellious also, that the LORD God might dwell there.

20 Blessed be the LORD, day by day He beareth our burden,
Even the God who is our salvation.   Selah

21 God is unto us a God of deliverances;
And unto GOD the LORD belong the issues of death.

22 Surely God will smite through the head of His enemies,
The hairy scalp of him that goeth about in his guiltiness.

23 The LORD said: "I will bring back from Bashan,
I will bring them back from the depths of the sea;

24 That thy foot may wade through blood,
That the tongue of thy dogs may have its portion from thine enemies."

25 They see Thy goings, O God,
Even the goings of my God, my King, in holiness.

26 The singers go before, the minstrels follow after,
In the midst of damsels playing upon timbrels:

27 "Bless ye God in full assemblies,
Even the LORD, ye that are from the fountain of Israel."

28 There is Benjamin, the youngest, ruling them,
The princes of Judah their council,
The princes of Zebulun, the princes of Naphtali.

29 Thy God hath commanded thy strength;
Be strong, O God, Thou that hast wrought for us

30 Out of Thy temple at Jerusalem,
Whither kings shall bring presents unto Thee.

31 Rebuke the wild beast of the reeds,
The multitude of the bulls, with the calves of the peoples,
Every one submitting himself with pieces of silver;
He hath scattered the peoples that delight in war!

32 Nobles shall come out of Egypt;

Ethiopia shall hasten to stretch out
her hands unto God.

33 Sing unto God, ye kingdoms of the
earth;
O sing praises unto the LORD;

Selah

34 To Him that rideth upon the heavens
of heavens, which are of old;

Lo, He uttereth His voice, a mighty
voice.

35 Ascribe ye strength unto God;
His majesty is over Israel,
And His strength is in the skies.

36 Awful is God out of thy holy places;
The God of Israel, He giveth strength
and power unto the people;
Blessed be God.

❧

A Patriot's Tribute to God

The author of Psalm 68 is a lover of God and a passionate patriot. The God he believes in is almighty and powerfully acts in the world He created. Under His protection, Israel will triumph over her enemies, who, in the psalmist's view, are also the enemies of God: "God is for us a God of deliverance . . . God will smash the heads of His enemies" (v. 21, 22). God is the champion of the upright: "The righteous shall rejoice; they shall exult in the presence of God" (v. 4).

God is also the compassionate protector of the weak: "The father of orphans, the champion of widows. . . . God restores the lonely to their homes. . . . frees the prisoners" (v. 6, 7).

The sight of the sanctuary in Jerusalem, the procession of "singers, musicians and maidens playing upon timbrels" (v. 26), enraptures the psalmist. He prays for the end of war: "Scatter the people who delight in war" (v. 31). He would have all the nations unite in praise of God: "O kingdoms of the earth, sing to God, chant hymns to the Lord" (v. 33).

❧

Reflection: Gratitude

Joy, thanksgiving, and triumph are the happy themes of this psalm. Whatever the occasion, either a great victory or an abundant harvest, there was a jubilant celebration in Jerusalem. The psalmist may have been inspired by the pageantry that he witnessed in the temple: a procession of "singers in the lead, followed by musicians in the midst of young women playing upon timbrels" (v. 26). For the psalmist and his people, religion was predominantly a joyful celebration of God: "Let the righteous be glad, let them exalt before God; let them rejoice with gladness" (v. 4). What would make the faithful rejoice with gladness? Gratitude for sustenance and help. God cares for the needy and down-trodden: "O God, in Your goodness You did prepare for the poor" (v. 11). Recognition of God's help in dire circumstances: "God is unto us a God of deliverances" (v. 21). At all times, God is to be thanked for the gift of life: "God provides for us escape from death" (v. 21). Those who are aware of God's presence see themselves at the receiving end of God's gifts. The grateful cannot be sad. Gladness is the companion of appreciation. The Hebrew word for "giving thanks" also means "giving praise." George Herbert connected gratitude with praise, not a single expression of thanks, but a constant sense of gratitude:

> Thou that hast given so much to me,
> Give one thing more—a grateful heart;
> Not thankful when it pleaseth me,
> As if Thy blessings had spare days;
> But such a heart whose pulse may be Thy praise.

❧ PSALM 69 ❧

For the Leader; upon Shoshannim. [A Psalm] of David.

2 Save me, O God;
For the waters are come in even unto the soul.
3 I am sunk in deep mire, where there is no standing;
I am come into deep waters, and the flood overwhelmeth me.
4 I am weary with my crying; my throat is dried;
Mine eyes fail while I wait for my God.
5 They that hate me without a cause are more than the hairs of my head;
They that would cut me off, being mine enemies wrongfully, are many;
Should I restore that which I took not away?
6 O God, Thou knowest my folly;
And my trespasses are not hid from Thee.
7 Let not them that wait for Thee be ashamed through me, O LORD God of hosts;
Let not those that seek Thee be brought to confusion through me, O God of Israel.

8 Because for Thy sake I have borne reproach;

Confusion hath covered my face.
9 I am become a stranger unto my brethren,
And an alien unto my mother's children.
10 Because zeal for Thy house hath eaten me up,
And the reproaches of them that reproach Thee are fallen upon me.
11 And I wept with my soul fasting,
And that became unto me a reproach.
12 I made sackcloth also my garment,
And I became a byword unto them.
13 They that sit in the gate talk of me;
And I am the song of the drunkards.

14 But as for me, let my prayer be unto Thee, O LORD, in an acceptable time;
O God, in the abundance of Thy mercy,
Answer me with the truth of Thy salvation.
15 Deliver me out of the mire, and let me not sink;
Let me be delivered from them that hate me, and out of the deep waters.
16 Let not the waterflood overwhelm me,
Neither let the deep swallow me up;

And let not the pit shut her mouth
upon me.

17 Answer me, O LORD, for Thy mercy
is good;
According to the multitude of Thy
compassions turn Thou unto me.

18 And hide not Thy face from Thy
servant;
For I am in distress; answer me
speedily.

19 Draw nigh unto my soul, and redeem
it;
Ransom me because of mine enemies.

20 Thou knowest my reproach, and my
shame, and my confusion;
Mine adversaries are all before Thee.

21 Reproach hath broken my heart; and I
am sore sick;
And I looked for some to show compassion, but there was none;
And for comforters, but I found none.

22 Yea, they put poison into my food;
And in my thirst they gave me vinegar
to drink.

23 Let their table before them become a
snare;
And when they are in peace, let it
become a trap.

24 Let their eyes be darkened, that they
see not;
And make their loins continually to
totter.

25 Pour out Thine indignation upon
them,
And let the fierceness of Thine anger
overtake them.

26 Let their encampment be desolate;
Let none dwell in their tents.

27 For they persecute him whom Thou
hast smitten;
And they tell of the pain of those
whom Thou hast wounded.

28 Add iniquity unto their iniquity;
And let them not come into Thy
righteousness.

29 Let them be blotted out of the book
of the living,
And not be written with the
righteous.

30 But I am afflicted and in pain;
Let Thy salvation, O God, set me up
on high.

31 I will praise the name of God with a
song,
And will magnify Him with thanksgiving.

32 And it shall please the LORD better
than a bullock
That hath horns and hoofs.

33 The humble shall see it, and be glad;
Ye that seek after God, let your heart
revive.

34 For the LORD hearkeneth unto the
needy,
And despiseth not His prisoners.

35 Let heaven and earth praise Him,
The seas, and every thing that moveth
therein.

36 For God will save Zion, and build the
cities of Judah;
And they shall abide there, and have it
in possession.

37 The seed also of His servants shall
inherit it;
And they that love His name shall
dwell therein.

Suffering for the Sake of God

Good deeds, as you must know, are not always rewarded, that is, not
immediately and not necessarily in the way you would expect. The
author of Psalm 69 identifies himself as a person whose zeal for God
has gotten him into lots of trouble (see v. 10). It has made him the target of insult and abuse: "For Your sake I have been put to shame" (v. 8).

The psalmist does not claim to be perfect: "O God, You know my folly and my wrongdoing are not hidden from you" (v. 6). He has shown remorse by weeping and fasting (see v. 11–12), and prays for mercy (see v. 14). The victim of malicious talk (see v. 13), deserted by friends, he is heartbroken: "I looked for someone to show compassion, but there is none; and for comforters, but I found none" (v. 21).

In great despair, he wishes his enemies dead: "Let them be blotted out of the book of the living" (v. 29). In his suffering, he begs for God's help: "I am lowly and in pain. Let Your help keep me safe" (v. 30).

But God's help is slow in coming. The psalmist makes a pathetic appeal for speedy relief: "Answer me, O God, for Your mercy is good; according to Your great compassion turn to me; do not hide Your face from your servant, for I am in distress; answer me speedily" (v. 18).

The psalmist learns from his own experience that piety and faithfulness to God do not guarantee you a bed of roses. Still, he clings to his faith even if his loyalty goes unrewarded for the time being: "I will praise the name of God with a song, and will magnify Him with thanksgiving" (v. 31).

∞

Reflection: The Book of Life

In an offhand remark, the psalmist mentions an important concept of faith: "The book of life." The psalmist has harsh words for certain malicious persons who gloat over the suffering of people who have already been punished by God. Such persons, lacking all compassion, do not deserve to live: "Let them be blotted out of the book of life and not be written with the righteous" (v. 29). The idea of God's Book of Life has profound implications: All forms of life, all persons, are bound together in unity as are the pages of a book. Every living thing contributes something to the total story of life. God is the Scribe in control of the Book of Life. We are alive as long as we are recorded in it; we die when blotted out. Underlying the observance of *Rosh Hashanah*, the Jewish New Years Festival, is the belief that all human beings pass for review and judgment before God at the start of a new year, to be either inscribed or blotted out in the Book of Life. From this notion comes the custom of sending to family and friends new year's greetings with the message: "May you be inscribed in the Book of Life." It is further assumed that God's sentence is suspended for ten days, during which the decree may be reversed through prayer, repentance, and charity, culminating on *Yom Kippur*, the Day of Atonement.

∾ PSALM 70 ∾

For the Leader. [A Psalm] of David;
  to make memorial.

2 O God, to deliver me,
  O LORD, to help me, make haste.
3 Let them be ashamed and abashed
  That seek after my soul;
  Let them be turned backward and
    brought to confusion
  That delight in my hurt.
4 Let them be turned back by reason of
  their shame

That say: "Aha, aha."
5 Let all those that seek Thee rejoice
  and be glad in Thee;
And let such as love Thy salvation say
  continually:
  "Let God be magnified."
6 But I am poor and needy;
  O God, make haste unto me;
  Thou art my help and my deliverer;
  O LORD, tarry not.

∾

Don't Be Ashamed to Ask for Help

A survey found that among motorists who have lost their way, women are more likely than men to stop and ask for help with directions. Are men ashamed to ask for help? The author of Psalm 70 does not hesitate to implore God for help when hard-pressed by adversaries: "O God, hasten to deliver me; rush to my rescue!" (v. 2).

Indeed, the psalmist suggests we should be glad to seek God and eager to receive His help: "Let all who seek You do so with gladness and joy" (v. 5). He is not ashamed to admit his need for help: "I am poor and needy. O God, hurry! You are my helper and my rescuer; O God, do not delay" (v. 6).

∾

Reflection: Hope and Patience

It is not easy to wait patiently for help when you are in trouble and worse may yet be on the way. The psalmist is in a perilous situation. He describes himself as "poor and needy" (v. 6). He wants God to hurry with His help: "O God, help me, make haste. . . . O God, make haste for me . . . O God, delay not" (v. 2, 6).

What enables one in illness or some other distress to wait for relief? Three things will give you the strength of patience. It helps if you have overcome other difficulties before. As Nietzsche said, "We take unto ourselves the strength of that which we have overcome." You will say to yourself: "I've done it before, I can do it again," and carry on as best you can. Hope is another source of strength enabling you to bear your burden. The saying "As long as there is life, there is hope" is equally true in reverse: "As long as there is hope, there is life." Believers in God have the great advantage of looking to God with hope, as did the psalmist even in his desperate situation: "You are my help and my deliverer" (v. 6).

Finally, we need the will to endure. There are problems in life for which no solution is at hand. All there is to do is hold out and wait for a change. When the German lyrical poet Rainer Maria Rilke was asked to sum up his view of life, he answered: "To endure it, that's all." If you wait long enough, the problem may vanish. Help may come in some unexpected way.

Note that Psalm 70 duplicates, with minor variations, Psalm 40:14–18.

❧ Psalm 71 ❧

In Thee, O Lord, have I taken
  refuge;
Let me never be ashamed.
2 Deliver me in Thy righteousness,
  and rescue me;
Incline Thine ear unto me, and save
  me.
3 Be Thou to me a sheltering rock,
  whereunto I may continually
  resort,
Which Thou hast appointed to save
  me;
For Thou art my rock and my
  fortress.

4 O my God, rescue me out of the
  hand of the wicked,
Out of the grasp of the unrighteous
  and ruthless man.
5 For Thou art my hope;
O Lord God, my trust from my
  youth.
6 Upon Thee have I stayed myself
  from birth;
Thou art He that took me out of my
  mother's womb;
My praise is continually of Thee.
7 I am as a wonder unto many;

But Thou art my strong refuge.
8 My mouth shall be filled with Thy
  praise,
And with Thy glory all the day.
9 Cast me not off in the time of old
  age;
When my strength faileth, forsake
  me not.
10 For mine enemies speak concerning
  me,
And they that watch for my soul take
  counsel together,
11 Saying: "God hath forsaken him;
Pursue and take him; for there is
  none to deliver."
12 O God, be not far from me;
O my God, make haste to help me.
13 Let them be ashamed and consumed
  that are adversaries to my soul;
Let them be covered with reproach
  and confusion that seek my hurt.

14 But as for me, I will hope continually,
And will praise Thee yet more and
  more.
15 My mouth shall tell of Thy
  righteousness,
And of Thy salvation all the day;

For I know not the numbers thereof.

16I will come with Thy mighty acts, O
Lord God;
I will make mention of Thy right-
eousness, even of Thine only.

17O God, Thou hast taught me from
my youth;
And until now do I declare Thy
wondrous works.

18And even unto old age and hoary
hairs, O God, forsake me not;
Until I have declared Thy strength
unto the next generation,
Thy might to every one that is to
come;

19Thy righteousness also, O God,
which reacheth unto high heaven;
Thou who hast done great things,
O God, who is like unto Thee?

20Thou, who hast made me to see
many and sore troubles,
Wilt quicken me again, and bring me
up again from the depths of the
earth.

21Thou wilt increase my greatness,
And turn and comfort me.

22I also will give thanks unto Thee
with the psaltery,
Even unto Thy truth, O my God;
I will sing praises unto Thee with the
harp,
O Thou Holy One of Israel.

23My lips shall greatly rejoice when I
sing praises unto Thee;
And my soul, which Thou hast
redeemed.

24My tongue also shall tell of Thy
righteousness all the day;
For they are ashamed, for they are
abashed, that seek my hurt.

⚮

We Grow More Dependent
upon God with Age

Every living creature is more or less dependent on others. At every
stage of life we require some kind of help, and more so as we grow old.
The author of Psalm 71, having reached old age, looks back on his life.
He acknowledges dependence on God while still unborn: "While yet
in the womb, I depended on You" (v. 6). Now, in old age, he hopes that
God will not abandon him: "Cast me not off in old age; forsake me not
when I am failing in strength" (v. 9).

His confidence in God is based on the numberless times he experienced God's help: "I shall daily tell of Your righteousness and deliverances though I know not how to number them" (v. 15). Now he
beseeches God to help him against enemies who consider him a
pushover because of his diminished strength in old age: "Mine enemies
talk against me; they watch me and agree, 'God has forsaken him, pursue and get him, for no one will save him'" (v. 10–11). But he feels
assured that the God Who has seen him through so many troubles in
the past will again empower him to cope with this crisis: "You who have
made me survive many problems and troubles will again strengthen me
and lift me up from the depths" (v. 20).

Reflection: Trust

The essential bond that holds people together in relationships is trust. What is trust made of? This psalm gives us some of the answer. Its author has many fears, yet he trusts that God Who was with him throughout life will be with him through old age. He is a person of faith, but not blind faith. He trusts God because his whole life is a record of God's help and beneficence: "You are my hope, O God, my trust from my youth. . . . I depended on you from birth. . . . while yet in my mother's womb" (v. 5, 6).

Trust looks toward the future with one eye while the other sees the past. You confidently cross a bridge if you have safely done so before. You trust a dealer whose past service was satisfactory. Old friends are best because they have been tested the longest. You trust the spouse whose love and faithfulness you have experienced over the years. Similarly, the psalmist turns to God with trust that He will uphold him in the future as He has done in the past. On the strength of his whole life's experience, he is hopeful in his prayer that God will be with Him in old age: "Cast me not off in old age; when I am failing in strength, forsake me not" (v. 9).

❧ PSALM 72 ❧

[A Psalm] of Solomon.

Give the king Thy judgments, O
    God,
And Thy righteousness unto the
    king's son;
2 That he may judge Thy people with
    righteousness,
And Thy poor with justice.
3 Let the mountains bear peace to the
    people,
And the hills, through righteousness.
4 May he judge the poor of the people,
And save the children of the needy,
And crush the oppressor.
5 They shall fear Thee while the sun
    endureth,
And so long as the moon, through-
    out all generations.

6 May he come down like rain upon
    the mown grass,
As showers that water the earth.
7 In his days let the righteous
    flourish,
And abundance of peace, till the
    moon be no more.

8 May he have dominion also from sea
    to sea,
And from the River unto the ends of
    the earth.
9 Let them that dwell in the wilderness
    bow before him;
And his enemies lick the dust.
10 The kings of Tarshish and of the isles
    shall render tribute;
The kings of Sheba and Seba shall
    offer gifts.

11 Yea, all kings shall prostrate themselves before him;
All nations shall serve him.
12 For he will deliver the needy when
he crieth;
The poor also, and him that hath no
helper.
13 He will have pity on the poor and
needy,
And the souls of the needy he will
save.
14 He will redeem their soul from
oppression and violence,
And precious will their blood be in
his sight;
15 That they may live, and that he may
give them of the gold of Sheba,
That they may pray for him
continually,
Yea, bless him all the day.
16 May he be as a rich cornfield in the
land upon the top of the
mountains;

May his fruit rustle like Lebanon;
And may they blossom out of the
city like grass of the earth.
17 May his name endure for ever;
May his name be continued as long
as the sun;
May men also bless themselves by
him;
May all nations call him happy.

18 Blessed be the LORD God, the God
of Israel,
Who only doeth wondrous things;
19 And blessed be His glorious name
for ever;
And let the whole earth be filled with
His glory.
Amen, and Amen.

20 The prayers of David the son of
Jesse are ended.

❧

Characteristics of an Ideal National Leader

The author of Psalm 72, by describing the kind of king he would want
for Israel, tells us something about the dominant ideals of his nation in
biblical times. He stresses four characteristics of the ideal king:

1. *Justice:* "May he judge Your people with righteousness" (v. 2).
2. *Concern for the Poor:* "May he treat justly the poor of the people
   and save the children of the needy" (v. 4).
3. *Love of Peace:* "May the righteous flourish in his days with abundant peace" (v. 7).
4. *Overcomes Oppression:* "He will save them from oppression and
   violence, for their blood will be precious in his sight"
   (v. 14).

❧

Reflection: Leadership

Hero worship has brought untold misery upon mankind. When people
follow their hero uncritically, unable or unwilling to recognize flaws in
his character and mistakes in his leadership, calamity lies ahead. A

Russian proverb wisely warns: "The toe of the star-gazer is often stubbed." We must take care that admiration for our star not blind us to reality with all its perils. When we idealize a leader, our sound judgment is at risk. It is remarkable that, unlike kings of other nations, who are glorified as conquerors, this psalm praises the king of Israel as a ruler of justice, peace, compassion, and liberator from oppression. In the psalmist's judgment, the king does not have license to do as he wishes. He, too, is subject to the same moral standards under God's laws that apply to all. He must be just, compassionate, and peace-loving and battle against oppression and violence.

❧ PSALM 73 ❧

A Psalm of Asaph.

Surely God is good to Israel,
Even to such as are pure in heart.
2 But as for me, my feet were almost gone;
My steps had well nigh slipped.
3 For I was envious at the arrogant,
When I saw the prosperity of the wicked.
4 For there are no pangs at their death,
And their body is sound.
5 In the trouble of man they are not;
Neither are they plagued like men.
6 Therefore pride is as a chain about their neck;
Violence covereth them as a garment.
7 Their eyes stand forth from fatness;
They are gone beyond the imaginations of their heart.
8 They scoff, and in wickedness utter oppression;
They speak as if there were none on high.
9 They have set their mouth against the heavens,
And their tongue walketh through the earth.
10 Therefore His people return hither;
And waters of fulness are drained out by them.

11 And they say: "How doth God know?
And is there knowledge in the Most High?"
12 Behold, such are the wicked;
And they that are always at ease increase riches.
13 Surely in vain have I cleansed my heart,
And washed my hands in innocency;
14 For all the day have I been plagued,
And my chastisement came every morning.

15 If I had said: "I will speak thus",
Behold, I had been faithless to the generation of Thy children.
16 And when I pondered how I might know this,
It was wearisome in mine eyes;
17 Until I entered into the sanctuary of God,
And considered their end.
18 Surely Thou settest them in slippery places;
Thou hurlest them down to utter ruin.
19 How are they become a desolation in a moment!
They are wholly consumed by terrors.
20 As a dream when one awaketh,

So, O LORD, when Thou arousest
   Thyself, Thou wilt despise their
   semblance.
21For my heart was in a ferment,
   And I was pricked in my reins.
22But I was brutish, and ignorant;
   I was as a beast before Thee.

23Nevertheless I am continually with
   Thee;
   Thou holdest my right hand.
24Thou wilt guide me with Thy
   counsel,
   And afterward receive me with glory.
25Whom have I in heaven but Thee?

And beside Thee I desire none upon
   earth.
26My flesh and my heart faileth;
   But God is the rock of my heart and
   my portion for ever.
27For, lo, they that go far from Thee
   shall perish;
   Thou dost destroy all them that go
   astray from Thee.
28But as for me, the nearness of God is
   my good;
   I have made the LORD God my
   refuge,
   That I may tell of all Thy works.

✳

When Good Things Happen
to Bad People

You are in good company if you are shocked by the fact that so many good things happen to bad people. It doesn't square with the doctrine of God's justice. In the Bible, prophets such as Jeremiah and sages such as the authors of the book of Job and Ecclesiastes were perplexed by the suffering of many an innocent person and the prosperity of notorious sinners. Psalm 73 wrestles with this problem: "As for me, I almost strayed off course and stumbled in my envy of the wayward, seeing how well off the wicked are" (v. 2).

It irks the psalmist that the wicked seem to be "untouched by the troubles that befall people and spared the afflictions which come to the rest of mankind" (v. 5). Moreover, "they scoff and hatch evil schemes . . . and say, 'how does God know?'" (v. 8, 11). Far from fearing punishment, these wanton sinners "are always relaxed and getting richer" (v. 12). It sickens the psalmist to make these observations (see v. 14–16). Embittered, he wonders if his uprightness is all for nothing: "What is the point of keeping my heart pure and washing my hands in innocence?" (v. 13).

He recovers his faith when, on a visit to the sanctuary, it occurs to him that those scoundrels are allowed to rise to such heights only to fall that much harder: "How suddenly are they ruined" (v. 19). Now he blames himself for his impatience and lack of trust in God: "I was an ignorant fool and behaved like a beast before You" (v. 22).

What really matters to him now is his closeness to God, which is denied to the wicked. It is the exclusive reward of the righteous: "As for me, I am always with You. You hold my hand and You will guide me with Your counsel" (v. 23–24). The psalmist at last feels rewarded and contented: "Whom have I in heaven but You? And having You, I want nothing else on earth. . . . As for me, the nearness of God is my good" (v. 25, 28).

❈

Reflection: Envy

We are all in the habit of making comparisons. We compare ourselves with others in appearance, in skill at games, in business and professional success. But take the advice of Cervantes, later repeated by Shakespeare: "All comparisons are odious." When you compare yourself with someone else, you run a moral risk. If you compare unfavorably, you will be envious; if the other person compares unfavorably, you will consider the other inferior and be contemptuous. Envy is the problem in Psalm 73, as stated from the start: "As for me, I almost strayed off course, and stumbled in my envy of the wayward, seeing how well off the wicked are" (v. 2–3).

Is envy a minor or a major sin? Don't belittle it, considering its destructiveness, not least of which is the pain it gives to the envious person himself. The envious literally eat their hearts out. Twenty-five hundred years ago, the Greek philosopher Antithenes already recognized the corrosive effect of envy: "As iron is eaten away by rust, so the envious are consumed by their own passion." Even earlier, the Bible referred to envy as a disease: "Envy is rottenness of the bones" (Proverbs 14:30). The first crime in human history, according to the Bible, was caused by envy. Cain killed his brother Abel because Abel's offering to God was received more favorably than his own.

How does the psalmist cope with this malicious passion of envy? He managed to do so in prayerful reflection in the Sanctuary of God (see v. 17). There he gained new insight into himself. He discovered that the material prosperity of others, always subject to sudden loss, was not so important to him after all. What mattered most to him was the feeling of being in God's presence: "As for me, I am always with You. You hold my hand and You will guide me with Your counsel. . . . beside You I desire none upon earth . . . as for me, the nearness of God is my good" (v. 23–25, 28). The psalmist's experience illustrates the saying of Samuel Johnson: "Envy is proportionate to desire." If you can change your desire, that is, reorder your priorities and no longer want what you had envied, envy dies a natural death.

❧ PSALM 74 ❧

Maschil of Asaph.

Why, O God, hast Thou cast us off
for ever?
Why doth Thine anger smoke
against the flock of Thy pasture?
2 Remember Thy congregation, which
Thou hast gotten of old,
Which Thou hast redeemed to be
the tribe of Thine inheritance;
And mount Zion, wherein Thou hast
dwelt.
3 Lift up Thy steps because of the perpetual ruins,
Even all the evil that the enemy hath
done in the sanctuary.
4 Thine adversaries have roared in the
midst of Thy meeting-place;
They have set up their own signs for
signs.
5 It seemed as when men wield
upwards
Axes in a thicket of trees.
6 And now all the carved work thereof
together
They strike down with hatchet and
hammers.
7 They have set Thy sanctuary on fire;
They have profaned the dwelling-
place of Thy name even to the
ground.
8 They said in their heart: "Let us
make havoc of them altogether";
They have burned up all the meeting-
places of God in the land.
9 We see not our signs;
There is no more any prophet;
Neither is there among us any that
knoweth how long.
10 How long, O God, shall the adversary reproach?
Shall the enemy blaspheme Thy
name for ever?
11 Why withdrawest Thou Thy hand,
even Thy right hand?
Draw it out of Thy bosom and consume them.

12 Yet God is my King of old,
Working salvation in the midst of the
earth.
13 Thou didst break the sea in pieces by
Thy strength;
Thou didst shatter the heads of the
sea-monsters in the waters.
14 Thou didst crush the heads of
leviathan,
Thou gavest him to be food to the
folk inhabiting the wilderness.
15 Thou didst cleave fountain and
brook;
Thou driedst up ever-flowing rivers.
16 Thine is the day, Thine also the
night;
Thou hast established luminary and
sun.
17 Thou hast set all the borders of the
earth;
Thou hast made summer and winter.

18 Remember this, how the enemy hath
reproached the LORD,
And how a base people have blas-
phemed Thy name.
19 O deliver not the soul of Thy turtle-
dove unto the wild beast;
Forget not the life of Thy poor for
ever.
20 Look upon the covenant;
For the dark places of the land are
full of the habitations of violence.
21 O let not the oppressed turn back in
confusion;
Let the poor and needy praise Thy
name.
22 Arise, O God, plead Thine own
cause;
Remember Thy reproach all the day
at the hand of the base man.
23 Forget not the voice of Thine
adversaries,
The tumult of those that rise up
against Thee which ascendeth
continually.

❦

Eyewitness to Destruction

It is easy to hold on to faith when all goes well, but difficult when disaster strikes. The author of Psalm 74 witnessed the collapse of his nation and the destruction of his beloved city of Jerusalem and somehow managed to cling to his faith in God. He describes the devastation of the city and the temple. Wielding axes and hatchets, the conquerors smashed to pieces the artistic interior of the sanctuary and burned it to the ground. He records with horror: "They have set Your sanctuary on fire!" (v. 7). In great anguish he cries out: "How long, O God, shall the enemy go on disgracing and scorning Your name?" (v. 10).

Having seen the slaughter and destruction with his very eyes, he nevertheless affirms his faith: "Yet, God is my king of old, working salvation throughout the land" (v. 12). How could he say this while the temple was still aflame? The conquerors of Jerusalem could destroy the temple but not God. God remains the creator and ruler of the universe: "Yours is the day and Yours is the night. You have established the light and the sun" (v. 16). The psalmist draws hope from his belief that God is above the wreckage done on earth. He has not lost control of the world, and with His help, everything is possible.

❦

Reflection: Making a Comeback

One of life's first lessons is that "you can't win them all." From earliest childhood to old age, even the ablest and most successful will, at times, suffer frustration, rejection, and defeat. The second lesson to learn is that no defeat is final. Every setback can be the beginning of a comeback. Psalm 74 tells of a devastating defeat. Sorrow over the humiliation and destruction of Jerusalem breaks the psalmist's heart, but not his spirit. Amidst the ruins of the city, he proclaims unbroken faith in God's saving power: "Yet, God is my king of old, working salvation throughout the land" (v. 12). He counts on restoration and rebuilding. In defeat it is good to remember Elbert Hubbard's saying: "There is no failure except in no longer trying." The key to victory or defeat is within yourself, as Longfellow said so well:

> Not in the clamor of the crowded street,
> Not in the shouts and plaudits of the throng,
> But in ourselves, are triumph and defeat.

❧ PSALM 75 ❧

For the Leader; Al-tashheth. A
Psalm of Asaph, a Song.

2We give thanks unto Thee, O God,
We give thanks, and Thy name is
near;
Men tell of Thy wondrous works.

3"When I take the appointed time,
I Myself will judge with equity.
4When the earth and all the inhabi-
tants thereof are dissolved,
I Myself establish the pillars of it."
Selah

5I say unto the arrogant: "Deal not
arrogantly";
And to the wicked: "Lift not up the
horn."
6Lift not up your horn on high;
Speak not insolence with a haughty
neck.

7For neither from the east, nor from
the west,
Nor yet from the wilderness, cometh
lifting up.
8For God is judge;
He putteth down one, and lifteth up
another.
9For in the hand of the LORD there is
a cup, with foaming wine, full of
mixture,
And He poureth out of the same;
Surely the dregs thereof, all the
wicked of the earth shall drain
them, and drink them.
10But as for me, I will declare for ever,
I will sing praises to the God of
Jacob.
11All the horns of the wicked also will I
cut off;
But the horns of the righteous shall
be lifted up.

❧

The World Will Not Fall Apart

If you have lived long enough, you will probably remember some crisis when the world seemed to spin out of control. The author of Psalm
75, speaking in the name of God, reassures us that God won't let the
world fall apart: "When the earth and all its inhabitants are about to be
dissolved, I shall firmly set up its pillars" (v. 4). God will take control of
world events and decide who will be on top: "For God is judge. He
puts this one down and raises that one up" (v. 8). Fortified in faith, the
psalmist faces the future without fear: "As for me, I will sing praises to
the God of Jacob. . . . the righteous shall be empowered" (v. 10, 11).

❧

Reflection: "With Firmness in the Right"

Thomas Paine had harsh words for American patriots who were luke-
warm in support of the American Revolution. He railed against those
halfhearted patriots, "the summer soldiers and the sunshine patriots."
Abraham Lincoln likewise called for strong commitment and resolve in

support of the Union's cause. In his second inaugural address to the war-weary nation, he said: "With firmness in the right, as God gave us to see the right, let us strive to finish the work we are in." Psalm 75 is a clarion call to the people of Israel not to weaken and not to waiver, but to stand firm in faith that God will uphold the pillars, that is, the principles and laws of His moral order, even "when the earth and all its inhabitants are about to be dissolved" (v. 4). Justice will prevail, "for God is judge" (v. 8). In troubled times such as ours, as terrorists aim to destroy our country and would tear down our whole civilization, we need the psalmist's confidence that "the righteous shall be empowered" (v. 11).

❧ PSALM 76 ❧

For the Leader; with string-music. A Psalm of Asaph, a Song.

2 In Judah is God known;
His name is great in Israel.
3 In Salem also is set His tabernacle,
And His dwelling-place in Zion.
4 There He broke the fiery shafts of the bow;
The shield, and the sword, and the battle.   Selah

5 Glorious art Thou and excellent, coming down from the mountains of prey.
6 The stout-hearted are bereft of sense, they sleep their sleep;
And none of the men of might have found their hands.
7 At Thy rebuke, O God of Jacob, They are cast into a dead sleep, the riders also and the horses.

8 Thou, even Thou, art terrible;
And who may stand in Thy sight when once Thou art angry?
9 Thou didst cause sentence to be heard from heaven;
The earth feared, and was still,
10 When God arose to judgment, To save all the humble of the earth.
                    Selah

11 Surely the wrath of man shall praise Thee;
The residue of wrath shalt Thou gird upon Thee.
12 Vow, and pay unto the LORD your God;
Let all that are round about Him bring presents unto Him that is to be feared;
13 He minisheth the spirit of princes;
He is terrible to the kings of the earth.

❧

God Is with the Humble

The author of Psalm 76 is jubilant about Israel's stunning victory over an enemy who had unleashed an attack against Jerusalem. The enemy was repelled, and the psalmist gives all the credit to God: "There He broke the fiery arrows of the bow, the shields and swords of war" (v. 4).

The psalmist interprets his people's victory as an act of God. He sees God as the savior of the weak, and this time the weak are represented by Israel: "When God rises to judgment, it is to save the humble of the earth" (v. 10).

Reflection: Providence

It is by no means obvious why God would favor the humble of the earth, as the psalmist asserts. Come to think of it, why should God bother with any of us, big or small, strong or weak, proud or humble? Are we, whose life flees away as a shadow, important enough for God to bother with? With trillions of worlds whirling about space and unimaginably many living beings in this world, why would God reach down to any one of us to drag us out of the mire of troubles? Why would our paltry needs merit the attention of the Master of the universe? Human logic cannot make the case for divine providence; neither can the human mind conceive how God can hear the billions of prayers recited daily in a thousand tongues. We can neither explain nor deny with certainty God's receptivity to our prayers and needs. The philosopher Pascal was sure of one thing: the human mind is not equal to such questions. Said Pascal: "If you say that man is too little for God to speak to him, you must be very big to be able to judge." The prophet Isaiah dealt with these questions best of all by teaching us that there is no comparison between the mind of man and the mind of God: "My thoughts are not your thoughts, neither are your ways My ways, says God" (Isaiah 55:8).

PSALM 77

For the Leader; for Jeduthun. A Psalm of Asaph.

2I will lift up my voice unto God, and cry;
I will lift up my voice unto God, that He may give ear unto me.
3In the day of my trouble I seek the LORD;
With my hand uplifted, [mine eye] streameth in the night without ceasing;
My soul refuseth to be comforted.
4When I think thereon, O God, I must moan;
When I muse thereon, my spirit fainteth.   Selah
5Thou holdest fast the lids of mine eyes;
I am troubled, and cannot speak.
6I have pondered the days of old,
The years of ancient times.
7In the night I will call to remembrance my song;

I will commune with mine own
  heart;
And my spirit maketh diligent
  search:
8"Will the LORD cast off for ever?
  And will He be favourable no more?
9Is His mercy clean gone for ever?
  Is His promise come to an end for
  evermore?
10Hath God forgotten to be gracious?
  Hath He in anger shut up His
  compassions?"   Selah
11And I say: "This is my weakness,
  That the right hand of the Most
  High could change.
12I will make mention of the deeds of
  the LORD;
  Yea, I will remember Thy wonders of
  old.
13I will meditate also upon all Thy
  work,
  And muse on Thy doings."
14O God, Thy way is in holiness;
  Who is a great god like unto God?
15Thou art the God that doest
  wonders;

Thou hast made known Thy
  strength among the peoples.
16Thou hast with Thine arm redeemed
  Thy people,
  The sons of Jacob and Joseph.
            Selah
17The waters saw Thee, O God;
  The waters saw Thee, they were in
  pain;
  The depths also trembled.
18The clouds flooded forth waters;
  The skies sent out a sound;
  Thine arrows also went abroad.
19The voice of Thy thunder was in the
  whirlwind;
  The lightnings lighted up the
  world;
  The earth trembled and shook.
20Thy way was in the sea,
  And Thy path in the great waters,
  And Thy footsteps were not
  known.
21Thou didst lead Thy people like a
  flock,
  By the hand of Moses and Aaron.

∞

Seeking God in Days of Trouble

How do you know that God cares for you? One way of finding out is to ask God for help: "I raise my voice unto God that He may listen to me. In the day of trouble I seek the Lord" (v. 2, 3). Will God help? The psalmist looks back on past experience: "I am thinking of days gone by and years long past" (v. 6). He remembers: "I will mention the acts of the Lord; I remember Your wonders of old" (v. 12). Now he asks: "Will God reject and show no more favors?" (v. 8). God has not changed. He is today what He has always been: "You are the God that does wonders; You have shown Your power among the peoples. . . . You redeemed Your people, the sons of Jacob and Joseph" (v. 15–16). The psalmist's hope for the future is based on past experience. The God Who gave us all that we are will not stop giving.

Reflection: Memory

The psalmist is in distress. Suffering robs him of sleep at night: "You hold mine eyes waking" (v. 5). His mind fills with memories of better days, which raise the disturbing question, Why have things changed? Is God abandoning him? Will God no longer be favorable and gracious (see v. 8–10)? Do our memories help or hurt? Both answers are true. Some memories embarrass and shame us; others make us proud. Some memories of what might have been in our lives fill us with regret; we blame ourselves for missed opportunities. Especially painful are memories of our victimization, which make us burn with resentment; on the other hand, there are memories of help and kindness that fill us with gratitude. Memories of our own success in the past may boost our self-confidence but also dishearten us as we realize how deeply we have fallen. There is a difference between memories of our own actions and the works of God. Remembering what we have done may both gladden and sadden us. But the memory of God's work is always awe-inspiring and uplifting. As the psalmist ponders the work of God, he forgets himself and all his troubles. He is full of praise for God's mighty acts: "I will mention the deeds of God; I will remember Your wonders of old." (See v. 12–21.)

❧ PSALM 78 ❧

Maschil of Asaph.

Give ear, O my people, to my
  teaching;
Incline your ears to the words of my
  mouth.
²I will open my mouth with a parable;
I will utter dark sayings concerning
  days of old.
³That which we have heard and
  known,
And our fathers have told us,
⁴We will not hide from their children,
Telling to the generation to come
  the praises of the LORD,
And His strength, and His wondrous
  works that He hath done.

⁵For He established a testimony in
  Jacob,
And appointed a law in Israel,
Which He commanded our
  fathers,
That they should make them
  known to their children;
⁶That the generation to come might
  know them, even the children that
  should be born;
Who should arise and tell them to
  their children,
⁷That they might put their confidence in God,
And not forget the works of God,
But keep His commandments;
⁸And might not be as their fathers,

A stubborn and rebellious generation;
A generation that set not their heart
aright,
And whose spirit was not stedfast
with God.

9 The children of Ephraim were as
archers handling the bow,
That turned back in the day of battle.
10 They kept not the covenant of God,
And refused to walk in His law;
11 And they forgot His doings,
And His wondrous works that He
had shown them.
12 Marvellous things did He in the
sight of their fathers,
In the land of Egypt, in the field of
Zoan.
13 He cleaved the sea, and caused them
to pass through;
And He made the waters to stand as
a heap.
14 By day also He led them with a
cloud,
And all the night with a light of fire.
15 He cleaved rocks in the wilderness,
And gave them drink abundantly as
out of the great deep.
16 He brought streams also out of the
rock,
And caused waters to run down like
rivers.

17 Yet went they on still to sin against
Him,
To rebel against the Most High in
the desert.
18 And they tried God in their heart
By asking food for their craving.
19 Yea, they spoke against God;
They said: "Can God prepare a table
in the wilderness?
20 Behold, He smote the rock, that
waters gushed out,
And streams overflowed;
Can He give bread also?
Or will He provide flesh for His
people?"

21 Therefore the LORD heard, and was
wroth;
And a fire was kindled against Jacob,
And anger also went up against
Israel;
22 Because they believed not in God,
And trusted not in His salvation.
23 And He commanded the skies above,
And opened the doors of heaven;
24 And He caused manna to rain upon
them for food,
And gave them of the corn of
heaven.
25 Man did eat the bread of the mighty;
He sent them provisions to the full.
26 He caused the east wind to set forth
in heaven;
And by His power He brought on
the south wind.
27 He caused flesh also to rain upon
them as the dust,
And winged fowl as the sand of the
seas;
28 And He let it fall in the midst of
their camp,
Round about their dwellings.
29 So they did eat, and were well filled;
And He gave them that which they
craved.
30 They were not estranged from their
craving,
Their food was yet in their mouths,
31 When the anger of God went up
against them,
And slew of the lustieth among
them,
And smote down the young men of
Israel.

32 For all this they sinned still,
And believed not in His wondrous
works.
33 Therefore He ended their days as a
breath,
And their years in terror.
34 When He slew them, then they
would inquire after Him,
And turn back and seek God
earnestly.

35 And they remembered that God was
  their Rock,
  And the Most High God their
  Redeemer.
36 But they beguiled Him with their
  mouth,
  And lied unto Him with their
  tongue.
37 For their heart was not stedfast with
  Him,
  Neither were they faithful in His
  covenant.
38 But He, being full of compassion,
  forgiveth iniquity, and destroyeth
  not;
  Yea, many a time doth He turn His
  anger away,
  And doth not stir up all His wrath.
39 So He remembered that they were
  but flesh,
  A wind that passeth away, and
  cometh not again.

40 How oft did they rebel against Him
  in the wilderness,
  And grieve Him in the desert!
41 And still again they tried God,
  And set bounds to the Holy One of
  Israel.
42 They remembered not His hand,
  Nor the day when He redeemed
  them from the adversary.
43 How He set His signs in Egypt,
  And His wonders in the field of
  Zoan;
44 And turned their rivers into blood,
  So that they could not drink their
  streams.
45 He sent among them swarms of flies,
  which devoured them;
  And frogs, which destroyed them.
46 He gave also their increase unto the
  caterpillar,
  And their labour unto the locust.
47 He destroyed their vines with hail,
  And their sycamore-trees with frost.
48 He gave over their cattle also to the
  hail,
  And their flocks to fiery bolts.

49 He sent forth upon them the fierceness of His anger,
  Wrath, and indignation, and trouble,
  A sending of messengers of evil.
50 He levelled a path for His anger;
  He spared not their soul from
  death,
  But gave their life over to the
  pestilence;
51 And smote all the first-born in
  Egypt,
  The first-fruits of their strength in
  the tents of Ham;
52 But He made His own people to go
  forth like sheep,
  And guided them in the wilderness
  like a flock.
53 And He led them safely, and they
  feared not;
  But the sea overwhelmed their
  enemies.
54 And He brought them to His holy
  border,
  To the mountain, which His right
  hand had gotten.
55 He drove out the nations also before
  them,
  And allotted them for an inheritance
  by line,
  And made the tribes of Israel to
  dwell in their tents.

56 Yet they tried and provoked God, the
  Most High,
  And kept not His testimonies;
57 But turned back, and dealt treacherously like their fathers;
  They were turned aside like a deceitful bow.
58 For they provoked Him with their
  high places,
  And moved Him to jealousy with
  their graven images.
59 God heard, and was wroth,
  And He greatly abhorred Israel;
60 And He forsook the tabernacle of
  Shiloh,
  The tent which He had made to
  dwell among men;

61And delivered His strength into
  captivity,
  And His glory into the adversary's
  hand.
62He gave His people over also unto
  the sword;
  And was wroth with His inheritance.
63Fire devoured their young men;
  And their virgins had no marriage-
  song.
64Their priests fell by the sword;
  And their widows made no
  lamentation.

65Then the LORD awaked as one
  asleep,
  Like a mighty man recovering from
  wine.
66And He smote His adversaries
  backward;
  He put upon them a perpetual
  reproach.

67Moreover He abhorred the tent of
  Joseph,
  And chose not the tribe of Ephraim;
68But chose the tribe of Judah,
  The mount Zion which He loved.
69And He built His sanctuary like the
  heights,
  Like the earth which He hath
  founded for ever.
70He chose David also His servant,
  And took him from the sheepfolds;
71From following the ewes that give
  suck He brought him,
  To be shepherd over Jacob His people, and Israel His inheritance.
72So he shepherded them according to
  the integrity of his heart;
  And led them by the skilfulness of
  his hands.

∞

Does History Teach Us Anything?

If the lessons of history are not to be wasted, we must do two things: remember the past and draw the right conclusions from what happened in the past. Disaster has struck. God "has turned over his people to the sword . . . fire devoured their young men . . . their priests fell by the sword" (v. 62–63). A morally superior people will not wish to strike back at the enemy without some soul-searching and admission of their own faults, which may have caused the calamity. That is just what the author of Psalm 78 is doing: "Listen, O my people, to my teaching. . . . that future generations might know . . ." (v. 1, 6).

A national catastrophe—the destruction of the northern Israelite kingdom and the exile of the survivors, the "ten lost tribes"—prompts the psalmist, who lived in the southern kingdom of Judah, to review all of Hebrew history. In verses 13 through 55, he retells highlights of the liberation from Egyptian bondage, the exodus, the journey through the wilderness, and the conquest of Canaan. It is a story full of wonders that convinced the Hebrews that they were saved and guided by God. The psalmist clearly states the purpose of this historical review: "That they might put their confidence in God and not forget the works of God, and keep His commandments" (v. 7).

He warns his people not to repeat the mistakes of past generations, whose backsliding into idolatry and violations of the covenant with God brought on destruction: "Let them not be like their fathers, a wayward and rebellious generation who did not have their heart in the right place and whose spirit was not true to God" (v. 8). Thus the lesson to be learned from history is clear: Faithfulness to God and His commandments is the price for survival: "For He established a decree in Jacob, and taught Israel, our ancestors, to make it known to their children" (v. 5).

∽

Reflection: Models

Psalm 78 includes a sentence that sounds somewhat shocking: "Let them not be like their fathers" (v. 8). This seems to contradict a basic moral principle in the Bible, respect for parents. Does not the fifth commandment say loud and clear, "Honor your father and your mother"? Should not children respect and emulate parents and elders? Why the exceptional warning in Psalm 78 *not* to be like the parents? Much of the psalm records various transgressions of previous generations, not to be followed by the new generation. Parents must set good examples or be disqualified as teachers of their children. You should note an important point suggested by the wording of the familiar passage from chapter 6:7–8 in the book of Deuteronomy, which enjoins the parents to teach God's commandments to the children: "And these words, which I command you this day, shall be upon your heart and you shall teach them diligently unto your children." How is the parent to teach? Not in the classroom but all day long, at home, at bedtime, and in the morning: "When you sit down in your house, when you walk by the way, when you lie down and when you rise up" (v. 7). In other words, parents should be role models for their children in daily life, from morning until nightfall. The primary task of parenthood is not only to correct, rebuke, and discipline children but also to exemplify right conduct, as Joseph Joubert said: "Children have more need of models than of critics." The alarming rise of juvenile delinquency must be charged to the absence of good role models at home, as has been pointed out by H. G. Hutchinson: "The most difficult job teenagers have today is learning good conduct without seeing any."

❧ Psalm 79 ❧

A Psalm of Asaph.

O God, the heathen are come into
 Thine inheritance;
They have defiled Thy holy temple;
They have made Jerusalem into
 heaps.
2 They have given the dead bodies of
 Thy servants to be food unto the
 fowls of the heaven,
The flesh of Thy saints unto the
 beasts of the earth.
3 They have shed their blood like
 water
Round about Jerusalem, with none
 to bury them.
4 We are become a taunt to our neighbours,
A scorn and derision to them that are
 round about us.

5 How long, O LORD, wilt Thou be
 angry for ever?
How long will Thy jealousy burn
 like fire?
6 Pour out Thy wrath upon the
 nations that know Thee not,
And upon the kingdoms that call not
 upon Thy name.
7 For they have devoured Jacob,
And laid waste his habitation.

8 Remember not against us the
 iniquities of our forefathers;
Let Thy compassions speedily come
 to meet us;
For we are brought very low.

9 Help us, O God of our salvation, for
 the sake of the glory of Thy name;
And deliver us, and forgive our sins,
 for Thy name's sake.
10 Wherefore should the nations say:
 "Where is their God?"
Let the avenging of Thy servants'
 blood that is shed
Be made known among the nations
 in our sight.
11 Let the groaning of the prisoner
 come before Thee;
According to the greatness of Thy
 power set free those that are
 appointed to death;
12 And render unto our neighbours
 sevenfold into their bosom
Their reproach, wherewith they have
 reproached Thee, O LORD.
13 So we that are Thy people and the
 flock of Thy pasture
Will give Thee thanks for ever;
We will tell of Thy praise to all
 generations.

❧

Search Your Own Soul When Disaster Strikes

When disaster strikes, it is only human to rage against those who have
done it to you. The author of Psalm 79 is horrified at the destruction
of Jerusalem, the desecration of the temple, and the slaughter of his
people: "O God, . . . they have desecrated Your holy Temple. They
have turned Jerusalem into heaps. . . . They have shed blood like water
round about Jerusalem" (v. 1, 3). He bursts out in fury against the per-
petrators of these atrocities: "Pour out Your wrath upon the nations
that do not know You!" (v. 6).

But then he confesses his own people's culpability. Admitting that
his ancestors and his own generation are not without blame, he begs

God for forgiveness and mercy: "Remember not against us the iniquities of our forefathers; let Your compassion speedily reach us. . . . and deliver us, and forgive our sins, for the sake of Your name" (v. 8, 9).

∞

Reflection: Faultfinding

It has been well said that victory has many fathers, but defeat is an orphan. People are quick to claim credit for success but don't want to share responsibility for failure. When confronted by problems, we wonder who is to blame and usually point fingers at others. A wise rabbi said: "God gave us two eyes, one to see the other person's virtues and the other to see our own faults." If we must find fault, let us begin with our own. Blaming others whenever we are in trouble is the sure mark of immaturity. "Conscience," explained the little girl, "is something in me that tells me when my brother Johnny is doing wrong." It says something about the superior character of the psalmist that in his rage against enemies who destroyed his country, he admitted his own people's faults and begged God, "remember not against us the iniquities of our forefathers. . . . and forgive our sins" (v. 8–9). Facing up to one's own faults is the first step in overcoming them.

∞ PSALM 80 ∞

For the Leader; upon Shoshannim.
　A testimony. A Psalm of Asaph.

2Give ear, O Shepherd of Israel,
　Thou that leadest Joseph like a flock;
　Thou that art enthroned upon the
　　cherubim, shine forth.
3Before Ephraim and Benjamin and
　　Manasseh, stir up Thy might,
　And come to save us.
4O God, restore us;
　And cause Thy face to shine, and we
　　shall be saved.

5O LORD God of hosts,
　How long wilt Thou be angry
　　against the prayer of Thy people?
6Thou hast fed them with the bread
　of tears,

And given them tears to drink in
　　large measure.
7Thou makest us a strife unto our
　　neighbours;
　And our enemies mock as they
　　please.
8O God of hosts, restore us;
　And cause Thy face to shine, and we
　　shall be saved.
9Thou didst pluck up a vine out of
　　Egypt;
　Thou didst drive out the nations,
　　and didst plant it.
10Thou didst clear a place before it,
　And it took deep root, and filled the
　　land.
11The mountains were covered with
　　the shadow of it,

And the mighty cedars with the boughs thereof.
12 She sent out her branches unto the sea,
And her shoots unto the River.
13 Why hast Thou broken down her fences,
So that all they that pass by the way do pluck her?
14 The boar out of the wood doth ravage it,
That which moveth in the field feedeth on it.

15 O God of hosts, return, we beseech Thee;
Look from heaven, and behold, and be mindful of this vine,

16 And of the stock which Thy right hand hath planted,
And the branch that Thou madest strong for Thyself.
17 It is burned with fire, it is cut down;
They perish at the rebuke of Thy countenance.
18 Let Thy hand be upon the man of Thy right hand,
Upon the son of man whom Thou madest strong for Thyself.
19 So shall we not turn back from Thee;
Quicken Thou us, and we will call upon Thy name.
20 O Lord God of hosts, restore us;
Cause Thy face to shine, and we shall be saved.

❧

It Takes Two to Make Peace

Reconciliation is not a one-way affair. It is not enough that the offender apologizes; the offended party needs to accept the apology and pardon the offense. Both sides must want to restore a good relationship. This is the message of Psalm 80. The people of Israel have offended God, their "Shepherd" (v. 2). But now they have suffered long enough for their transgression. It is time for God to calm His anger and receive the people's prayers: "O Lord . . . how long will You angrily shut off the prayer of your people?" (v. 5). Four times the psalmist beseeches God to favor His people again: "O God, restore us; shine upon us and we shall be saved" (v. 4, also 8, 15, and 20). In conclusion, he makes a pledge as inducement for God to grant forgiveness: "We shall not slide back from You. Preserve us alive and we shall pray to You" (v. 19).

❧

Reflection: Forgiveness

This psalm is about forgiveness. The psalmist addresses his ardent plea to God, as so many of us do in prayer. But should we not examine our own hearts if we can forgive those who offended against us? Intentionally or unintentionally, we inflict distress upon one another. Because of the imperfections of human nature, all our relationships are vulnerable, and none more so than family relations. Forgiveness is the only means of healing an injured relationship. The gift of forgiveness goes both ways. The offender and the offended benefit. If you as the injured party withhold forgiveness, your ongoing resentment hijacks your peace of mind, as Laurence Sterne pointed out: "A man who values a good night's rest will not lie down with enmity in his heart, if he can help it." You cannot force an enemy into reconciliation, but your apology will give it a powerful start. An apology may be the most rewarding thing you ever do. If you need another push to apologize or forgive, remember that sooner or later, each of us becomes an offender, as George Herbert said: "He who cannot forgive breaks the bridge over which he himself must pass."

⸙ PSALM 81 ⸙

For the Leader; upon the Gittith. [A Psalm] of Asaph.

2 Sing aloud unto God our strength;
Shout unto the God of Jacob.
3 Take up the melody, and sound the timbrel,
The sweet harp with the psaltery.
4 Blow the horn at the new moon,
At the full moon for our feastday.
5 For it is a statute for Israel,
An ordinance of the God of Jacob.
6 He appointed it in Joseph for a testimony,
When He went forth against the land of Egypt.
The speech of one that I knew not did I hear:

7 "I removed his shoulder from the burden;
His hands were freed from the basket.
8 Thou didst call in trouble, and I rescued thee;
I answered thee in the secret place of thunder;
I proved thee at the waters of Meribah.   Selah
9 Hear, O My people, and I will admonish thee:
O Israel, if thou wouldest hearken unto Me!

10 There shall no strange god be in thee;
Neither shalt thou worship any foreign god.
11 I am the LORD thy God,
Who brought thee up out of the land of Egypt;
Open thy mouth wide, and I will fill it.

12 But My people hearkened not to My voice;
And Israel would none of Me.
13 So I let them go after the stubbornness of their heart,
That they might walk in their own counsels.
14 Oh that My people would hearken unto Me,
That Israel would walk in My ways!
15 I would soon subdue their enemies,
And turn My hand against their adversaries.
16 The haters of the LORD should dwindle away before Him;
And their punishment should endure for ever.
17 They should also be fed with the fat of wheat;
And with honey out of the rock would I satisfy thee."

〰

Free to Choose or Reject God

Powers other than your own control much of your life, but there is one area in which you enjoy freedom of choice: your faith in God! Faith cannot be compelled. It must be an expression of your free will. The psalmist points to the example of his people. Recalling the events of the exodus, he imagines hearing a mysterious voice, presumably the voice of God: "I heard an unfamiliar speech" (v. 6).

Verses 7 through 15 report what the psalmist believed to have been a message from God, how Israel was redeemed from Egyptian bondage and received commandments, which, however, they disobeyed: "But My people would not listen to me . . . Israel would not obey Me" (v. 12). What follows underscores an important feature of the biblical God concept. Faith in God is not to be compelled. It should be a free response to God. This means we are also free to reject God: "I let them go after their willful hearts that they might follow their own minds" (v. 13).

〰

Reflection: Pray with Joy

C. S. Lewis, the Anglican Oxford and Cambridge scholar, lived and worked in an environment of gentlemanly reserve, but he admired the Hebrew spirit of "cheerful spontaneity" that rings forth from the Psalms. Referring to the opening verses of Psalm 81, "Sing unto God . . . shout . . . take up the melody and sound the timbrel, the harp and the lyre . . . blow the horn" (v. 2–4), Lewis made this comment in *Reflections on the Psalms*:

> Let's have a song, bring the tambourine, "bring the merry harp with the lute," we're going to sing merrily and make a joyful noise . . . mere music is not enough . . . clap hands . . . let us have clashing cymbals and dances too . . . We Anglicans have a terrible concern about good taste.

There is no biblical justification for the hushed solemnity, whispered prayers, and restrained emotions so typical of many a church service. We can learn from the robust piety of the psalmists that it is all right to release your feelings in worship; to sing and clap your hands and even dance, as a happy response to God's presence. What God said to Abraham goes for all of Abraham's spiritual descendants:

"Be whole-hearted" (Genesis 17:1). Give God all the feelings of your heart. You can do so in silence but also in the uninhibited expression of jubilation.

❧ Psalm 82 ❧

A Psalm of Asaph.

God standeth in the congregation of
  God;
In the midst of the judges He judgeth:
2 "How long will ye judge unjustly,
And respect the persons of the wicked?
                     Selah
3 Judge the poor and fatherless;
Do justice to the afflicted and
  destitute.
4 Rescue the poor and needy;
Deliver them out of the hand of the
  wicked.

5 They know not, neither do they
  understand;
They go about in darkness;
All the foundations of the earth are
  moved.
6 I said: Ye are godlike beings,
And all of you sons of the Most High.
7 Nevertheless ye shall die like men,
And fall like one of the princes."

8 Arise, O God, judge the earth;
For Thou shalt possess all the nations.

❧

"Arise, O God, Judge the Earth"

The author of Psalm 82 shares with us his vision of God, champion of the poor and needy. He looks to God for justice: "Do justice to the afflicted and destitute" (v. 3). If corruption disqualifies the judges, the psalmist hopes that God Himself will act as judge: "Arise, O God, judge the earth; for all the nations belong to You" (v. 8).

❧

Reflection: How Long?

"How long" (v. 2), cries the psalmist, will justice be perverted? The cry has been taken up by countless believers in God. How long will evil-doers prosper? How long must the poor, the ill, the innocent sufferer wait for relief and deliverance? How long must we wait for violence and terror to cease? Waiting is a proof of faith. We wait for that which we have reason to expect. It would be futile to wait for the impossible. We wait only for the possible, for healing, justice, peace, and the liberation of the oppressed. These are all possibilities that justify waiting for their fulfillment. We would not yearn for justice, brotherhood, and peace if God had not implanted in our souls the sensitivities that make for justice, brotherhood, and peace. Our waiting is a station on the way. Let us trust that hopes cherished by so many will be fulfilled—in God's own good time.

❧ Psalm 83 ❧

A Song, a Psalm of Asaph.

2 O God, keep not Thou silence;
  Hold not Thy peace, and be not still, O God.
3 For, lo, Thine enemies are in an uproar;
  And they that hate Thee have lifted up the head.
4 They hold crafty converse against Thy people,
  And take counsel against Thy treasured ones.
5 They have said: "Come, and let us cut them off from being a nation;
  That the name of Israel may be no more in remembrance."
6 For they have consulted together with one consent;
  Against Thee do they make a covenant;
7 The tents of Edom and the Ishmaelites;
  Moab, and the Hagrites;
8 Gebal, and Ammon, and Amalek;
  Philistia with the inhabitants of Tyre;
9 Assyria also is joined with them;
  They have been an arm to the children of Lot.   Selah

10 Do Thou unto them as unto Midian;
   As to Sisera, as to Jabin, at the brook Kishon;
11 Who were destroyed at En-dor;
   They became as dung for the earth.
12 Make their nobles like Oreb and Zeeb,
   And like Zebah and Zalmunna all their princes;
13 Who said: "Let us take to ourselves in possession
   The habitations of God."
14 O my God, make them like the whirling dust;
   As stubble before the wind.
15 As the fire that burneth the forest,
   And as the flame that setteth the mountains ablaze;
16 So pursue them with Thy tempest,
   And affright them with Thy storm.
17 Fill their faces with shame;
   That they may seek Thy name, O LORD.
18 Let them be ashamed and affrighted for ever;
   Yea, let them be abashed and perish;
19 That they may know that it is Thou alone whose name is the LORD,
   The Most High over all the earth.

❧

Enduring the Silence of God

The greater your faith in God, the more puzzling is God's silence in the presence of outrageous human conduct. The psalmist feared for the survival of his people, Israel, undergoing attack by enemies resolved to exterminate them: "They say: 'Let us wipe them out as a nation so that Israel's name will be remembered no more'" (v. 5). The psalmist waits impatiently for God's response: "O God, keep not silent" (v. 2). He would have God repel the enemies of his people: "O God, make them like the whirling dust, like straw driven by the wind" (v. 14). Maybe those pagan enemies of Israel, in defeat, will acknowledge God: "Fill them with shame so that they may seek Your name, O God" (v. 17). Despite God's silence, the psalmist clings to his faith. He ends his prayer with the declaration: "They will know that You alone are the Lord, the most high over all the earth" (v. 19).

Reflection: Unanswered Prayer

People of faith must wrestle, one time or the other, with the problem of God's silence, as did the psalmist: "O God, keep not silent; be not quiet; do not rest still" (v. 2). You reach out to God in your deepest need, in fear and in pain, and nothing happens. There is no relief. You wonder: "Did I connect? Did my prayer reach God? When will God answer or give me a sign that help is coming?" You repeat your prayers—and all you get is the silence of God. It is as though your letter to a friend came back from the post office with the notation "addressee unknown." How can you explain it? One possible explanation: God hears you and will act, but not now. Think of your early childhood. You asked your mother for something, pulled at her apron, and she rebuffed you: "not now—wait till later." Another explanation: The problem is not God's silence or absence, but your lack of perception. You can't get God's response because your spiritual receiving set is not properly attuned. God is not silent—you may be deaf. Finally, faith does not guarantee an understanding of God's action or inaction. On the contrary, as Isaiah taught us, we must submit to One whose ways and thoughts are beyond our grasp: "For as the heavens are higher than the earth, so are My ways higher than your ways and My thoughts higher than your thoughts" (Isaiah 55:9).

❧ PSALM 84 ❧

For the Leader; upon the Gittith. A Psalm of the sons of Korah.

2 How lovely are Thy tabernacles, O LORD of hosts!
3 My soul yearneth, yea, even pineth for the courts of the LORD;
My heart and my flesh sing for joy unto the living God.
4 Yea, the sparrow hath found a house, and the swallow a nest for herself, Where she may lay her young;
Thine altars, O LORD of hosts, My King, and my God—.

5 Happy are they that dwell in Thy
   house,
 They are ever praising Thee.   Selah

6 Happy is the man whose strength is in
   Thee;
 In whose heart are the highways.
7 Passing through the valley of Baca
   they make it a place of springs;
 Yea, the early rain clotheth it with
   blessings.
8 They go from strength to strength,
 Every one of them appeareth before
   God in Zion.

9 O Lord God of hosts, hear my
   prayer;
 Give ear, O God of Jacob.   Selah

10 Behold, O God our shield,
   And look upon the face of Thine
   anointed.
11 For a day in Thy courts is better than
   a thousand;
 I had rather stand at the threshold of
   the house of my God,
 Than to dwell in the tents of
   wickedness.
12 For the Lord God is a sun and a
   shield;
 The Lord giveth grace and glory;
 No good thing will He withhold from
   them that walk uprightly.
13 O Lord of hosts,
 Happy is the man that trusteth in
   Thee.

A Day of Joy in the Sanctuary

Worship experiences differ from person to person and from time to time. One day you are inspired by the service in the sanctuary; the next time, it doesn't grab you at all. The author of Psalm 84 is ecstatic about a service at the temple in Jerusalem. That visit to the sanctuary made God come alive for him: "My soul yearns for the courts of the Lord. My soul and body sing for joy to the living God" (v. 3). It is a happy experience: "Happy are those who dwell in Your house; they are forever praising You" (v. 5). No place means as much to him as the sanctuary: "A day in Your courts is better than a thousand elsewhere" (v. 11). Such feelings of joy are possible only for one who brings to the sanctuary faith and trust in God: "O Lord of hosts, happy is the person who trusts in You" (v. 13).

Reflection: Personal God

The prayer of this psalmist is not a request but a declaration of love for the *living* God: "My body and soul sing for joy to the living God" (v. 3). In his view, God is not an idea, a concept, or a theory but a living presence. What make the psalmist so happy? It is the feeling of being at home with God that gives him a deep sense of security like that of a bird returning to the nest: "The sparrow has found a house and the swallow a nest for herself where she may place her young" (v. 4). He looks up to God with awe and reverence as the supreme ruler of the universe, "O Lord of hosts" (v. 4), but immediately adds the personal touch: "My King and My God" (v. 4). This expresses his renewed sense of intimate connection with God gained from prayer. For the psalmist, a visit to the sanctuary is meeting with his beloved. He asks God for nothing. Knowing that God is near empowers him: "Those who appear before God go from strength to strength" (v. 8).

❧ PSALM 85 ❧

For the Leader. A Psalm of the sons of Korah.

2 LORD, Thou hast been favourable unto Thy land,
Thou hast turned the captivity of Jacob.
3 Thou hast forgiven the iniquity of Thy people,
Thou hast pardoned all their sin.
                                    Selah
4 Thou hast withdrawn all Thy wrath;
Thou hast turned from the fierceness of Thine anger.
5 Restore us, O God of our salvation,
And cause Thine indignation toward us to cease.
6 Wilt Thou be angry with us for ever?
Wilt Thou draw out Thine anger to all generations?
7 Wilt Thou not quicken us again,
That Thy people may rejoice in Thee?

8 Show us Thy mercy, O LORD,
And grant us Thy salvation.

9 I will hear what God the LORD will speak;
For He will speak peace unto His people, and to His saints;
But let them not turn back to folly.
10 Surely His salvation is nigh them that fear Him;
That glory may dwell in our land.
11 Mercy and truth are met together;
Righteousness and peace have kissed each other.
12 Truth springeth out of the earth;
And righteousness hath looked down from heaven.
13 Yea, the LORD will give that which is good;
And our land shall yield her produce.
14 Righteousness shall go before Him,
And shall make His footsteps a way.

❧

Spiritual Foundations of Peace

Judging by the way news is reported, it would seem that only politics and military power count in the quest for peace and security. The Bible, however, stresses another approach rarely mentioned in the media—the moral conditions that make for peace. Psalm 85 has something important to say about the way to peace: "I will hear what God, the Lord, will speak. He promises peace to His people. . . . Mercy and truth are met together, justice and peace kiss each other" (v. 9, 11). In order to keep quarrels from exploding into bloody conflicts, one must get to the bottom of the problem in the light of truth, and show compassion to all who are hurt in the struggle. This is a moral approach. Furthermore, we need to understand that justice and peace are inseparable. They "kiss each other."

Reflection: The Sense of Justice

How do we develop our sense of justice? Is it rooted in nature? There is no evidence for compassion or justice in the animal world. Nature is more of a slaughterhouse than a courtroom. The prevailing rules seem to be the survival of the fittest and dog eat dog. Alfred, Lord Tennyson described nature as brutal and bloody: "Nature, red in tooth and claw." Does justice grow out of human nature? Certainly not, in view of the fact that man kills more of his own kind than does any other species on earth. Is justice a product of rational thinking? The rationalist philosopher David Hume sharply rejected that notion, arguing that it is quite rational for a person to have more concern over a cut in his little finger than for the welfare of all humanity. Does the universe reflect any kind of justice? Maurice Maeterlinck saw nothing of the sort: "Justice is the very last thing of all wherewith the universe concerns itself. It is equilibrium that absorbs its attention." The psalmist's answer to the question of where justice comes from is: "Truth springs out of the earth; justice looks down from heaven" (v. 12). Whereas scientific knowledge is gained from observation of the earth, our sense of justice is God-inspired, a heavenly gift. The prophet Micah says it plainly: "It has been *told* you, O man, what is good and what God requires of you: Only to do justly, to love mercy and walk humbly before God" (Micah 6:8). The point is that justice and the foundations of ethics are not natural products and did not grow out of man's head, but were conveyed to the human mind by God's revelation.

❧ PSALM 86 ❧

A Prayer of David.

Incline Thine ear, O LORD, and
   answer me;
For I am poor and needy.
2 Keep my soul, for I am godly;
   O Thou my God, save Thy servant
   that trusteth in Thee.

3 Be gracious unto me, O LORD;
   For unto Thee do I cry all the day.
4 Rejoice the soul of Thy servant;
   For unto Thee, O LORD, do I lift up
   my soul.
5 For Thou, LORD, art good, and ready
   to pardon,

And plenteous in mercy unto all them
  that call upon Thee.

⁶Give ear, O LORD, unto my prayer;
  And attend unto the voice of my
  supplications.
⁷In the day of my trouble I call upon
  Thee;
  For Thou wilt answer me.
⁸There is none like unto Thee among
  the gods, O LORD,
  And there are no works like Thine.
⁹All nations whom Thou hast made
  shall come and prostrate themselves
  before Thee, O LORD;
  And they shall glorify Thy name.
¹⁰For Thou art great, and doest wondrous things;
  Thou art God alone.
¹¹Teach me, O LORD, Thy way, that I
  may walk in Thy truth;
  Make one my heart to fear Thy name.
¹²I will thank Thee, O LORD my God,
  with my whole heart;

And I will glorify Thy name for evermore.
¹³For great is Thy mercy toward me;
  And Thou hast delivered my soul
  from the lowest netherworld.

¹⁴O God, the proud are risen up against
  me,
  And the company of violent men have
  sought after my soul,
  And have not set Thee before them.
¹⁵But Thou, O LORD, art a God full of
  compassion and gracious,
  Slow to anger, and plenteous in mercy
  and truth.
¹⁶O turn unto me, and be gracious unto
  me;
  Give Thy strength unto Thy servant,
  And save the son of Thy handmaid.
¹⁷Work in my behalf a sign for good;
  That they that hate me may see it,
  and be put to shame,
  Because Thou, LORD, hast helped me,
  and comforted me.

❧

Pray for the Power of Decision

If you have difficulty making decisions, you are probably inwardly
divided. You either face several options or struggle with your own conflicting desires, and can't make up your mind which way to go. This
could also happen in our religious life. We sometimes offer prayers
with mixed feelings, faith alternating with doubt. Psalm 86 is a moving
prayer that includes the striking words "unify my heart" (v. 11). We do
not know over which issues the psalmist was inwardly divided, but he
did face some kind of a crisis: "In the day of trouble, I call upon You"
(v. 7).

What follows is a petition for enlightenment: "Teach me, O Lord,
Your way that I may walk in Your truth" (v. 11). He awaits God's guidance in order to reach that unity of mind and purpose that is indispensable for decisive action. Such guidance would enable him to act,
boosted by God's strength: "Graciously turn unto me; give of Your
strength to Your servant" (v. 16). It is a sure sign that your prayer has
been answered if it becomes clear to you which way to go and you are
of one mind to do so.

✑

Reflection: Human Nature Divided

The words "unify my heart" in this psalm (v. 12) should have a place in everyone's personal prayer. The human being is notoriously in conflict with himself. "Two souls dwell, alas! in my breast," exclaims the hero of Goethe's drama *Faust*. An ancient Jewish legend says that on the second day of creation, God made the angels with their perfect, innate goodness. Later, He made beasts with their animal desires. But God was not pleased with either. So he fashioned man, a combination of angel and beast, free to follow good and evil. David, crushed by his burden of guilt, prayed, "create me a *clean* heart" (Psalm 51:12). It was an impossible request, since no human being can be completely purged of all evil. The author of Psalm 86 is more realistic, asking God only to "*unify*" his heart. Unity of heart can last only as long as our good impulse dominates and keeps under control the evil impulse within us. Considering human nature, we must be in a constant state of moral vigilance, for which a high degree of spiritual discipline is required: daily prayer and regular study, the immersion of the mind in God's teachings so that we can act resolutely and wholeheartedly. Therefore the psalmist prefaced his wish for an undivided heart with the prayer, "Teach me, O God, Your way, that I may walk in Your truth" (v. 11).

✑ PSALM 87 ✑

A Psalm of the sons of Korah; a Song.

His foundation is in the holy
  mountains.
2 The LORD loveth the gates of Zion
More than all the dwellings of Jacob.
3 Glorious things are spoken of Thee,
O city of God.   Selah
4 "I will make mention of Rahab and
  Babylon as among them that know
  Me;
Behold Philistia, and Tyre, with
  Ethiopia;

This one was born there."
5 But of Zion it shall be said: "This man
  and that was born in her;
And the Most High Himself doth
  establish her."
6 The LORD shall count in the register
  of the peoples:
"This one was born there."   Selah
7 And whether they sing or dance,
All my thoughts are in thee.

Jerusalem, Future Spiritual Home of All Peoples

The author of Psalm 87, an ardent lover of Jerusalem, envisages a time when all peoples will enjoy spiritual citizenship in the Holy City: "The Lord shall count in the register of all peoples each one as being born there" (v. 6).

Reflection: Jerusalem

The author of this very short psalm was visionary about the future role of Jerusalem. At the time he wrote it, Jerusalem was the capital of a ministate, often under foreign domination by one of the neighboring superpowers. Yet he foresees a time when all nations will claim spiritual citizenship in his city of God. The psalmist reaffirms the prophecy of Isaiah: "Many peoples shall go and say: 'Come, let us go up to the mountain of the Lord, to the House of the God of Jacob, and He will teach us of His ways and we will walk in His paths.' For out of Zion shall go forth the law and the word of the Lord from Jerusalem" (Isaiah 2:3). For the first one thousand years of the city's history, only Jews—one to three million at the most—looked to Jerusalem as their spiritual center. Later, many hundreds of millions of Christians added their claim of spiritual citizenship in Jerusalem, as recorded in countless writings, poems, and songs, such as this medieval composition based on St. Augustine:

> Jerusalem, my happy home,
> Would God I were in thee
> Would God my woes were at an end.
> Thy joys that I might see!

We are not yet at the point when all of mankind regards Jerusalem as their spiritual center, but the psalmist's vision is moving closer to fulfillment.

PSALM 88

A Song, a Psalm of the sons of
Korah; for the Leader; upon
Mahalath Leannoth. Maschil of
Heman the Ezrahite.

2 O LORD, God of my salvation,
What time I cry in the night before
Thee,
3 Let my prayer come before Thee,
Incline Thine ear unto my cry.

4 For my soul is sated with troubles,
And my life draweth nigh unto the
grave.
5 I am counted with them that go down
into the pit;
I am become as a man that hath no
help;
6 Set apart among the dead,
Like the slain that lie in the grave,
Whom Thou rememberest no more;
And they are cut off from Thy hand.

7 Thou hast laid me in the nethermost
pit,
In dark places, in the deeps.
8 Thy wrath lieth hard upon me,
And all Thy waves Thou pressest
down.   Selah
9 Thou hast put mine acquaintance far
from me;
Thou hast made me an abomination
unto them;
I am shut up, and I cannot come
forth.
10 Mine eye languisheth by reason of
affliction;

I have called upon Thee, O LORD,
every day,
I have spread forth my hands unto
Thee.
11 Wilt Thou work wonders for the
dead?
Or shall the shades arise and give
Thee thanks?   Selah
12 Shall Thy mercy be declared in the
grave?
Or Thy faithfulness in destruction?
13 Shall Thy wonders be known in the
dark?
And Thy righteousness in the land of
forgetfulness?

14 But as for me, unto Thee, O LORD,
do I cry,
And in the morning doth my prayer
come to meet Thee.
15 LORD, why casteth Thou off my soul?
Why hidest Thou Thy face from me?
16 I am afflicted and at the point of
death from my youth up;
I have borne Thy terrors, I am
distracted.
17 Thy fierce wrath is gone over me;
Thy terrors have cut me off.
18 They came round about me like water
all the day;
They compassed me about together.
19 Friend and companion hast Thou put
far from me,
And mine acquaintance into darkness.

Prayer in Hopeless Situations

What can one pray for in a hopeless situation? The author of Psalm 88
feels near death: "My life approaches the grave" (v. 4). He sees no hope:
"I have become a man for whom there is no help" (v. 5). His distress is
deepened by the desertion of friends: "You have removed from me
mine acquaintances" (v. 9).

The amazing thing about this desperately suffering man awaiting death in total isolation—perhaps in a leper colony—is his persistence in prayer. He continues praying, although so far it has not helped: "As for me, I implore You, O Lord; in the morning my prayer comes to meet You" (v. 14). Not receiving God's help, he asks sarcastically: "Will You work wonders for the dead? Will Your loving-kindness be talked about in the grave?" (v. 11, 12). He feels rejected: "Lord, why do You cast me off?" (v. 15). Is it a touch of irony or indestructible devotion that makes him exclaim, despite God's silence, "O Lord, God of my salvation"? (v. 2).

♋

Reflection: Hope

What comfort and encouragement can one give to one who considers himself hopeless? Whatever the condition, remember Napoleon's saying, "There are no hopeless situations, only men who grow hopeless about them." No situation is unalterable. Everything can change momentarily. The unexpected can happen any time. A Yiddish story tells of a poor tenant farmer who could not pay rent to the Polish count who owned vast stretches of land. The poor farmer pleaded with the count to extend his time for payment by another year. The capricious count agreed on a strange condition: "I'll give you another year if you will teach my dog to speak Polish. If not, I shall drive you off the farm a year from now." The poor farmer, seeing no alternative, agreed to these impossible terms and rushed home with the dog. When he told his wife about the deal, she said: "Have you lost your mind? Do you think you can teach the animal to speak?" The husband replied: "Of course not. But anything can happen in a year's time: The dog may die; the count may die; the count may change his mind. Meanwhile, we'll have another year with bread to eat." No truer words were ever spoken than "anything can happen."

In 1905, a handful of Jews, escaping from oppression and misery in Eastern Europe, gathered on the sand dunes outside of Jaffa to dedicate their settlement. In defiance of those who thought that their project was hopeless, they named the place Tel Aviv, meaning "Hill of Hope." Now greater Tel Aviv, with its population of over one million, is one of the most progressive and prosperous cities in the Middle East. Everyone can build his hill of hope, even in the most barren stretches of life. If you can't see hope with your eyes open, shut them and dream of tomorrow.

❧ Psalm 89 ❧

Maschil of Ethan the Ezrahite.
2 I will sing of the mercies of the Lord
    for ever;
To all generations will I make known
    Thy faithfulness with my mouth.
3 For I have said: "For ever is mercy
    built;
In the very heavens Thou dost
    establish Thy faithfulness.
4 I have made a covenant with My
    chosen,
I have sworn unto David My servant:
5 For ever will I establish thy seed,
And build up thy throne to all
    generations."   Selah

6 So shall the heavens praise Thy
    wonders, O Lord,
Thy faithfulness also in the assembly
    of the holy ones.
7 For who in the skies can be compared
    unto the Lord,
Who among the sons of might can be
    likened unto the Lord,
8 A God dreaded in the great council of
    the holy ones,
And feared of all them that are round
    about Him?
9 O Lord God of hosts,
Who is a mighty one, like unto Thee,
    O Lord?
And Thy faithfulness is round about
    Thee.
10 Thou rulest the proud swelling of the
    sea;
When the waves thereof arise, Thou
    stillest them.
11 Thou didst crush Rahab, as one that
    is slain;
Thou didst scatter Thine enemies
    with the arm of Thy strength.
12 Thine are the heavens, Thine also the
    earth;
The world and the fulness thereof,
    Thou hast founded them.
13 The north and the south, Thou hast
    created them;

Tabor and Hermon rejoice in Thy
    name.
14 Thine is an arm with might;
Strong is Thy hand, and exalted is
    Thy right hand.
15 Righteousness and justice are the
    foundation of Thy throne;
Mercy and truth go before Thee.
16 Happy is the people that know the
    joyful shout;
They walk, O Lord, in the light of
    Thy countenance.
17 In Thy name do they rejoice all the
    day;
And through Thy righteousness are
    they exalted.
18 For Thou art the glory of their
    strength;
And in Thy favour our horn is
    exalted.
19 For of the Lord is our shield;
And of the Holy One of Israel is our
    king.

20 Then Thou spokest in vision to Thy
    godly ones,
And saidst: "I have laid help upon one
    that is mighty;
I have exalted one chosen out of the
    people.
21 I have found David My servant;
With My holy oil have I anointed
    him;
22 With whom My hand shall be
    established;
Mine arm also shall strengthen him.
23 The enemy shall not exact from him;
Nor the son of wickedness afflict him.
24 And I will beat to pieces his
    adversaries before him,
And smite them that hate him.
25 But My faithfulness and My mercy
    shall be with him;
And through My name shall his horn
    be exalted.
26 I will set his hand also on the sea,
And his right hand on the rivers.

27 He shall call unto Me: Thou art my
Father,
My God, and the rock of my
salvation.
28 I also will appoint him first-born,
The highest of the kings of the earth.
29 For ever will I keep for him My
mercy,
And My covenant shall stand fast with
him.
30 His seed also will I make to endure
for ever,
And his throne as the days of heaven.
31 If his children forsake My law,
And walk not in Mine ordinances;
32 If they profane My statutes,
And keep not My commandments;
33 Then will I visit their transgression
with the rod,
And their iniquity with strokes.
34 But My mercy will I not break off
from him,
Nor will I be false to My faithfulness.
35 My covenant will I not profane,
Nor alter that which is gone out of
My lips.
36 Once have I sworn by My holiness:
Surely I will not be false unto David;
37 His seed shall endure for ever,
And his throne as the sun before Me.
38 It shall be established for ever as the
moon;
And be stedfast as the witness in the
sky."   Selah

39 But Thou hast cast off and rejected,
Thou hast been wroth with Thine
anointed.
40 Thou hast abhorred the covenant of
Thy servant;
Thou hast profaned his crown even to
the ground.
41 Thou hast broken down all his fences;
Thou hast brought his strongholds to
ruin.
42 All that pass by the way spoil him;

He is become a taunt to his neighbours.
43 Thou hast exalted the right hand of
his adversaries;
Thou hast made all his enemies to
rejoice.
44 Yea, Thou turnest back the edge of
his sword,
And hast not made him to stand in
the battle.
45 Thou hast made his brightness to
cease,
And cast his throne down to the
ground.
46 The days of his youth hast Thou
shortened;
Thou hast covered him with shame.
Selah
47 How long, O LORD, wilt Thou hide
Thyself for ever?
How long shall Thy wrath burn like
fire?
48 O remember how short my time is;
For what vanity hast Thou created all
the children of men!
49 What man is he that liveth and shall
not see death,
That shall deliver his soul from the
power of the grave?   Selah
50 Where are Thy former mercies, O
LORD,
Which Thou didst swear unto David
in Thy faithfulness?
51 Remember, LORD, the taunt of Thy
servants;
How I do bear in my bosom [the
taunt of] so many peoples;
52 Wherewith Thine enemies have
taunted, O LORD,
Wherewith they have taunted the
footsteps of Thine anointed.

53 Blessed be the LORD for evermore.
Amen, and Amen.

∞

Punishment Is Not Rejection

Surely there are times when you are angry with someone very dear to you. Such a disturbance may temporarily damage the relationship, but not to the point of rupture. Usually, after rebukes and expressions of regret, there is forgiveness and reconciliation, and the relationship is restored.

The author of Psalm 89 thinks of a similar pattern in God's relationship with us. What if God is offended by the misconduct of His people, or persons, who are in covenant with Him? Fundamental to the psalmist's view of God is his belief in the everlasting loving-kindness of God: "I will sing of the loving-kindness of God forever" (v. 2). He is in charge of the whole cosmos: "To You belong the heavens and the earth, the world and its fullness. You have founded them" (v. 12). Closely joined with God's power are His moral attributes: "Righteousness and justice are the foundations of Your throne, loving-kindness and faithfulness go before You" (v. 15). If God enters into a covenant, He will faithfully keep it: "I shall not violate My covenant nor change that which has passed My lips" (v. 35).

However, when those who violate the terms of His covenant offend God, there will be swift and painful punishment (see verses 39–46). The psalmist understands the devastation Israel suffered as God's punishment, even though in his judgment the punishment was excessive and too long: "How long, O Lord, will You keep away from us? How long shall Your anger keep burning like fire?" (v. 47).

Very touching is the psalmist's mention of the brevity of his life, hinting that if God is going to bring redemption, it had better be soon so that he may live to see it: "O remember how short my time is" (v. 48). Out of the intimacy of his relationship with God, he dares to challenge Him: "Where is Your former loving-kindness, O Lord?" (v. 50). But this does not change his absolute devotion to God, for he ends his prayer with the words, "Blessed be the Lord forever" (v. 53).

∞

Reflection: The Problem of Evil

When promises are made and not kept, what happens to the relationship? This is the psalmist's problem as he tries to understand God's dealings with His people. God entered into an everlasting covenant to protect Israel, in return for its faithful observance of His commandments. True, Israel has transgressed, but the death and destruction rained upon the nation violate the standards of justice, loving-kindness, and faithfulness that are supposed to be the foundations of God's throne: "Righteousness and justice are the foundations of Your throne, loving-kindness and faithfulness go before You" (v. 15). When experience contradicts the expectations of faith, what happens to the faith? The psalmist is at a loss to explain why things happened the way they did. Despite disappointment and dissatisfaction, he will not renounce his faith. He ends his reflection blessing God: "Blessed be the Lord forever" (v. 53).

People of faith still wrestle with the same problem that confounded the psalmist. Shocked by the brutalities of evildoers and the innocent suffering of so many, we too must wonder, Where are the mercies of God? Where is His justice? Why would God in His goodness let so much wrongdoing plague mankind? We are no wiser than was the psalmist in his day. We, too, cannot explain the tolerance of evil in God's world. Neither can we repudiate faith in God. A world without God is even less acceptable than a world in which God, for reasons unknown to us, allows evil to cause so much pain and suffering. Mysteries becloud our judgment.

❧ PSALM 90 ❧

A Prayer of Moses the man of God.

LORD, Thou hast been our dwelling-
  place in all generations.
2 Before the mountains were brought
  forth,
  Or ever Thou hadst formed the earth
  and the world,
  Even from everlasting to everlasting,
  Thou art God.
3 Thou turnest man to contrition;
  And sayest: "Return, ye children of
  men."
4 For a thousand years in Thy sight
  Are but as yesterday when it is past,
  And as a watch in the night.
5 Thou carriest them away as with a
  flood; they are as a sleep;
  In the morning they are like grass
  which groweth up.
6 In the morning it flourisheth, and
  groweth up;

In the evening it is cut down, and
  withereth.

7 For we are consumed in Thine anger,
  And by Thy wrath are we hurried
  away.
8 Thou hast set our iniquities before
  Thee,
  Our secret sins in the light of Thy
  countenance.
9 For all our days are passed away in
  Thy wrath;
  We bring our years to an end as a tale
  that is told.
10 The days of our years are threescore
  years and ten,
  Or even by reason of strength
  fourscore years;
  Yet is their pride but travail and
  vanity;
  For it is speedily gone, and we fly
  away.

11 Who knoweth the power of Thine
  anger,
  And Thy wrath according to the fear
  that is due unto Thee?
12 So teach us to number our days,
  That we may get us a heart of wisdom.

13 Return, O LORD; how long?
  And let it repent Thee concerning
  Thy servants.
14 O satisfy us in the morning with Thy
  mercy;
  That we may rejoice and be glad all
  our days.

15 Make us glad according to the days
  wherein Thou hast afflicted us,
  According to the years wherein we
  have seen evil.
16 Let Thy work appear unto Thy
  servants,
  And Thy glory upon their children.
17 And let the graciousness of the LORD
  our God be upon us;
  Establish Thou also upon us the work
  of our hands;
  Yea, the work of our hands establish
  Thou it.

"As a Tale That Is Told"

Can you take a realistic measure of life without falling into despair? Life is full of contradictions: It is a gift—which is taken away. It is growth—and decline. It offers pleasures—and pain. Among the many billions of people, no two are alike, but all share the same ending. All we are vanishes in death, or so it seems to us. Two mysteries envelop life: what we were before birth and what we shall be after death. Psalm 90 speaks to us about the realities of life. Our brief morning of life begins with an amazing power for growth: "In the morning it flourishes and grows up" (v. 6). But soon we go into decline: "In the evening it is cut down and withers" (v. 6).

The psalmist measures our normal life span: "The days of our years are seventy years, or given the strength, eighty years" (v. 10). But even when lived to its limit, life is a mere flicker out of eternity: "It is speedily gone" (v. 10). Because our time is so short, we must not foolishly waste it. To make proper use of our lifetime, we need wisdom: "So teach us to number our days that we may get us a heart of wisdom" (v. 12).

But regardless of how we live our lives, wisely or foolishly, what remains when it is all over is as insubstantial "as a tale that is told" (v. 9). This, however, is not the full story. Man has a place with the Eternal: "God, You have been our dwelling place in all generations" (v. 1). In some unfathomable way we are connected with the God Who "formed the earth and the world" (v. 2).

In God's presence, time has no meaning: "A thousand years in Your sight are but as yesterday when it is past" (v. 4). Thus, assured of our share in God's eternity, the psalmist turns his attention to the possibilities for happiness that compensate us for the suffering we must endure in our brief earthly existence: "Give us joy for as long as You have afflicted us, the years in which we have seen evil" (v. 15).

The psalmist finds meaning in life to the extent that one partakes in God's work. Life is neither a comedy nor a tragedy. It is an assignment. We are witness to and part of God's work, which reflects glory upon His creatures: "May Your work be seen by Your servants and Your glory be reflected by their children. May the favor of our God be upon us. Establish upon us the work of our hands" (v. 16, 17).

∞

Reflection: Death

Do you fear death? Few of those who do, say so. They prefer not to think of it, or drop the subject as soon as it comes up. Others are morbidly obsessed with death and think of it all the time. Most people, though not focused consciously on the topic of death, are aware of an undercurrent of anxiety that surfaces sporadically into consciousness as a vague fear. According to the philosopher Francis Bacon, "Men fear death as children fear to go in the dark." Darkness is threatening because we do not know what it conceals. For the seventeenth-century poet John Dryden, death is frightening because we don't know what it is: "Death in itself is nothing, but we fear/To be we know not what, we know not where." Psalm 90 realistically and boldly faces death. Its author seeks no escape into fantasies about survival in some other form or return to life by way of resurrection. What explains his calm acceptance of death? The answer lies in the very first sentence: "God, You have been our dwelling place in all generations" (v. 1). He looks to God as his eternal home. Death is for him a homecoming to God's presence. He is with God always.

∞ PSALM 91 ∞

O thou that dwellest in the covert of
   the Most High,
And abidest in the shadow of the
   Almighty;
2 I will say of the LORD, who is my
   refuge and my fortress,
My God, in whom I trust,
3 That He will deliver thee from the
   snare of the fowler,
And from the noisome pestilence.

4 He will cover thee with His pinions,
   And under His wings shalt thou take
      refuge;
   His truth is a shield and a buckler.

5 Thou shalt not be afraid of the terror
      by night,
   Nor of the arrow that flieth by day;
   6 Of the pestilence that walketh in
      darkness,

Nor of the destruction that wasteth at
noonday.

7 A thousand may fall at thy side,
And ten thousand at thy right hand;
It shall not come nigh thee.
8 Only with thine eyes shalt thou
behold,
And see the recompense of the
wicked.

9 For thou hast made the LORD who is
my refuge,
Even the Most High, thy habitation.
10 There shall no evil befall thee,
Neither shall any plague come nigh
thy tent.

11 For He will give His angels charge
over thee,
To keep thee in all thy ways.

12 They shall bear thee upon their
hands,
Lest thou dash thy foot against a
stone.
13 Thou shalt tread upon the lion and
asp;
The young lion and the serpent shalt
thou trample under feet.

14 "Because he hath set his love upon
Me, therefore will I deliver him;
I will set him on high, because he
hath known My name.
15 He shall call upon Me, and I will
answer him;
I will be with him in trouble;
I will rescue him, and bring him to
honour.
16 With long life will I satisfy him,
And make him to behold My
salvation."

❧

Do Not Fear!

Could you count the number of times you escaped death, sometimes
very narrowly? The author of Psalm 91 shares with us his feeling of
being protected by God every step of his life: "I say of God, He is my
refuge and my fortress, my God in whom I trust" (v. 2). Living under
God's protection, there is no reason to fear. The psalmist speaks to
those who live in constant awareness of God: "If you have made God,
who is my refuge, the most high, your dwelling place, no evil shall
befall you" (v. 9, 10). Only transgressors should be afraid: "You will see
with your own eyes the recompense of the wicked"(v. 8).

Speaking, as it were, through the lips of the psalmist, God promises
deliverance to anyone who loves Him: "Because he set his love upon
Me, I shall deliver him. I shall protect him. He shall call upon Me and
I shall answer. I shall be with him in trouble and rescue him in honor"
(v. 14, 15).

❧

Reflection: Old Age

Psalm 91 reflects the deep sense of security the faithful finds in his relationship with God. He feels sheltered against all kinds of perils. Either
during prayer or in the silent meditation of his heart, the psalmist enters

into dialogue with God. He perceives God's reassurance: "I will be with him in trouble" (v. 15). God will bless him also with long life: "With long life will I satisfy him" (v. 16). In this context, "satisfy" is to be understood as "give contentment." We should all crave the blessing of contentment in old age. Unfortunately, old age is more often than not a time of discontent. It is associated with dependence, disability, and being sidelined from important affairs in the community, social life, and even the family. We live in a culture that glorifies youth, not age.

Although no one wants to die young, we are ambivalent about old age. We want to live longer, but not be older, or, as Harry Emerson Fosdick said it so well: "It is magnificent to grow old, if one keeps young." However, given reasonably good health, there is no age limit to creativity, intellectual growth, and leadership ability. William Gladstone was Great Britain's prime minister at the age of eighty-three; Konrad Adenauer served as Germany's chancellor until close to ninety; Benjamin Franklin worked on the American constitution at eighty; Oliver Wendell Holmes retired from the U.S. Supreme Court at almost ninety-one; Michelangelo worked on his sculptures into his eighties. Each age has its special strength and beauty, and so does old age.

∾ PSALM 92 ∾

A Psalm, a Song. For the sabbath day.

2 It is a good thing to give thanks unto the LORD,
  And to sing praises unto Thy name, O Most High;
3 To declare Thy lovingkindness in the morning,
  And Thy faithfulness in the night seasons,
4 With an instrument of ten strings, and with the psaltery;
  With a solemn sound upon the harp.

5 For Thou, LORD, hast made me glad through Thy work;
  I will exult in the works of Thy hands.
6 How great are Thy works, O LORD!
  Thy thoughts are very deep.
7 A brutish man knoweth not,

Neither doth a fool understand this.
8 When the wicked spring up as the grass,
  And when all the workers of iniquity do flourish;
  It is that they may be destroyed for ever.

9 But Thou, O LORD, art on high for evermore.
10 For, lo, Thine enemies, O LORD,
  For, lo, Thine enemies shall perish:
  All the workers of iniquity shall be scattered.
11 But my horn hast Thou exalted like the horn of the wild-ox;
  I am anointed with rich oil.
12 Mine eye also hath gazed on them that lie in wait for me,
  Mine ears have heard my desire of the evil-doers that rise up against me.

13 The righteous shall flourish like the
   palm-tree;
   He shall grow like a cedar in
   Lebanon.
14 Planted in the house of the LORD,
   They shall flourish in the courts of
   our God.

15 They shall still bring forth fruit in old
   age;
   They shall be full of sap and richness;
16 To declare that the LORD is upright,
   My Rock, in whom there is no
   unrighteousness.

In the Long Run, Good Will Triumph

If you are caught up in the petty details of your life, you might miss seeing the bigger picture—the grandeur and majesty of the whole, the world in its totality. The author of Psalm 92 has that larger perspective. He sees himself as part of an awesome world that surpasses our understanding: "How great are Your works, O God; Your thoughts are very deep" (v. 6).

We may be troubled by what appear to us as defects in God's creation, such as the freedom of evildoers to do their mischief. But in the long run they are doomed: "When the wicked spring up as grass and when all the workers of iniquity flourish, it is that they may be destroyed for ever. . . . Behold, Your enemies, O God, shall perish; all the workers of iniquity shall be scattered" (v. 8, 10). The triumph of righteousness may be delayed, but it will happen: "The righteous shall flourish like the palm-tree" (v. 13). Their reward is assured: "They shall bring forth fruit in old age" (v. 15); therefore, "it is good to give thanks to God" (v. 1).

Reflection: Gratitude

The psalmist exclaims, "It is good to give thanks to God" (v. 2)—good for whom? Do we know what God gains from our thanksgiving? We can only guess that God is pleased to have our thanksgiving, as we are pleased to receive thanks from anyone to whom we showed favor. But this is projecting our mentality upon God. Considering that each of us is less than a speck of dust in the universe, it is difficult to imagine that God gains anything from our words of thanksgiving. What good there is in thanksgiving to God goes entirely to the person who gives thanks.

Gratitude opens the door to contentment, and contentment induces happiness. The American poet John Greenleaf Whittier made the keen observation that gratitude focuses on the good we enjoy in the present:

No longer forward nor behind
I look in hope or fear,
But grateful, take the good I find,
The best of now and here.

To put yourself in a better mood, all you need to do is to count the things you appreciate. Gratitude is the twin of appreciation. Whether you give thanks to God or to human beings, you will be the first to benefit from thanksgiving.

❧ Psalm 93 ❧

The LORD reigneth; He is clothed in majesty;
The LORD is clothed, He hath girded Himself with strength;
Yea, the world is established, that it cannot be moved.
2 Thy throne is established of old;
Thou art from everlasting.

3 The floods have lifted up, O LORD,
The floods have lifted up their voice;
The floods lift up their roaring.
4 Above the voices of many waters,
The mighty breakers of the sea,
The LORD on high is mighty.

5 Thy testimonies are very sure,
Holiness becometh Thy house,
O LORD, for evermore.

❧

The World Shall Not Be Moved

Look around you, and you will see everything in motion and changing. Might the earth someday collapse and disappear? The author of Psalm 93 insists that regardless of instability and fluctuations, God's world will abide: "Your throne is established of old; You are eternal" (v. 2). Unfazed by the roaring sea is the eternal God, Who rules nature and guides man by laws: "Your decrees are most enduring" (v. 5).

❧

Reflection: Uncertainty

One of life's predicaments is uncertainty. Everything within us and in the world about us is constantly changing, as was already noted twenty-five hundred years ago by the Greek philosopher Heraclites: "Nothing endures but change. . . . You could not step twice into the same river, for other waters are ever flowing unto you." Our works are castles in the sand, quickly washed away by ever-rolling waves. In his insecurity, the psalmist reaches out to the only certainty he knows, the God Who rules the universe: "Your throne is established of old; You are eternal"

(v. 2). Storms may rage and floods may sweep over the Earth, but above the roaring sea, the psalmist sees his rock of ages: "God on high is mighty" (v. 4). If all instruments should fail, the pilot can still set the course of his ship by the unchanging North Star. So may we set the course of our life by the unchanging truth of God's commands: "Your decrees are most enduring" (v. 5).

❧ PSALM 94 ❧

O LORD, Thou God to whom vengeance belongeth,
Thou God to whom vengeance belongeth, shine forth.
2 Lift up Thyself, Thou Judge of the earth;
Render to the proud their recompense.

3 LORD, how long shall the wicked,
How long shall the wicked exult?
4 They gush out, they speak arrogancy;
All the workers of iniquity bear themselves loftily.
5 They crush Thy people, O LORD,
And afflict Thy heritage.
6 They slay the window and the stranger,
And murder the fatherless.
7 And they say: "The LORD will not see,
Neither will the God of Jacob give heed."
8 Consider, ye brutish among the people;
And ye fools, when will ye understand?
9 He that planted the ear, shall He not hear?
He that formed the eye, shall He not see?
10 He that instructeth nations, shall not He correct,
Even He that teacheth man knowledge?
11 The LORD knoweth the thoughts of man,
That they are vanity.

12 Happy is the man whom Thou instructest, O LORD,
And teachest out of Thy law;
13 That Thou mayest give him rest from the days of evil,
Until the pit be digged for the wicked.
14 For the LORD will not cast off His people,
Neither will He forsake His inheritance.
15 For right shall return unto justice,
And all the upright in heart shall follow it.

16 Who will rise up for me against the evil-doers?
Who will stand up for me against the workers of iniquity?
17 Unless the LORD had been my help,
My soul had soon dwelt in silence.
18 If I say: "My foot slippeth",
Thy mercy, O LORD, holdeth me up.
19 When my cares are many within me,
Thy comforts delight my soul.
20 Shall the seat of wickedness have fellowship with Thee,
Which frameth mischief by statute?
21 They gather themselves together against the soul of the righteous,
And condemn innocent blood.
22 But the LORD hath been my high tower,
And my God the rock of my refuge.
23 And He hath brought upon them their own iniquity,
And will cut them off in their own evil;
The LORD our God will cut them off.

〰

The Day of Reckoning Will Come

If you believe in the biblical God of justice and righteousness, you must be perplexed by the presence and proliferation of evil in a world subject to God's rule. Are evildoers free to do their mischief with impunity?

Psalm 94 argues for a God Who knows what is happening in human affairs and will bring evildoers to justice. The psalm opens up with a declaration of God as judge: "O God of retribution, make Your appearance, rise up, Judge of the earth, give the arrogant their recompense" (v. 1, 2). The psalmist is troubled by the freedom of the wicked to do evil: "God, how long shall the wicked rejoice. . . . They crush Your people . . . They slay the widow and stranger and murder the orphan" (v. 3, 5, 6). Most galling is their taunt: "They say, 'God will not see'" (v. 7).

The psalmist reasons in response that the Creator must Himself possess the capacities for perception with which He endowed His creatures: "He that planted the ear, shall He not hear? He that formed the eye, shall He not see? He that instructed nations, shall not He correct? . . . The Lord knows the thoughts of man" (v. 9. 10, 11). God has given instructions to mankind for their happiness: "Happy is the man whom You instruct, O God, and teach out of Your law" (v. 12). As for the evildoers, their day of reckoning will come when the righteous are vindicated: "For right shall return unto justice and all the upright in heart shall follow it" (v. 15).

The psalmist admits that the religious problem with which he was wrestling made him waver, but God upheld his faith: "When I thought, 'I am slipping,' Your loving-kindness, O God, upheld me" (v. 18). After thinking it through, he now finds it inconceivable that God could have any association with corruption: "Shall the seat of injustice have partnership with You?" (v. 20). He feels assured that evil will destroy itself in the long run: "He will make evil rebound on them and destroy them through their own iniquity" (v. 23).

〰

Reflection: Rehabilitation

This psalm furnishes a good example of the power of personal experience in shaping one's beliefs. After straying from the right path, the psalmist experienced the forgiveness and mercy of God: "When I thought, 'I am slipping,' Your loving-kindness, O God, upheld me" (v. 18). Yes, God the Judge brings sinners to justice. But by instructing them out of his teachings (see v. 12), He gives them a chance for rehabilitation. God will discipline, but "God will not cast off His people" (v. 14). Our pursuit of justice should aim at the rehabilitation of the wrongdoer. St. Leonard's House of Chicago, a rehabilitation center, declared: "One can discard a warped chair, but one cannot discard a warped man. One can junk a car that doesn't function, but one cannot junk a man who doesn't. . . . We cannot throw away broken men. For we are made our brother's keeper . . . and in God's name we try to straighten and repair." We are all prone to err and go astray. But no one is beyond redemption. "The saints are sinners who keep trying," said Robert Louis Stevenson. Jews and Christians are one in their regard for the repentant sinner. The Talmudic sage Abbahu went as far as to say: "Where penitents stand, the wholly righteous cannot stand." The seventeenth-century French Cardinal de Retz expressed the same thought in different words: "The person who can own up to his errors is greater than he who merely knows how to avoid making them." The strongest argument for giving the transgressor a second chance is the ever-present possibility of moral and spiritual renewal. As Susan Coolidge suggested in her poem:

> Every day is a fresh beginning;
> Listen my soul, to the glad refrain,
> And, spite of old sorrow and older sinning,
> And puzzles forecasted and possible pain,
> Take heart with the day, and begin again.

❧ Psalm 95 ❧

O come, let us sing unto the LORD;
Let us shout for joy to the Rock of our salvation.
2 Let us come before His presence with thanksgiving,
Let us shout for joy unto Him with psalms.
3 For the LORD is a great God,
And a great King above all gods;
4 In whose hand are the depths of the earth;
The heights of the mountains are His also.
5 The sea is His, and He made it;
And His hands formed the dry land.
6 O come, let us bow down and bend the knee;
Let us kneel before the LORD our Maker;
7 For He is our God,
And we are the people of His pasture, and the flock of His hand.
To-day, if ye would but hearken to His voice!
8 "Harden not your heart, as at Meribah,
As in the day of Massah in the wilderness;

9When your fathers tried Me,
Proved Me, even though they saw My work.
10For forty years was I wearied with that generation,
And said: It is a people that do err in their heart,

And they have not known My ways;
11Wherefore I swore in My wrath,
That they should not enter into My rest."

※

God Waits for You at All Times, Even Today

It is good etiquette for a guest to come with a gift for the host. Similarly, the psalmist, entering the sanctuary, wants to express thanksgiving and appreciation to the host of living things: "Let us come before His presence with thanksgiving" (v. 2). God cares for us as does the shepherd for his flock: "Let us kneel before God, our Maker. For He is our God and we are the people of His pasture" (v. 7). Then comes a mystifying sentence: "Today, if you would only listen to His voice" (v. 7). What is it that should be done *today*? Its meaning might be that we can enter into close relationship with God at any moment if only we obey His commandments.

※

Reflection: Today!

The arresting words "*Today*, if you would only listen" (v. 7) might well be addressed to every person. Most people try to plan ahead and mark their calendar accordingly. Some make detailed lists of things to do for each day of the week ahead. All this makes good sense as long as you know that of all the days, today is most important.

After the death of a saintly rabbi, one of his disciples was asked, "What was most important to your teacher?" He answered: "Whatever he happened to be doing at the moment." Attend first and foremost to the task at hand; give full attention to each person you encounter today, and never stop thanking God for this moment, this hour, and this day of your life. Alcoholics Anonymous once published a statement entitled "Just for Today." Its opening sentence is: "*Just for today*, I will try to live through this day only, and not tackle my whole life problem at once." America's beloved humorist and sage Will Rogers was once asked by a deeply troubled friend: "Will, if you had only forty-eight hours to live, how would you spend them?" "One at a time" was his answer. You will be most effective and gratified if you live and do your work each hour, without the burden of all the tomorrows on your mind.

❧ Psalm 96 ❧

O sing unto the LORD a new song;
Sing unto the LORD, all the earth.
2 Sing unto the LORD, bless His name;
Proclaim His salvation from day to
day.
3 Declare His glory among the nations,
His marvellous works among all the
peoples.

4 For great is the LORD, and highly to
be praised;
He is to be feared above all gods.
5 For all the gods of the peoples are
things of nought;
But the LORD made the heavens.
6 Honour and majesty are before Him;
Strength and beauty are in His
sanctuary.
7 Ascribe unto the LORD, ye kindreds of
the peoples,
Ascribe unto the LORD glory and
strength.
8 Ascribe unto the LORD the glory due
unto His name;
Bring an offering, and come into His
courts.

9 O worship the LORD in the beauty of
holiness;
Tremble before Him, all the earth.

10 Say among the nations: "The LORD
reigneth."
The world also is established that it
cannot be moved;
He will judge the peoples with
equity.
11 Let the heavens be glad, and let the
earth rejoice;
Let the sea roar, and the fulness
thereof;
12 Let the field exult; and all that is
therein;
Then shall all the trees of the wood
sing for joy;
13 Before the LORD, for He is come;
For He is come to judge the earth;
He will judge the world with
righteousness,
And the peoples in His faithfulness.

❧

All Belongs to God and
God Belongs to All

Regular worshippers want to repeat the prayers with which they are
familiar but also, on occasion, appreciate a fresh prayer and a new
song. It must have been some special occasion that prompted the
author of Psalm 96 to "sing unto God a new song" (v. 1). In a broad
spirit of universalism, he calls on all mankind to join in the adoration
of God: "Sing unto God all the earth. . . . Declare His glory among the
nations, His marvelous works among all the peoples" (v. 1, 3). He
refers to mankind as "the families of nations" and would have them all
attribute to God glory and strength (v. 7). He is ready to share his faith
with all mankind: "Say among the nations, 'God reigns'" (v. 10). God
wants justice not only for His people, Israel, but for all nations:
"He has come to rule the world with justice and the peoples in His
faithfulness" (v. 13).

❧

Reflection: Daily Wonders

This psalm is jubilant in the extreme. The heavens, the earth and the sea, even the fields and the trees are called to unite with all nations in praise of almighty God. Why this universal chorus of rejoicing? Because the same God who "established the world that it cannot move, will judge the peoples with equity" (v. 10). Do not think of God's majesty only in connection with the creation that shaped the universe. God is also present in the ordinary, commonplace events of daily life, as suggested by the psalmist: "Proclaim His salvation from day to day" (v. 2). We are surrounded daily by countless marvels. Should we not wonder at the seed that falls into the ground and grows into a mighty oak tree or beautiful flower? The poet Alfred Lord Tennyson, upon seeing a flower grow out of the crevice of a wall, immortalized his amazement at the life force burgeoning in nature:

> Flower in the crannied wall,
> I pluck you out of the crannies,
> I hold you here, root and all, in my hand,
> Little flower—but *if* I could understand
> What you are, root and all, and all in all,
> I should know what God and man is.

"From day to day" we are sustained by the mysterious force of life; "from day to day" we witness the miracles of body and mind: the power of healing, the birth of a child whose babbling sounds become intelligent speech, the mystery of love that binds a couple in a lifetime covenant, and, not least of all, God's gift of genius, which enables man to harness the forces of nature and rule over all other creatures on Earth. Only the spiritually blind will not see the miracles and wonders that surround us from day to day.

❧ PSALM 97 ❧

The LORD reigneth; let the earth rejoice;
Let the multitude of isles be glad.
2 Clouds and darkness are round about Him;
Righteousness and justice are the foundation of His throne.

3 A fire goeth before Him,
And burneth up His adversaries round about.
4 His lightnings lighted up the world;
The earth saw, and trembled.
5 The mountains melted like wax at the presence of the LORD,

At the presence of the LORD of the
  whole earth.
6 The heavens declared His
  righteousness,
And all the peoples saw His glory.

7 Ashamed be all they that serve graven
  images,
That boast themselves of things of
  nought;
Bow down to Him, all ye gods.
8 Zion heard and was glad,
And the daughters of Judah rejoiced;

Because of Thy judgments, O LORD.
9 For Thou, LORD, art most high above
  all the earth;
Thou art exalted far above all gods.

10 O ye that love the LORD, hate evil;
He preserveth the souls of His saints;
He delivered them out of the hand of
  the wicked.
11 Light is sown for the righteous,
And gladness for the upright in heart.
12 Be glad in the LORD, ye righteous;
And give thanks to His holy name.

The Almighty Is All Good

The religions of the biblical tradition envisage God not only as almighty but also as all good. God is the source and model of our ethical ideals. Accordingly, the author of Psalm 97 acknowledges God as ruler of the world, clouded in mystery, yet just in all His actions: "God reigns, let the earth rejoice . . . clouds and darkness are round about Him; righteousness and justice are the foundations of His throne" (v. 1, 2). Religion and morality should go together: "O you lovers of God, hate evil" (v. 10). God enlightens the minds of the faithful so that they are glad to do right: "Light is sown for the righteous and gladness for the upright in heart" (v. 11).

Reflection: Morality and Its Source

Since time immemorial, people have debated various definitions of right and wrong. Where do our ideas of right and wrong come from? There are many different and contradictory answers offered by moral philosophers. This confusing clash of moral theories inspired the rhyme of the nineteenth-century Irish poet Thomas Moore:

> I find the doctors and the sages
> Have differed in all climes and ages,
> And two in fifty scarce agree
> On what is pure morality

The Bible has no doubt whatever about what is moral and what is the source of such knowledge. From the first to the last pages of the Bible, God is named as the moral lawgiver who, through the mouth of

Moses and the prophets, defined right and wrong. Biblical morality is absolute and supernatural. Psalm 97 confirms the biblical view that God and morality are inseparable: "Righteousness and justice are the foundations of His throne" (v. 2). In the end, the psalm glorifies the righteous as living in the light that is "sown" for them. The point is that the righteous person receives moral enlightenment from a higher source. The light of our moral intelligence is not spun out of our own heads, but is something given to us by God. In that light, we see the way we should walk in life. Biblical morality is not subject to the whims and fads of changing political powers, institutions, and special-interest groups. Its essential principles are good for all times. The psalm ends joyously with the assurance that there will be "gladness for the upright in heart" (v. 11).

❧ Psalm 98 ❧

A Psalm.

O sing unto the LORD a new song;
For He hath done marvellous things;
His right hand, and His holy arm, hath
wrought salvation for Him.
2 The LORD hath made known His
salvation;
His righteousness hath He revealed in
the sight of the nations.
3 He hath remembered His mercy and
His faithfulness toward the house of
Israel;
All the ends of the earth have seen the
salvation of our God.

4 Shout unto the LORD, all the earth;
Break forth and sing for joy, yea, sing
praises.

5 Sing praises unto the LORD with the
harp;
With the harp and the voice of
melody.
6 With trumpets and sound of the horn
Shout ye before the King, the LORD.

7 Let the sea roar, and the fulness
thereof;
The world, and they that dwell
therein;
8 Let the floods clap their hands;
Let the mountains sing for joy
together;
9 Before the LORD, for He is come to
judge the earth;
He will judge the world with
righteousness,
And the peoples with equity.

The God of Israel Is the God of Mankind

It is not given to human beings to see God, but we are able to recognize the effects of His deeds. You can detect His saving power in your own life and perceive God-given moral power shaping history in the long run, if not at a specific point in time: "God has made known His salvation. His righteousness has He revealed in the sight of the nations" (v. 2).

The psalmist sees the hand of God in the amazing preservation of the people of Israel: "He has remembered His loving-kindness and faithfulness toward the people of Israel. All the world has seen the salvation of our God" (v. 3). He ends his reflection with the declaration that the God of Israel is the God of all mankind, Who "will rule the world with justice and the peoples with equity" (v. 9).

❧

Reflection: New Prayers and New Songs

This psalm makes the case for innovation in worship: "Sing unto God a new song" (v. 1). What is wrong with the old, familiar hymns, prayers, and songs? Nothing at all. Traditions of worship unite the generations and should be preserved. But there is also need for new forms of religious expression. Why change? Does God change? God does not change, but we, human beings, change. Our ideas change, our circumstances change, our problems change, our needs change, and our moods change. These changes call for new prayers and songs. When Hannah, childless and despondent, went to the sanctuary in Shiloh, "she was in bitterness of soul and prayed unto God and wept sorely" (I Samuel 1:10). She then continued in silent prayer, just moving her lips, giving Eli, the priest, the impression that she was drunk. After the birth of her son, Samuel, she returned to the sanctuary full of joy and prayed: "My heart exults in God" (I Samuel 2:1). This time she was in the mood to offer a triumphant prayer of thanksgiving. We would imagine that an Olympic athlete, giving thanks to God for winning a gold medal, will pray quite differently from a gravely ill person on his deathbed. New prayers and songs don't have to replace the old. They simply enrich our forms of religious expression.

❧ PSALM 99 ❧

The LORD reigneth; let the peoples tremble;
He is enthroned upon the cherubim;
let the earth quake.

2 The LORD is great in Zion;
And He is high above all the peoples.

3 Let them praise Thy name as great and awful;
Holy is He.

4 The strength also of the king who loveth justice—

Thou hast established equity,
Thou hast executed justice and righteousness in Jacob.
5 Exalt ye the LORD our God,
And prostrate yourselves at His
footstool;
Holy is He.

6 Moses and Aaron among His priests,
And Samuel among them that call
upon His name,
Did call upon the LORD, and He
answered them.

7 He spoke unto them in the pillar of
cloud;
They kept His testimonies, and the
statute that He gave them.
8 O LORD our God, Thou didst answer
them;
A forgiving God wast Thou unto
them,
Though Thou tookest vengeance of
their misdeeds.
9 Exalt ye the LORD our God,
And worship at His holy hill;
For the LORD our God is holy.

❧

God Is Forgiving Yet Exacts Retribution

The author of Psalm 99 hopes that the God whom he came to love as the God in Zion, the God of Israel, will also be revered by all nations: "God is great in Zion; and He is high above all the peoples. Let them praise Your name as great and awesome; holy is He" (v. 2, 3). He gave His people "decrees and laws" (v. 7). Though He exacts retribution for misdeeds, He is a forgiving God (see v. 8).

❧

Reflection: Holy

The word "holy" occurs four times in this psalm. It is one of those words that are often used and little understood. Clearly, it refers to God's most distinctive attribute, but what does it mean? As used in the Bible, the word "holy" points to the awesomeness of God, Who is to be approached and spoken to only with great caution. The innermost chamber of the ancient temple in Jerusalem, the Holy of Holies, was closed to all except the high priest, and he could enter it only once each year, on the Day of Atonement. God's holiness is associated with moral purity. One should come near God "with clean hands and a pure heart" (Psalm 24:4). That is why Jews and Christians practice a symbolic purification ritual, the washing of hands, before worship services or before reciting certain blessings. "Holy" is the term by which we describe the absolute difference between God and man. God is the "wholly Other," namely, unlike any other being in the world. "Holy" stands for the ultimate mystery of God, to be revered and worshipped even if not understood.

❧ Psalm 100 ❧

A Psalm of thanksgiving.

Shout unto the LORD, all the earth.
2 Serve the LORD with gladness;
Come before His presence with
    singing.
3 Know ye that the LORD He is God;
It is He that hath made us, and we are
    His,
His people, and the flock of His
    pasture.

4 Enter into His gates with thanksgiving,
And into His courts with praise;
Give thanks unto Him, and bless His
    name.
5 For the LORD is good; His mercy
    endureth for ever;
And His faithfulness unto all
    generations.

❧

Serve God with Joy

Certain religious sects and movements have at times given religion the image of harshness and grim severity. This does not apply to biblical religion. Overwhelmingly, the people of the Bible adored God as a loving Father, shepherd, and protector and worshipped Him with joy. Thus, the author of Psalm 100 calls on all the world to approach God with happiness: "Serve God with gladness; come before His presence with singing" (v. 2). There is good reason to be joyful in God's presence: "Know that it is God Who made us and we are His people and the flock of His pasture" (v. 3). The right mood in which to worship God is not fear, but appreciation and praise: "Enter His gates with thanksgiving and His courts with praise . . . For God is good; His loving-kindness endures for ever and His faithfulness unto all generations" (v. 4–5).

❧

Reflection: How to Serve God

This short psalm of only five verses radiates thanksgiving and joy. Both moods are closely related. Joy always accompanies gratitude. However, we may not see the connection the psalmist makes between service and gladness: "Serve God with gladness" (v. 2). It would be a mistake to limit our understanding of "service of God" to worship *services*. Such a narrow view would be deplorable. Every religion based on the Bible teaches that God wants to be served not only with prayer, but by our way of life, by good deeds, by help given to the needy, by love extended to our neighbor, even by kindness to animals, as expressions of reverence for life created by God. The service we should render to

God is not confined to a special occasion or holiday. We should be serving God day by day with our lives. The psalmist calls on us to do so with gladness, willingly, and in the spirit of gratitude, as long as God grants us life.

❧ PSALM 101 ❧

A Psalm of David.

I will sing of mercy and justice;
Unto Thee, O LORD, will I sing
   praises.
2 I will give heed unto the way of
   integrity;
Oh when wilt Thou come unto me?
I will walk within my house in the
   integrity of my heart.

3 I will set no base thing before mine
   eyes;
I hate the doing of things crooked;
It shall not cleave unto me.
4 A perverse heart shall depart from me;
I will know no evil thing.

5 Whoso slandereth his neighbour in
   secret, him will I destroy;
Whoso is haughty of eye and proud of
   heart, him will I not suffer.
6 Mine eyes are upon the faithful of the
   land, that they may dwell with me;
He that walketh in a way of integrity,
   he shall minister unto me.

7 He that worketh deceit shall not dwell
   within my house;
He that speaketh falsehood shall not
   be established before mine eyes.
8 Morning by morning will I destroy all
   the wicked of the land;
To cut off all the workers of iniquity
   from the city of the LORD.

A Code of Ethics for Politicians

Do you distrust politicians? Do you hold a low opinion of their ethical standards? Psalm 101, if taken to heart by public servants, might raise them to a higher level of integrity. It sets moral standards for leaders. Officials in authority should punish slanderers: "Whoever slanders his neighbor in secret, him will I destroy" (v. 5). In the context of contemporary life, all who misuse the media to smear and defame others should be held liable. Deceivers and liars should not be tolerated: "He who practices deceit and speaks falsehood shall not be established before Me" (v. 7). Only persons of integrity should serve the ruler and the public: "He that walks in the way of integrity, he shall serve me" (v. 6).

Reflection: Moral Leadership

Psalm 101, like many other psalms, links God with the highest moral standards. In this case, it is the king who ascribes to God faithful love and justice: "I will sing of faithful love and justice. Unto You, O God, I will sing praises" (v. 1). The king then lists the moral qualities he will expect of his officials. Wisely, the king means to achieve integrity in his government not merely by preaching or edicts, but by force of his personal example: "I will give heed unto the way of integrity. . . . I will walk within my house in the integrity of my heart. I will set no base thing before my eyes" (v. 2–3). He has harsh words of condemnation and threats of destruction for the corrupt and iniquitous: "I hate crooked dealings" (v. 3). The psalmist understands that evil must be rooted out so that the good may grow. A good gardener who loves flowers must hate the weeds.

❧ Psalm 102 ❧

A Prayer of the afflicted, when he fainteth, and poureth out his complaint before the LORD.

2 O LORD, hear my prayer,
And let my cry come unto Thee.
3 Hide not Thy face from me in the day of my distress;
Incline Thine ear unto me;
In the day when I call answer me speedily.

4 For my days are consumed like smoke,
And my bones are burned as a hearth.
5 My heart is smitten like grass, and withered;
For I forget to eat my bread.
6 By reason of the voice of my sighing
My bones cleave to my flesh.
7 I am like a pelican of the wilderness;
I am become as an owl of the waste places.
8 I watch, and am become
Like a sparrow that is alone upon the housetop.
9 Mine enemies taunt me all the day;
They that are mad against me do curse by me.
10 For I have eaten ashes like bread,
And mingled my drink with weeping.

11 Because of Thine indignation and Thy wrath;
For Thou hast taken me up, and cast me away.
12 My days are like a lengthening shadow;
And I am withered like grass.

13 But Thou, O LORD, sittest enthroned for ever;
And Thy name is unto all generations.
14 Thou wilt arise, and have compassion upon Zion;
For it is time to be gracious unto her, for the appointed time is come.
15 For Thy servants take pleasure in her stones,
And love her dust.
16 So the nations will fear the name of the LORD,
And all the kings of the earth Thy glory;
17 When the LORD hath built up Zion,
When He hath appeared in His glory;
18 When He hath regarded the prayer of the destitute,
And hath not despised their prayer.

19 This shall be written for the generation to come;
And a people which shall be created shall praise the LORD.

20 For He hath looked down from the height of His sanctuary;
From heaven did the LORD behold the earth;

21 To hear the groaning of the prisoner;
To loose those that are appointed to death;

22 That men may tell of the name of the LORD in Zion,
And His praise in Jerusalem;

23 When the peoples are gathered together,
And the kingdoms, to serve the LORD.

24 He weakened my strength in the way;
He shortened my days.

25 I say: "O my God, take me not away in the midst of my days,

Thou whose years endure throughout all generations.

26 Of old Thou didst lay the foundation of the earth;
And the heavens are the work of Thy hands.

27 They shall perish, but Thou shalt endure;
Yea, all of them shall wax old like a garment;
As a vesture shalt Thou change them, and they shall pass away;

28 But Thou art the selfsame,
And Thy years shall have no end.

29 The children of Thy servants shall dwell securely,
And their seed shall be established before Thee."

❧

Hope in Times of Despair

When you are ruined in the collapse of your community due to some terrible disaster, where can you find relief and new hope? The author of Psalm 102 survived the destruction of Jerusalem as a captive in exile. He feels totally abandoned by God, Who, it seems, pays no attention to his misery: "Hide not Your face from me in the day of my distress" (v. 3). He expresses his distress in graphic language (see v. 4, 10), yet, undeterred by God's silence, the psalmist envisages the future rebuilding of devastated Jerusalem with God's help (see v. 17). His prayers will not be in vain (v. 18), because God must be aware of the suffering of His people (see v. 20–21). Still young in years, he begs God to prolong his life: "O my God, take me not away in the midst of my days, You Whose years endure throughout all generations" (v. 25). Conscious of his own mortality, he is in awe of God's eternity. God will outlast all of creation (see v. 26–28). The psalmist hopes that future generations will see redemption: "The children of Your servants shall dwell securely and their offspring shall be established in Your presence" (v. 29). Not every prayer is answered at the moment, but the mere process of worship may lift our mood from despair to hope.

❧

Reflection: Fear of Death

The Viennese physician and playwright Arthur Schnitzler was of the opinion that thoughts of our own death are always with us, emerging from the depth of our soul into consciousness at various times: "Is there a reasonable person who at any significant moment does not deep in his soul think of anything but death?" In Psalm 102, a gravely ill person, still in the midst of life, comes face to face with his mortality. He feels the sun of his life sinking; soon night will fall: "My days are like a lengthening shadow and I am withered like grass" (v. 12). He is a physical and emotional wreck. His body is wasting away (v. 4); he has no appetite (v. 5); he feels deserted, like a "lonely sparrow on the housetop" (v. 8). He has the symptoms of deep depression, imagining enemies rejoicing over his travails and weeping incessantly (v. 9–10). Surprisingly, he endures his agony without screaming against his bitter fate and the prospect of death, as Dylan Thomas did in his poem "Do Not Go Gentle into That Good Night."

How could the psalmist accept his condition with so little bitterness and protest? Ordinarily, the more severe the illness and pain, the more self-centered becomes the patient. He becomes obsessed with the symptoms of his illness and the fear of death. The psalmist, however, escapes from such sickly morbidity. He forgets himself by shifting his attention to the needs of others. He prays to God for his ravaged city and people (v. 14), and feels for the destitute and for the groaning of the imprisoned (v. 18, 21). We all know the adage "God helps those who help themselves." The psalmist's experience would change it to "As you help others, you help yourself."

❧ PSALM 103 ❧

[A Psalm] of David.

Bless the LORD, O my soul;
And all that is within me, bless His holy name.
2 Bless the LORD, O my soul,
And forget not all His benefits;
3 Who forgiveth all thine iniquity;
Who healeth all thy diseases;
4 Who redeemeth thy life from the pit;
Who encompasseth thee with loving-kindness and tender mercies;
5 Who satisfieth thine old age with good things;
So that thy youth is renewed like the eagle.

6 The LORD executeth righteousness,
And acts of justice for all that are oppressed.
7 He made known His ways unto Moses,
His doings unto the children of Israel.
8 The LORD is full of compassion and gracious,
Slow to anger, and plenteous in mercy.
9 He will not always contend;
Neither will He keep His anger for ever.
10 He hath not dealt with us after our sins,

Nor requited us according to our
   iniquities.
11 For as the heaven is high above the
   earth,
   So great is His mercy toward them
   that fear Him.
12 As far as the east is from the west,
   So far hath He removed our
   transgressions from us.
13 Like as a father hath compassion
   upon his children,
   So hath the LORD compassion upon
   them that fear Him.
14 For He knoweth our frame;
   He remembereth that we are dust.
15 As for man, his days are as grass;
   As a flower of the field, so he
   flourisheth.
16 For the wind passeth over it, and it is
   gone;
   And the place thereof knoweth it no
   more.
17 But the mercy of the LORD is from

everlasting to everlasting upon them
   that fear Him,
   And His righteousness unto children's
   children;
18 To such as keep His covenant,
   And to those that remember His
   precepts to do them.

19 The LORD hath established His
   throne in the heavens;
   And His kingdom ruleth over all.
20 Bless the LORD, ye angels of His,
   Ye mighty in strength, that fulfil His
   word,
   Hearkening unto the voice of His
   word.
21 Bless the LORD, all ye His hosts;
   Ye ministers of His, that do His
   pleasure.
22 Bless the LORD, all ye His works,
   In all places of His dominion;
   Bless the LORD, O my soul.

❧

Thank God That All Is Well

This psalm will put you in a good mood. It is full of praise and thanks-giving. The psalmist blesses God as the source of many benefits: "Bless God, O my soul, and forget not all His benefits, Who forgives all your iniquities and heals all your diseases" (v. 2–3). God's loving-kindness saves us from destruction (see v. 6). He acts righteously and deals justly with all who are oppressed (see v. 6). He is forgiving and compassion-ate (see v. 3 and 8–11): "For He knows our nature and remembers that we are dust" (v. 14). In contrast with man's mortality, whose "days are as grass" (v. 15), "God's loving-kindness is from everlasting to everlast-ing . . . and His kingdom rules over all" (v. 17, 19). The psalm ends with a rousing call on all creation to praise God: "Bless God all you who are His works" (v. 22).

❧

Reflection: Physical and Moral Renewal

Almost every line in this psalm has become part of the prayer books of different denominations. In its totality, the psalm offers us a key to serenity in the face of old age, moral failure, and mortality. Even though "we are dust" (v. 14), we are everlastingly linked to the mercy of God (v. 17). Daily, and through old age, we experience the miracle of healing by the One "Who heals all your diseases" (v. 3). We recover strength "so that your youth is renewed like the eagle" (v. 5). We retain the capacity for happiness even in old age because God "satisfies your old age with good things" (v. 3). God has made known His will, yet, knowing our limitations ("He knows our frame," v. 14), He "forgives all your iniquity" (v. 3). When we err and sin, His mercy is without end. He loves us as a father: "Like a father has compassion upon his children, so has God compassion upon them that revere Him" (v. 13). Considering how utterly insignificant and short-lived man is ("His days are as grass; as a flower of the field, so he flourishes; the wind passes over it, and it is gone . . ."), God's unceasing love for us passes our understanding. The nineteenth-century rabbi Nathan David Slidovtzer ingeniously interpreted verse 12, "As far as the east is from the west, so far has He removed our transgressions from us." When a person stands facing east, he can face the opposite direction, west, just by turning around. Likewise, a sinner needs but a simple mental turnabout to be far removed from his transgression. The point of the rabbi's interpretation is that a radical change in a person's character need not require long years of reeducation. A fundamentally new outlook on life may instantly produce a moral transformation. What might such a fundamentally new viewpoint be? The recognition of the brevity of life or the realization of one's unworthiness ("What a fool am I!"). It might result from an extraordinary experience in prayer inducing the worshipper to trust God and find the peace of surrender to God's will.

❧ PSALM 104 ❧

Bless the LORD, O my soul.
O LORD my God, Thou art very
    great;
Thou art clothed with glory and
    majesty.
2 Who coverest Thyself with light as
    with a garment,
Who stretchest out the heavens like a
    curtain;
3 Who layest the beams of Thine upper
    chambers in the waters,
Who makest the clouds Thy chariot,
Who walkest upon the wings of the
    wind;

4 Who makest winds Thy messengers,
    The flaming fire Thy ministers.

5 Who didst establish the earth upon its
    foundations,
    That it should not be moved for ever
    and ever;
6 Thou didst cover it with the deep as
    with a vesture;
    The waters stood above the mountains.
7 At Thy rebuke they fled,
    At the voice of Thy thunder they
    hasted away—

8 The mountains rose, the valleys sank
   down—
   Unto the place which Thou hadst
   founded for them;
9 Thou didst set a bound which they
   should not pass over,
   That they might not return to cover
   the earth.

10 Who sendest forth springs into the
    valleys;
    They run between the mountains;
11 They give drink to every beast of the
    field,
    The wild asses quench their thirst.
12 Beside them dwell the fowl of the
    heaven,
    From among the branches they sing.
13 Who waterest the mountains from
    Thine upper chambers;
    The earth is full of the fruit of Thy
    works.

14 Who causeth the grass to spring up
    for the cattle,
    And herb for the service of man;
    To bring forth bread out of the earth,
15 And wine that maketh glad the heart
    of man,
    Making the face brighter than oil,
    And bread that stayeth man's heart.
16 The trees of the LORD have their fill,
    The cedars of Lebanon, which He
    hath planted;
17 Wherein the birds make their nests;
    As for the stork, the fir-trees are her
    house.
18 The high mountains are for the wild
    goats;
    The rocks are a refuge for the conies.

19 Who appointedst the moon for
    seasons;
    The sun knoweth his going down.
20 Thou makest darkness, and it is night,
    Wherein all the beasts of the forest do
    creep forth.
21 The young lions roar after their prey,
    And seek their food from God.
22 The sun ariseth, they slink away,

And couch in their dens.
23 Man goeth forth unto his work
    And to his labour until the evening.
24 How manifold are Thy works, O
    LORD!
    In wisdom hast Thou made them all;
    The earth is full of Thy creatures.
25 Yonder sea, great and wide,
    Therein are creeping things innumer-
    able,
    Living creatures, both small and
    great.
26 There go the ships;
    There is leviathan, whom Thou hast
    formed to sport therein.
27 All of them wait for Thee,
    That Thou mayest give them their
    food in due season.
28 Thou givest it unto them, they gather
    it;
    Thou openest Thy hand, they are sat-
    isfied with good.
29 Thou hidest Thy face, they vanish;
    Thou withdrawest their breath, they
    perish,
    And return to their dust.
30 Thou sendest forth Thy spirit, they
    are created;
    And Thou renewest the face of the
    earth.

31 May the glory of the LORD endure for
    ever;
    Let the LORD rejoice in His works!
32 Who looketh on the earth, and it
    trembleth;
    He toucheth the mountains, and they
    smoke.
33 I will sing unto the LORD as long as I
    live;
    I will sing praise to my God while I
    have any being.
34 Let my musing be sweet unto Him;
    As for me, I will rejoice in the LORD.
35 Let sinners cease out of the earth,
    And let the wicked be no more.
    Bless the LORD, O my soul.
    Hallelujah.

❦

"How Manifold Are Your Works, O God"

Can you remember certain sights that overwhelmed you? A spectacular view from a mountaintop? Standing at the seashore and seeing the sun go down? The author of Psalm 104 is aglow with wonder as he contemplates the panorama of nature. He is amazed at the infinite variety of animals that inhabit the earth: "How manifold are Your works, O God! In wisdom have You made them all; the earth is full of Your creatures" (v. 24). He acknowledges the total dependence of all living things upon God's life-giving power: "All of them wait for You that You may give them their food in due season. . . . You withdraw their spirit, they perish and return to dust" (v. 27, 29). There is *one* flaw in the universe, the presence of evildoers, and the psalmist prays for their elimination: "Let sinners cease from the earth and let the wicked be no more" (v. 35). He ends as he began, with the words "Bless God, O my soul" (v. 35).

❦

Reflection: Sin and Sinners

The eighteenth-century German philosopher Johann Gottfried Herder said, "It is worthwhile studying the Hebrew language for ten years in order to read Psalm 104 in the original." Psalm 104 depicts the panorama of creation. After promising to "sing unto God as long as I live" (v. 33), the psalmist has only one wish, and that is to see the removal of the blemish of evil upon God's work of creation: "Let sinners cease from the earth and let the wicked be no more" (v. 35). The Talmud reports that the great Rabbi Meir, a leading Jewish scholar of the second century, angered by the conduct of some lawless men, prayed that they might perish and quoted this verse: "Let sinners cease from the earth." His wife, Beruriah, overheard the curse and corrected her husband, quoting the same verse with a slight change of a Hebrew vowel to mean: "Let *sin* cease from the earth and the wicked will be no more." We should all hope for the eradication of the sources of sin rather than wish death upon the sinners.

PSALM 105

O give thanks unto the LORD, call
upon His name;
Make known His doings among the
peoples.
2 Sing unto Him, sing praises unto
Him;
Speak ye of all His marvellous works.
3 Glory ye in His holy name;
Let the heart of them rejoice that seek
the LORD.
4 Seek ye the LORD and His strength;
Seek His face continually.
5 Remember His marvellous works that
He hath done,
His wonders, and the judgments of
His mouth;
6 O ye seed of Abraham His servant,
Ye children of Jacob, His chosen ones.

7 He is the LORD our God;
His judgments are in all the earth.
8 He hath remembered His covenant
for ever,
The word which He commanded to a
thousand generations;
9 [The covenant] which He made with
Abraham,
And His oath unto Isaac;
10 And He established it unto Jacob for a
statute,
To Israel for an everlasting covenant;
11 Saying: "Unto thee will I give the
land of Canaan,
The lot of your inheritance."

12 When they were but a few men in
number.
Yea, very few, and sojourners in it,
13 And when they went about from
nation to nation,
From one kingdom to another
people,
14 He suffered no man to do them
wrong,
Yea, for their sake He reproved kings:
15 "Touch not Mine anointed ones,
And do My prophets no harm."

16 And He called a famine upon the land;
He broke the whole staff of bread.
17 He sent a man before them;
Joseph was sold for a servant;
18 His feet they hurt with fetters,
His person was laid in iron;
19 Until the time that his word came to
pass,
The word of the LORD tested him.
20 The king sent and loosed him;
Even the ruler of peoples, and set him
free.
21 He made him lord of his house,
And ruler of all his possessions;
22 To bind his princes at his pleasure,
And teach his elders wisdom.

23 Israel also came into Egypt;
And Jacob sojourned in the land of
Ham.
24 And He increased His people greatly,
And made them too mighty for their
adversaries.
25 He turned their heart to hate His
people,
To deal craftily with His servants.
26 He sent Moses His servant,
And Aaron whom He had chosen.
27 They wrought among them His manifold signs,
And wonders in the land of Ham.
28 He sent darkness, and it was dark;
And they rebelled not against His
word.
29 He turned their waters into blood,
And slew their fish.
30 Their land swarmed with frogs,
In the chambers of their kings.
31 He spoke, and there came swarms of
flies,
And gnats in all their borders.
32 He gave them hail for rain,
And flaming fire in their land.
33 He smote their vines also and their
fig-trees;
And broke the trees of their borders.
34 He spoke, and the locust came,

And the canker-worm without
number,

³⁵And did eat up every herb in their
land,

And did eat up the fruit of their
ground.

³⁶He smote also all the first-born in
their land,

The first-fruits of all their strength.

³⁷And He brought them forth with
silver and gold;

And there was none that stumbled
among His tribes.

³⁸Egypt was glad when they departed;

For the fear of them had fallen upon
them.

³⁹He spread a cloud for a screen;

And fire to give light in the night.

⁴⁰They asked, and He brought quails,

And gave them in plenty the bread of
heaven.

⁴¹He opened the rock, and waters
gushed out;

They ran, a river in the dry places.

⁴²For He remembered His holy word

Unto Abraham His servant;

⁴³And He brought forth His people
with joy,

His chosen ones with singing.

⁴⁴And He gave them the lands of the
nations,

And they took the labour of the
peoples in possession;

⁴⁵That they might keep His statutes,

And observe His laws.

Hallelujah.

Proof of God's Care for His People

Are you a seeker of God? Do you reach out to God in the hope that He
might take notice of you? The author of Psalm 105 has an encourag-
ing message for those who look for proof that God cares for His creatures: "Let the heart of those who seek God rejoice" (v. 3).

What is his message? Look back into history, and you will detect
many signs of God's favor. As a patriotic Israelite, the psalmist naturally
points to the history of his own people, with which he is most familiar.
He summarizes the amazing rise of the people of Israel from a single
patriarchal family to a people, their migration to Egypt, the liberation
from bondage in the Exodus, and the conquest of the Promised Land
(see v. 6–42). It is a story full of wonders. Why would God extend His
special care upon Israel? The psalmist's explanation sounds like a warning: "In order that they might keep His statutes and observe His teachings" (v. 45). The inference is that if Israel is unfaithful to its covenant
with God, He will withdraw His benefits.

Reflection: The High Value of Memory

The key word of this psalm is "remember." The psalmist remembers
highlights of his people's liberation from Egyptian bondage. He wants
his people, Israel, to remember their identity as a people in covenant
with God: "Remember His marvelous works. . . . He has remembered

His covenant for ever" (v. 5, 8). Every individual's sense of identity is built upon memory. It is the basis of all language, education, knowledge, and skill. Take away your memory, and you could not function. As for our conduct of life, memory is more than a storehouse of experience. It is a school. The Bible regards memory as our principal teacher: "Remember the days of old, consider the years of many generations; ask your father, and he will declare unto you, and your elders and they will tell you" (Deuteronomy 32:7). Memories of pleasure and pain, success and failure should teach us what to do and what not to do. The philosopher George Santayana warned us against the high cost of forgetting: "Those who cannot remember the past are condemned to repeat it." Memories are precious to us because in memory we relive the significant moments of our life. To that end, we collect souvenirs, take photos, keep scrapbooks, and write diaries. The Jewish philosopher Philo, a contemporary of Jesus, would draw on memory to expand our perspective on life and awaken our sense of responsibility: "In wealth, remember your poverty; in distinction, your insignificance . . . in peace, the dangers of war; in cities, the life of loneliness."

❧ PSALM 106 ❧

Hallelujah.
O give thanks unto the LORD; for He
　is good;
For His mercy endureth for ever.
2 Who can express the mighty acts of
　the LORD,
Or make all His praise to be heard?
3 Happy are they that keep justice,
That do righteousness at all times.
4 Remember me, O LORD, when Thou
　favourest Thy people;
O think of me at Thy salvation;
5 That I may behold the prosperity of
　Thy chosen,
That I may rejoice in the gladness of
　Thy nation,
That I may glory with Thine
　inheritance.

6 We have sinned with our fathers,
We have done iniquitously, we have
　dealt wickedly.
7 Our fathers in Egypt gave no heed
　unto Thy wonders;

They remembered not the multitude
　of Thy mercies;
But were rebellious at the sea, even at
　the Red Sea.
8 Nevertheless He saved them for His
　name's sake,
That He might make His mighty
　power to be known.
9 And He rebuked the Red Sea, and it
　was dried up;
And He led them through the depths,
　as through a wilderness.
10 And He saved them from the hand of
　him that hated them,
And redeemed them from the hand of
　the enemy.
11 And the waters covered their
　adversaries;
There was not one of them left.
12 Then believed they His words;
They sang His praise.

13 They soon forgot His works;
They waited not for His counsel;

14But lusted exceedingly in the
   wilderness,
   And tried God in the desert.
15And He gave them their request;
   But sent leanness into their soul.

16They were jealous also of Moses in
   the camp,
   And of Aaron the holy one of the
   LORD.
17The earth opened and swallowed up
   Dathan,
   And covered the company of Abiram.
18And a fire was kindled in their
   company;
   The flame burned up the wicked.

19They made a calf in Horeb,
   And worshipped a molten image.
20Thus they exchanged their glory
   For the likeness of an ox that eateth
   grass.
21They forgot God their saviour,
   Who had done great things in Egypt;
22Wondrous works in the land of Ham,
   Terrible things by the Red Sea.
23Therefore He said that He would
   destroy them,
   Had not Moses His chosen stood
   before Him in the breach,
   To turn back His wrath, lest He
   should destroy them.

24Moreover, they scorned the desirable
   land,
   They believed not His word;
25And they murmured in their tents,
   They hearkened not unto the voice of
   the LORD.
26Therefore He swore concerning
   them,
   That He would overthrow them in
   the wilderness;
27And that He would cast out their seed
   among the nations,
   And scatter them in the lands.

28They joined themselves also unto
   Baal of Peor,
   And ate the sacrifices of the dead.

29Thus they provoked Him with their
   doings,
   And the plague broke in upon them.
30Then stood up Phinehas, and
   wrought judgment,
   And so the plague was stayed.
31And that was counted unto him for
   righteousness,
   Unto all generations for ever.

32They angered Him also at the waters
   of Meribah,
   And it went ill with Moses because of
   them;
33For they embittered his spirit,
   And he spoke rashly with his lips.

34They did not destroy the peoples,
   As the LORD commanded them;
35But mingled themselves with the
   nations,
   And learned their works;
36And they served their idols,
   Which became a snare unto them;
37Yea, they sacrificed their sons and
   their daughters unto demons,
38And shed innocent blood, even the
   blood of their sons and of their
   daughters,
   Whom they sacrificed unto the idols
   of Canaan;
   And the land was polluted with blood.
39Thus were they defiled with their
   works,
   And went astray in their doings.
40Therefore was the wrath of the LORD
   kindled against His people,
   And He abhorred His inheritance.
41And He gave them into the hand of
   the nations;
   And they that hated them ruled over
   them.
42Their enemies also oppressed them,
   And they were subdued under their
   hand.
43Many times did He deliver them;
   But they were rebellious in their
   counsel,
   And sank low through their iniquity.
44Nevertheless He looked upon their
   distress,

When He heard their cry;
45 And He remembered for them His
   covenant,
   And repented according to the
   multitude of His mercies.
46 He made them also to be pitied
   Of all those that carried them captive.

47 Save us, O LORD our God,
   And gather us from among the
   nations,

That we may give thanks unto Thy
   holy name,
That we may triumph in Thy praise.

48 Blessed be the LORD, the God of
   Israel,
   From everlasting even to everlasting,
   And let all the people say: "Amen."
   Hallelujah.

❦

As Great as Their Sins,
So Great Was God's Forgiveness

This psalm, like Psalm 105, is a review of Israel's history, with this difference: Psalm 105 retells God's mighty acts in the liberation of Israel from Egyptian bondage, whereas Psalm 106 enumerates the many sins and betrayals of the people God had chosen as His partner in covenant: "Many times did He deliver them. But they were rebellious and sank low through their iniquities" (v. 43). Yet God was merciful and forgiving despite all their offenses: "Nevertheless, He looked upon their distresses, when He heard their cry; and He remembered His covenant for their benefit and relented according to His great loving-kindness" (v. 44–45).

❦

Reflection: Punished but Not Rejected

Have you ever broken off a relationship with a friend or a family member? Such estrangement often leaves both sides so embittered that the break becomes final and they never want to see each other or speak with one another again. It is not so in our relationship with God. According to the author of Psalm 106, if we offend against God by our sins, we shall provoke His anger and draw punishment, but God will not cut off the sinner. The psalmist illustrates his belief with a review of Israel's history of transgressions (see v. 6–40). Again and again the people showed ingratitude toward God and sinned against Him. As punishment, God let Israel suffer humiliation and defeat. But He did not reject His people: "He looked upon their distress when He heard their cry. He was mindful of His covenant and relented according to His great loving-kindness" (v. 44, 45). Could a husband or wife be equally forgiving to a spouse, on the strength of their covenant as life partners in marriage? In a marital dispute both sides suffer grievously. Many a marriage could be saved if spouses could only look "upon their distresses," forgive and relent with compassion, and maintain their covenant.

❧ PSALM 107 ❧

"O give thanks unto the LORD, for He is good,
For His mercy endureth for ever."
2 So let the redeemed of the LORD say,
Whom He hath redeemed from the hand of the adversary;
3 And gathered them out of the lands,
From the east and from the west,
From the north and from the sea.

4 They wandered in the wilderness in a desert way;
They found no city of habitation.
5 Hungry and thirsty,
Their soul fainted in them.
6 Then they cried unto the LORD in their trouble,
And He delivered them out of their distresses.
7 And He led them by a straight way,
That they might go to a city of habitation.
8 Let them give thanks unto the LORD for His mercy,
And for His wonderful works to the children of men!
9 For He hath satisfied the longing soul,
And the hungry soul He hath filled with good.

10 Such as sat in darkness and in the shadow of death,
Being bound in affliction and iron—
11 Because they rebelled against the words of God,
And contemned the counsel of the Most High.
12 Therefore He humbled their heart with travail,
They stumbled, and there was none to help—

13 They cried unto the LORD in their trouble,
And He saved them out of their distresses.
14 He brought them out of darkness and the shadow of death,
And broke their bands in sunder.
15 Let them give thanks unto the LORD for His mercy,
And for His wonderful works to the children of men!
16 For He hath broken the gates of brass,
And cut the bars of iron in sunder.

17 Crazed because of the way of their transgression,
And afflicted because of their iniquities—
18 Their soul abhorred all manner of food,
And they drew near unto the gates of death—
19 They cried unto the LORD in their trouble,
And He saved them out of their distresses;
20 He sent His word, and healed them,
And delivered them from their graves.
21 Let them give thanks unto the LORD for His mercy,
And for His wonderful works to the children of men!
22 And let them offer the sacrifices of thanksgiving,
And declare His works with singing.

23 They that go down to the sea in ships,
That do business in great waters—
24 These saw the works of the LORD,
And His wonders in the deep;

25 For He commanded, and raised the
   stormy wind,
   Which lifted up the waves thereof;
26 They mounted up to the heaven, they
   went down to the deeps;
   Their soul melted away because of
   trouble;
27 They reeled to and fro, and staggered
   like a drunken man,
   And all their wisdom was swallowed
   up—
28 They cried unto the LORD in their
   trouble,
   And He brought them out of their
   distresses.
29 He made the storm a calm,
   So that the waves thereof were still.
30 Then were they glad because they
   were quiet,
   And He led them unto their desired
   haven.
31 Let them give thanks unto the LORD
   for His mercy,
   And for His wonderful works to the
   children of men!
32 Let them exalt Him also in the assembly of the people,
   And praise Him in the seat of the
   elders.

33 He turneth rivers into a wilderness,
   And watersprings into a thirsty
   ground;

34 A fruitful land into a salt waste,
   For the wickedness of them that dwell
   therein.
35 He turneth a wilderness into a pool of
   water,
   And a dry land into watersprings.
36 And there He maketh the hungry to
   dwell,
   And they establish a city of habitation;
37 And sow fields, and plant vineyards,
   Which yield fruits of increase.
38 He blesseth them also, so that they
   are multiplied greatly,
   And suffereth not their cattle to
   decrease.

39 Again, they are minished and dwindle
   away
   Through oppression of evil and
   sorrow.
40 He poureth contempt upon princes,
   And causeth them to wander in the
   waste, where there is no way.
41 Yet setteth He the needy on high
   from affliction,
   And maketh his families like a flock.
42 The upright see it, and are glad;
   And all iniquity stoppeth her mouth.

43 Whoso is wise, let him observe these
   things,
   And let them consider the mercies of
   the LORD.

The Hard Knocks of Experience

Life's important lessons are not learned in classrooms or from books, but through experience. Which experiences are our most effective teachers? Pleasure and pain are among our best teachers. We are likely to repeat doing what gives us pleasure and refrain from doing what causes us pain. The author of Psalm 107 points to various times in history when the people of Israel, having gone wrong, suffered the consequences and, after enduring misery, were set on the right path by God: "He humbled their heart with distress; they stumbled and there was none to help them" (v. 12). It was in such crises that they turned to God: "They cried unto God in their trouble and He saved them out of their distresses" (v. 13). The psalmist closes with the thought that wise people will take to heart the lessons of history: "The upright see it and are glad; the mouth of wrongdoing is silenced. The wise will note these things and will consider the loving-kindness of God" (v. 42–43).

∽

Reflection: God as Savior

Psalm 107 is a ringing declaration of God's saving power. He rescues human beings in distress. The psalmist, however, does not speak in terms of abstract generalities about deliverance, redemption, and salvation. He is concrete and specific. He enumerates actual events and experiences that were perceived as God's saving acts: His people, saved from death by thirst and starvation during their perilous journey in the wilderness; prisoners, released from the dungeon, emerging from the shadow of death; the sick, brought back to health from the gates of death; the mariners, reeling to and fro and staggering in their ships, storm-tossed by the furious sea, returning safely to the harbor. You, too, must know of critical moments in your life. But do you know how often your life, unbeknownst to you, was in jeopardy? You may call your escape from danger chance or good luck. But that is not the way the psalmist sees it. He sees God's design everywhere, in nature and in the events of our life. He recognizes God's moral order in human affairs. Oppressors are brought low and the needy raised up high so that "the upright see it and are glad" (v. 42). The message of this psalm is God's response to human needs, for which no people can give more convincing witness than the people of Israel, who experienced redemption again and again in their history.

∽ PSALM 108 ∽

A Song, a Psalm of David.

2 My heart is stedfast, O God;
  I will sing, yea, I will sing praises,
    even with my glory.
3 Awake, psaltery and harp;
  I will awake the dawn.
4 I will give thanks unto Thee, O
    LORD, among the peoples;
  And I will sing praises unto Thee
    among the nations.

5 For Thy mercy is great above the
    heavens,
  And Thy truth reacheth unto the
    skies.
6 Be Thou exalted, O God, above the
    heavens;
  And Thy glory be above all the earth.
7 That Thy beloved may be delivered,
  Save with Thy right hand, and answer
    me.

8God spoke in His holiness, that I
   would exult;
   That I would divide Shechem, and
   mete out the valley of Succoth.
9Gilead is mine, Manasseh is mine;
   Ephraim also is the defence of my
   head;
   Judah is my sceptre.
10Moab is my washpot;
   Upon Edom do I cast my shoe;
   Over Philistia do I cry aloud.

11Who will bring me into the fortified
   city?
   Who will lead me unto Edom?
12Hast not Thou cast us off, O God?
   And Thou goest not forth, O God,
   with our hosts.
13Give us help against the adversary;
   For vain is the help of man.
14Through God we shall do valiantly;
   For He it is that will tread down our
   adversaries.

❧

The Joy of Being Sure

One of the trying, wearisome situations in life is to be unsure about what to think or do next. Pity the person who can't make up his mind about some important decision. The author of Psalm 108, wavering in his beliefs, finally overcomes the doubts that had plagued him and joyfully exclaims: "My heart is steady, O God; I will sing and chant with all my soul" (v. 2).

The psalmist's crisis was triggered by a clash between expectations, based on his faith in a loving God, and the cruel experiences of life. On one hand, he had believed that God would faithfully protect his people: "Your loving-kindness is higher than the heavens; Your faithfulness reaches unto the sky" (v. 5). On the other hand, the crushing defeat of his people filled him with fear that Israel had been rejected by God: "Have You not rejected us, O God? You did not go forth with our armies, O God" (v. 12).

For a while, the psalmist might have felt betrayed, but just the same he turned to God in prayer: "Help us against the enemy, for the help of man is worthless" (v. 13). Through prayer, he overcame his doubts and, again steady in faith, faced the future with confidence: "Through God we shall triumph, for He will crush our enemies" (v. 14).

Note that in Psalm 108, verses 2 to 6 correspond to Psalm 57, verses 8 to 12; verses 7 to 14 correspond to Psalm 60, verses 7 to 14.

❧

Reflection: Uncertainty in Life

What can you be absolutely sure of? We have heard of individuals who passed their annual physical checkup with flying colors, only to collapse and die as they walked out of the doctor's office. How certain is any promise made to you, or, for that matter, a promise you have made? Even your best intentions are subject to the unforeseen, as we are told in Robert Burns's proverbial statement about "the best laid schemes o' mice and men." The poet Samuel Taylor Coleridge awoke one morning with a lengthy poem clearly etched in his mind. He quickly began to write the first dozen lines of "Kubla Khan," and then the doorbell rang; a man from Porlock had come for some business. An hour or so later, Coleridge returned to his desk to finish the poem but, to his dismay, it had vanished from his memory. It is tantalizing to imagine how magnificent a poem his "Kubla Khan" might have been had not the interruption prevented its completion. There is a "man from Porlock" in everyone's life to overturn your plans and projects. You cannot rule out unexpected obstacles on your way, no matter what your goal. In the light of life's uncertainties, we can understand the psalmist's exhilaration at having reached a moment free of all doubt, a moment in which he can be wholehearted and of one mind: "My heart is steady, O God, I will sing praises" (v. 2). What is the psalmist so sure about? It is his faith that God's "mercy is great above the heavens" (v. 5) and that one may count on God that "Your beloved may be delivered" (v. 7).

❦ Psalm 109 ❦

For the Leader. A Psalm of David.

O God of my praise, keep not silence;
2For the mouth of the wicked and the mouth of deceit have they opened against me;
They have spoken unto me with a lying tongue.
3They compassed me about also with words of hatred,
And fought against me without a cause.
4In return for my love they are my adversaries;
But I am all prayer.
5And they have laid upon me evil for good,
And hatred for my love:

6"Set Thou a wicked man over him;
And let an adversary stand at his right hand.

7When he is judged, let him go forth condemned;
And let his prayer be turned into sin.
8Let his days be few;
Let another take his charge.
9Let his children be fatherless,
And his wife a widow.
10Let his children be vagabonds, and beg;
And let them seek their bread out of their desolate places.
11Let the creditor distrain all that he hath;
And let strangers make spoil of his labour.
12Let there be none to extend kindness unto him;
Neither let there be any to be gracious unto his fatherless children.
13Let his posterity be cut off;
In the generation following let their name be blotted out.

14Let the iniquity of his fathers be
  brought to remembrance unto the
  LORD,
  And let not the sin of his mother be
  blotted out.
15Let them be before the LORD
  continually,
  That He may cut off the memory of
  them from the earth.
16Because that he remembered not to
  do kindness,
  But persecuted the poor and needy
  man,
  And the broken in heart he was ready
  to slay.
17Yea, he loved cursing, and it came
  unto him;
  And he delighted not in blessing, and
  it is far from him.
18He clothed himself also with cursing
  as with his raiment,
  And it is come into his inward parts
  like water,
  And like oil into his bones.
19Let it be unto him as the garment
  which he putteth on,
  And for the girdle wherewith he is
  girded continually.”

20This would mine adversaries effect
  from the LORD,
  And they that speak evil against my
  soul.
21But Thou, O GOD the LORD, deal
  with me for Thy name’s sake;

  Because Thy mercy is good, deliver
  Thou me.
22For I am poor and needy,
  And my heart is wounded within me.
23I am gone like the shadow when it
  lengtheneth;
  I am shaken off as the locust.
24My knees totter through fasting;
  And my flesh is lean, and hath no
  fatness.
25I am become also a taunt unto them;
  When they see me, they shake their
  head.

26Help me, O LORD my God;
  O save me according to Thy mercy;
27That they may know that this is Thy
  hand;
  That Thou, LORD, hast done it.
28Let them curse, but bless Thou;
  When they arise, they shall be put to
  shame, but Thy servant shall
  rejoice.
29Mine adversaries shall be clothed with
  confusion,
  And shall put on their own shame as a
  robe.
30I will give great thanks unto the LORD
  with my mouth;
  Yea, I will praise Him among the
  multitude;
31Because He standeth at the right hand
  of the needy,
  To save him from them that judge his
  soul.

God Will Not Abandon the Weak and Needy

Imagine good friends turning against you for no reason at all. Your reaction would be far more vehement than mere disappointment. You would be hurt, resentful, and angry to the point of wanting to strike back at them. The author of Psalm 109 went through such a bitter experience. Friends he had trusted attacked him and spread lies about him: “The wicked and deceitful speak against me; they lie to me; they encircle me with words of hate and fight against me for no reason. In return for my love, they act as enemies toward me” (v. 2–4).

Exasperated, the psalmist heaps curses upon his adversaries (see v. 8–19). But after his outburst of bitterness and anger, he finds relief by leaving matters in God's hands: "Now, O God, act for me according to Your name; save me, because Your loving-kindness is good!" (v. 21). He describes his pathetic condition: "I am poor and needy and my heart is wounded" (v. 22).

While pouring out his heart before God, he recovers confidence that the ill will of his enemies will be offset by God's blessings: "Let them curse, but You will bless. When they rise, they shall be put to shame, but Your servant will rejoice" (v. 28). At the beginning, he was distressed by God's silence: "O God of my praise, keep not silent" (v. 1). In the end, he feels reassured that God will stand by him in time of need: "Because He stands at the right hand of the needy to save him from those who would condemn him" (v. 31).

∾

Reflection: Disappointed

Among life's most galling experiences is that of being betrayed by people one loves and trusts. It happened to the psalmist: "They have laid upon me evil for good and hatred for my love" (v. 5). Understandably, he laments: "My heart is wounded within me" (v. 22). How can one cope with the hurt of such a betrayal? The one thing you must not do is allow the disappointment in one relationship to make you distrustful of all relationships. One rotten apple in a bushel does not prove all others rotten. Do not fall into the error of Wordsworth, England's celebrated poet, who because of his own disappointing experiences soured on the whole world:

> Nothing is left which I can venerate,
> So that a doubt almost within me springs
> Of providence, such emptiness at length
> Seems at the heart of all things.

Worse than the hurt done to you by deceitful, dishonest, and corrupt individuals would be your self-punishment of turning your back on everybody. Benjamin Franklin advised that we be less judgmental about people, since their conduct most likely mirrors some of our own faults and foibles. The psalmist finds consolation in his reliance on God and His love and justice: "Let them curse, but You do bless" (v. 28).

❧ Psalm 110 ❧

A Psalm of David.

The LORD saith unto my lord: "Sit
   thou at My right hand,
Until I make thine enemies thy
   footstool."
2 The rod of thy strength the LORD will
   send out of Zion:
"Rule thou in the midst of thine
   enemies."
3 Thy people offer themselves willingly
   in the day of thy warfare;
In adornments of holiness, from the
   womb of the dawn,
Thine is the dew of thy youth.

4 The LORD hath sworn, and will not
   repent:
"Thou art a priest for ever
After the manner of Melchizedek."
5 The LORD at thy right hand
Doth crush kings in the day of His
   wrath.
6 He will judge among the nations;
He filleth it with dead bodies,
He crusheth the head over a wide
   land.
7 He will drink of the brook in the way;
Therefore will he lift up the head.

❧

Victory Belongs to God

We are quick to take full credit for achievements without acknowledging the help of others who enabled us to succeed. The psalmist, however, while paying tribute to the king for his leadership in time of war, recognizes God as the power that made the king's victory possible. It is God Who empowers us in all we do: "God will extend the scepter of your strength from Zion, saying, 'Rule over your enemies'" (v. 2). This does not mean that we should sit back and let God do our work. We must do all we can by our own means, as did the youth who volunteered for battle: "Your people volunteered on the day of warfare" (v. 3). Only then may you count on God to shape the course of events: "He will judge among the nations" (v. 6).

❧

Reflection: Whom Should We Thank?

A poetically gifted courtier wrote this psalm in praise of his king's stunning victories. However, he did not neglect to give credit to God, the power behind the king, Who enabled the king to achieve: "God will extend the scepter of your strength" (v. 2). Are you giving credit to all who gave their share to make your accomplishments possible? It would be a long list, beginning with parents, relatives, nurses, teachers, and friends, to which should be added people, known and unknown to you, who at various crossroads of your life gave you a helping hand. It has been well said that wherever a man climbs to the top, there's a woman standing and holding the ladder. Some people are exceptionally scrupulous in acknowledging every gift or favor they receive. The dramatist Charles Lederer was invited to watch the rehearsals for the Broadway play *Jumbo* by Ben Hecht and Charles MacArthur. When the comedian Jimmy Durante tried to steer the elephant past the sheriff, who was going to confiscate the animal, Lederer made a suggestion to the playwrights: "Have the sheriff say: 'Where are you going with that elephant?' And then let Jimmy say, 'What elephant?'" The suggestion was incorporated into the play and drew the biggest laugh in the show. Hecht and MacArthur acknowledged their friend's contribution with a credit in the program: "Joke by Charles Lederer." If you were to make a movie of each day of your life, you would have to add, at the end, credits for all your benefactors who provided information, advice, and help. Should not the list be topped by the One to Whom you owe life and whose benefits enabled you to make it through that day?

❧ PSALM III ❧

Hallelujah.

I will give thanks unto the LORD with my whole heart,
In the council of the upright, and in the congregation.
2 The works of the LORD are great,
Sought out of all them that have delight therein.
3 His work is glory and majesty;
And His righteousness endureth for ever.
4 He hath made a memorial for His wonderful works;
The LORD is gracious and full of compassion.
5 He hath given food unto them that fear Him;
He will ever be mindful of His covenant.
6 He hath declared to His people the power of His works,

In giving them the heritage of the nations.
7 The works of His hands are truth and justice;
All His precepts are sure.
8 They are established for ever and ever,
They are done in truth and uprightness.
9 He hath sent redemption unto His people;
He hath commanded His covenant for ever;
Holy and awful is His name.
10 The fear of the LORD is the beginning of wisdom;
A good understanding have all they that do thereafter;
His praise endureth for ever.

❦

Thank God!

You are fortunate if you are surrounded by positive-minded people who see the bright side of things. Such persons are generally cheerful and quick to express thanks and appreciation for anything you might do for them. Such a person was the author of Psalm 111, whose heart was filled with thanksgiving: "I will give thanks to God with my whole heart" (v. 1). He marvels at the glory and majesty of God's creation and sees in the bounties of the earth tokens of God's goodness and compassion. He rests assured that God will be faithful to His covenant: "He will ever be mindful of His covenant" (v. 5). On his part, the psalmist wants to do everything to prove his love for God and fears doing anything that might offend Him. Therefore, he ends the psalm with the words: "The fear of God is the beginning of wisdom" (v. 10).

❦

Reflection: The Fear of God

One of the most misunderstood biblical words is "fear" of God. It occurs in verse 10: "The fear of God is the beginning of wisdom." To better understand the real meaning of "fear of God," bear in mind the context. Psalm 111 is the first of a series, each beginning with the Hebrew word *Hallelujah*, which means "praise God." These *Hallelujah* psalms are Israel's love songs to God. When the psalmist speaks of the fear of God, he certainly does not mean that we should be terrorized by God. There is a difference between fear of God and being afraid of God. So what does it mean? Consider this: When we call a person "God-fearing," we merely want to say that the person is deeply attached to God and therefore careful in all he does. God-fearing means God-loving. What does fear have to do with love? The answer is that the more you love someone, the more you fear to offend or hurt that person by word or deed. You fear to lose the love and respect of the person you are attached to. Love is like a very precious object that you fear might get damaged or lost. So it is with a believer to whom the relationship with God is most precious. Therefore, he watches his every word, thought, and deed so as not to offend God. To fear God means to fear the loss of God's love.

Psalm 112

Hallelujah.

Happy is the man that feareth the
  LORD,
That delighteth greatly in His commandments.
2 His seed shall be mighty upon earth;
  The generation of the upright shall be
  blessed.
3 Wealth and riches are in his house;
  And his merit endureth for ever.
4 Unto the upright He shineth as a
  light in the darkness,
  Gracious, and full of compassion, and
  righteous.
5 Well is it with the man that dealeth
  graciously and lendeth,
  That ordereth his affairs rightfully.

6 For he shall never be moved;
  The righteous shall be had in everlasting remembrance.
7 He shall not be afraid of evil tidings;
  His heart is stedfast, trusting in the
  LORD.
8 His heart is established, he shall not
  be afraid,
  Until he gaze upon his adversaries.
9 He hath scattered abroad, he hath
  given to the needy;
  His righteousness endureth for ever;
  His horn shall be exalted in honour.
10 The wicked shall see, and be vexed;
  He shall gnash with his teeth, and
  melt away;
  The desire of the wicked shall perish.

A Composite Sketch of the Righteous

How would you define a good person? Consider the characteristics of the righteous as outlined in Psalm 112. Could such a person serve as your role model? Note what the psalmist puts first: "He reveres God and gladly performs His commandments" (v. 1). Though wealthy, the righteous is a shining example of kindness, compassion, and justice: "With all his wealth and riches, he is a person of righteousness; he shines as a light in darkness, gracious, compassionate, and just" (v. 3, 4). He is helpful and honest: "Things go well with that man who readily extends a loan and runs his business honestly" (v. 5). He is undeviating in his ways even in bad times, "unafraid of bad news, stout-hearted and trusting God" (v. 7). Generous to the needy, "he is powerful and respected" (v. 9). Evildoers can only glare in hate: "Their wishes come to nothing" (v. 10).

Reflection: Worries and Fears

To be human is to live with fears. Some are justified and some are not. Most afraid, and for good reason, are the very young, the very old, and the sick, because of their insecurity or frailty. Much of the emotional life of normal, average adults is also made up of worries, anxieties, and fears. These may be work-related, such as the fear of unsatisfactory performance or job insecurity; other fears arise from troubled relationships, impending financial loss, and exposure to crime and violence. A word has to be said in recognition of the value of fear. Fear makes us cautious. We install burglar alarms because of fear for our personal safety and property. The Renaissance genius Leonardo da Vinci said in praise of fear: "Just as courage imperils life, fear protects it." The American publisher Edgar Watson Howe considered fear to be a most effective teacher: "A good scare is worth more to a man than good advice."

However, many of our fears are not based on reality but are in our minds. The way to cope with fears is to recognize the difference between what is imagination and what is fact. The British naval commander Lord Mountbatten, as a small boy of five years, was afraid to go to bed alone in the dark. "There are wolves up there," he explained to his father. "But there are no wolves in this house," said the father reassuringly. Young Mountbatten replied: "I dare say there aren't, but I *think* there are." Most of our fears are only in our heads. They may possibly become reality, but not yet, not now. We must learn to master these anxious expectations and frightening anticipations lest they master us. Our psalmist sets an example to follow. He counsels us to order our affairs right, that is, to do whatever we can to prepare for what lies ahead, then be steadfast and trust God: "He shall never be moved; . . . he shall not be afraid of evil tidings; his heart is steadfast, trusting in the Lord. His heart is set, he shall not be afraid" (v. 6–7). In one of the darkest moments of World War II, Winston Churchill, trying to lift the morale of his countrymen, ended one of his great speeches with part of verse 7: "He shall not be afraid of evil tidings; his heart is steadfast, trusting in the Lord."

∾ PSALM 113 ∾

Hallelujah.
Praise, O ye servants of the LORD,
Praise the name of the LORD.
2 Blessed be the name of the LORD
From this time forth and for ever.
3 From the rising of the sun unto the
   going down thereof
  The LORD's name is to be praised.

4 The LORD is high above all nations,

His glory is above the heavens.
5 Who is like unto the LORD our God,
  That is enthroned on high,
6 That looketh down low
  Upon heaven and upon the earth?

7 Who raiseth up the poor out of the
  dust,
  And lifteth up the needy out of the
  dunghill;

8 That He may set him with princes,
 Even with the princes of His people.
9 Who maketh the barren woman to
 dwell in her house

As a joyful mother of children.
Hallelujah.

❧

Nothing Escapes God's Attention

Do you wonder if the God of the universe pays attention to each of His countless creatures? The author of Psalm 113 had no doubt about it. God, exalted above the heavens, "sees what is below in heaven and on earth" (v. 6), The rational mind cannot conceive how God does it, but people of faith believe it. The psalmists went even further in their trust that God not only knows each and every one but cares about everyone's well-being, hears their sighs, counts their tears, and answers their needs. In that faith, the psalmist asserts that God "raises up the poor out of the dust and lifts the needy out of the dunghill, to bring him up to the level of princes" (v. 7–8). It is in His power to "turn the barren woman into a joyful mother of children" (v. 9).

❧

Reflection: Coping with Depression

This psalm is good medicine for the discouraged, defeated, and depressed. The psalmist is jubilant and heaps praises on God. He would go on praising God, he says, "from sunrise to sunset" (v. 3). This psalm begins and ends with the word *Hallelujah*, praise God! What makes him so upbeat? He has come to believe that God knows and responds to human needs. He credits God for raising paupers to become companions of princes and for blessing the barren woman so that she becomes "a joyful mother of children" (v. 9). The message is: Don't despair. Consider how quickly things can change. A legend tells that King Solomon in his wisdom had a ring designed for him, inscribed with the words "This too will pass." Whenever he felt gloomy, he looked at his ring and was cheered by the thought that the cause for his gloom would pass, as does everything else. Nothing in life is permanent. As suddenly as our circumstances deteriorate, so suddenly could things improve.

❦ Psalm 114 ❦

When Israel came forth out of
   Egypt,
 The house of Jacob from a people of
   strange language;
2 Judah became His sanctuary,
 Israel His dominion.

3 The sea saw it, and fled;
 The Jordan turned backward.
4 The mountains skipped like rams,
 The hills like young sheep.

5 What aileth thee, O thou sea, that
   thou fleest?

Thou Jordan, that thou turnest
   backward?
6 Ye mountains, that ye skip like rams;
 Ye hills, like young sheep?

7 Tremble, thou earth, at the presence of
   the LORD,
 At the presence of the God of Jacob;
8 Who turned the rock into a pool of
   water,
 The flint into a fountain of waters.

❦

Seeing the World through Your Feelings

The author of Psalm 114 pictures his people's happiness at their liberation from Egyptian slavery: "When Israel came forth out of Egypt" (v. 1), they sang and danced for joy. And so it seemed to them, at that triumphant time, that the world was also singing and dancing with them: "The mountains skipped like rams, the hills like young sheep" (v. 4). We should note a striking sentence in this psalm: "Judah became His [God's] sanctuary, Israel His dominion" (v. 2). In the psalmist's view, his people, Judah, ought to be a place fit for God to dwell in. Synagogues and churches are convenient meeting places for congregational worship, but God's true dwelling is among the people, in their hearts and minds.

❦

Reflection: Mood Determines What You See

This psalm speaks of the sea and the river and the mountains. But it is not a realistic description of nature. Rather, it offers us insight into human nature. When you are happy, the whole world smiles with you. When you are angry or sad, even the clearest and sunniest sky offends you. Your mood largely determines what you see around you. "When Israel came forth out of Egypt" (v. 1), the liberated people sang and danced for joy. And so it seemed to them that the whole world was also singing and dancing with them. We see the world through lenses tinted by our feelings. It is the world *within* that determines our outlook upon the world around us. This highlights the importance of cultivating our inner life, for the key to happiness and peace is within.

❦ Psalm 115 ❦

Not unto us, O Lord, not unto us,
But unto Thy name give glory,
For Thy mercy, and for Thy truth's
   sake.
2 Wherefore should the nations say:
   "Where is now their God?"

3 But our God is in the heavens;
   Whatsoever pleased Him He hath
   done.
4 Their idols are silver and gold,
   The work of men's hands.
5 They have mouths, but they speak
   not;
   Eyes have they, but they see not;
6 They have ears, but they hear not;
   Noses have they, but they smell not;
7 They have hands, but they handle
   not;
   Feet have they, but they walk not;
   Neither speak they with their throat.
8 They that make them shall be like
   unto them;
   Yea, every one that trusteth in them.

9 O Israel, trust thou in the Lord!
   He is their help and their shield!
10 O house of Aaron, trust ye in the
   Lord!

He is their help and their shield!
11 Ye that fear the Lord, trust in the
   Lord!
   He is their help and their shield.

12 The Lord hath been mindful of us,
   He will bless—
   He will bless the house of Israel;
   He will bless the house of Aaron.
13 He will bless them that fear the
   Lord,
   Both small and great.
14 The Lord increase you more and
   more,
   You and your children.
15 Blessed be ye of the Lord,
   Who made heaven and earth.

16 The heavens are the heavens of the
   Lord;
   But the earth hath He given to the
   children of men.
17 The dead praise not the Lord,
   Neither any that go down into
   silence;
18 But we will bless the Lord
   From this time forth and for ever.
   Hallelujah.

❦

We Are in Charge of the Earth

This psalmist speaks of the human condition with humility and pride. He revels in his people's achievements, which honor God in the eyes of the nations: "Not to us, but to You, O God, bring glory for the sake of Your loving-kindness and faithfulness" (v. 1).

The pagans are puzzled by Israel's belief in a God who cannot be seen. The psalmist explains: "Our God is in the heavens; He does whatever pleases Him" (v. 3). He ridicules the pagans, whose idols are lifeless, impotent products of human craftsmanship (see v. 4–8). Most remarkable is the psalmist's view of God's partnership with mankind. God oversees the universe but has turned the earth over to human control: "The heavens are the heavens of God; but the earth He has given over to man" (v. 16). Implied in this mastery over the earth is the task of responsible management of our planet.

∽

Reflection: Mankind's Responsibility

Are we entitled to argue that almighty God, Creator and Ruler of the universe, should use His power to keep us out of trouble here on earth? This psalmist puts the responsibility for our welfare squarely upon our own shoulders. He is no less lavish than other psalmists in his praise of God. But after glorifying God, "Who made heaven and earth" (v. 15), he quickly adds: "The heavens are the heavens of God, but the earth has He given to the children of men" (v. 16). Imagine God saying to mankind: "Here is the earth. It is yours to keep and preserve. You are in charge as My deputies. Don't expect Me to solve your problems. Make your bed, and sleep in it!" With the assignment to rule the earth comes grave responsibility. The New Testament put it well: "To whomsoever much is given, of him much will be required" (Luke 12:48). Tragically, we human beings seem to be more bent on the destruction than the preservation of life, and when calamities catch up with our mismanagement of human affairs, many blame God: How could You, O God, let it happen? Why do You stand by at the death of so many? Before you challenge God to do mankind's repair work, remember the psalmist's statement: "The earth has He given to the children of men" (v. 16). It is our job, not God's, to keep the earth safe for all its inhabitants. Ambrose Bierce, in his cynical *Devil's Dictionary*, defines responsibility as "a detachable burden easily shifted to the shoulders of God, Fate, Fortune, Luck or one's neighbor. In the days of astrology it was customary to unload it upon a star." God not only set us above all other creatures to rule the earth, but He also made known to us the rules and principles that should guide our actions: "It has been told you, O man, what is good and what God requires of You, only to do justly, love mercy and walk humbly with your God" (Micah 6:8).

❦ Psalm 116 ❦

I love that the LORD should hear
My voice and my supplications.
2 Because He hath inclined His ear
    unto me,
Therefore will I call upon Him all my
    days.

3 The cords of death compassed me,
And the straits of the netherworld got
    hold upon me;
I found trouble and sorrow.
4 But I called upon the name of the
    LORD:
"I beseech Thee, O LORD, deliver my
    soul."
5 Gracious is the LORD, and righteous;
Yea, our God is compassionate.
6 The LORD preserveth the simple;
I was brought low, and He saved me.
7 Return, O my soul, unto thy rest;
For the LORD hath dealt bountifully
    with thee.
8 For Thou hast delivered my soul
    from death,
Mine eyes from tears,
And my feet from stumbling.
9 I shall walk before the LORD
In the lands of the living.

10 I trusted even when I spoke:
"I am greatly afflicted."
11 I said in my haste:
"All men are liars."

12 How can I repay unto the LORD
All His bountiful dealings toward me?
13 I will lift up the cup of salvation,
And call upon the name of the LORD.
14 My vows will I pay unto the LORD,
Yea, in the presence of all His people.

15 Precious in the sight of the LORD
Is the death of His saints.
16 I beseech Thee, O LORD, for I am
    Thy servant;
I am Thy servant, the son of Thy
    handmaid;
Thou hast loosed my bands.
17 I will offer to Thee the sacrifice of
    thanksgiving,
And will call upon the name of the
    LORD.
18 I will pay my vows unto the LORD,
Yea, in the presence of all His people;
19 In the courts of the LORD's house,
In the midst of thee, O Jerusalem.
Hallelujah.

❦

Pulled Back from the Brink of Death

This psalm exemplifies *crisis religion*, that is, a response to the immediate threat of death or some other dreadful peril: "The cords of death were all around me" (v. 3). In distress, the psalmist throws himself on God's mercy: "I beseech You, O God, save me" (v. 4). He is overjoyed as he emerges alive: "I shall walk before God in the lands of the living" (v. 9). He sees his new lease on life as God's doing: "I was down and out and He saved me" (v. 6).

While thanking God for his deliverance, he wants God to know that even during his affliction, he never lost faith in God: "I trusted even when I said, 'I am greatly afflicted'" (v. 10). Now he wonders: "How can I repay God for all His bounties?" (v. 12). The sanctuary meets his need to express publicly his gratitude to God: "My vows will I pay unto God in the presence of all His people in the courts of God's house" (v. 18–19).

⸺

Reflection: On Being a Listener

This psalm opens with a sentence that speaks for all of us: "I love it that God listens to my voice" (v. 1). The psalmist is overjoyed to have found a listening ear. Usually we stress the ability to speak. We are taught to choose words carefully. Schools hold oratorical contests. On a personal level, we appreciate a good listener more than a good talker. Eleanor Roosevelt advised people that to win friends, be a good listener. Voltaire said it most succinctly: "The ear is the road to the heart." The listener is appreciated for several reasons. By giving you attention, the listener assures you that you are worthy and that you are a person of interest. To be listened to makes you feel accepted and almost gives you the feeling of being liked. A listener draws you out and encourages the unfolding and expansion of your true self. You might define friendship as that relationship which permits two persons to be comfortable when silent together. A perceptive young woman told a man who liked her: "We do not know each other well enough; we have not yet been silent together." The fourth-century Greek philosopher Zeno of Citium summed it all up in his saying: "The reason why we have two ears and only one mouth is so that we may listen more and talk less."

⸺ **PSALM 117** ⸺

O praise the LORD, all ye nations;
  Laud Him, all ye peoples.
2 For His mercy is great toward us;

And the truth of the LORD endureth
  for ever.
  Hallelujah.

⸺

Let All Nations Praise God!

This shortest of the 150 psalms has a mighty message or, you might call it, vision: Let all mankind unite in the praise of God, since His mercy extends to all humanity and His faithfulness endures forever: "O praise God, all you nations; glorify Him, all you peoples!" (v. 1).

❦

Reflection: Mankind's Unity

A long view of history suggests that mankind is moving toward ever-larger units, from families to clans, to tribes, to nations. Beginning some four thousand years ago, superpowers united, by conquest, groups of nations in their empires. It was a unity achieved by the sword and sooner or later fragmented by the sword, through uprisings and wars waged by rival powers. Not until the twentieth century was the attempt made to unite the nations politically, and not by force, in an international body, first the League of Nations after World War I and then the United Nations after World War II. The Bible was the first to voice the vision of all nations uniting spiritually, not by conquest but by consent, in adoration of the one and only God. Tragically, emerging world religions also adopted the bloody methods of empire-building by waging holy wars, crusades, and jihads. Only in recent decades have the major religions of the world been turning from armed conflict and persecution to interfaith dialogue. We need to build more bridges of understanding in order to realize the vision of all peoples voluntarily uniting in the worship of God, each in their own way yet sharing a common faith in God.

❦ PSALM 118 ❦

"O give thanks unto the LORD, for He is good,
For His mercy endureth for ever.
2 So let Israel now say,
For His mercy endureth for ever,
3 So let the house of Aaron now say,
For His mercy endureth for ever.
4 So let them now that fear the LORD say,
For His mercy endureth for ever.

5 Out of my straits I called upon the LORD;
He answered me with great enlargement.
6 The LORD is for me; I will not fear;
What can man do unto me?
7 The LORD is for me as my helper;
And I shall gaze upon them that hate me.

8 It is better to take refuge in the LORD
Than to trust in man.
9 It is better to take refuge in the LORD
Than to trust in princes.
10 All nations compass me about;
Verily, in the name of the LORD I will cut them off.
11 They compass me about, yea, they compass me about;
Verily, in the name of the LORD I will cut them off.
12 They compass me about like bees;
They are quenched as the fire of thorns;
Verily, in the name of the LORD I will cut them off.
13 Thou didst thrust sore at me that I might fall;
But the LORD helped me.
14 The LORD is my strength and song;

And He is become my salvation.

15 The voice of rejoicing and salvation is
  in the tents of the righteous;
  The right hand of the LORD doeth
  valiantly.
16 The right hand of the LORD is
  exalted;
  The right hand of the LORD doeth
  valiantly.
17 I shall not die, but live,
  And declare the works of the LORD.
18 The LORD hath chastened me sore;
  But He hath not given me over unto
  death.
19 Open to me the gates of
  righteousness;
  I will enter into them, I will give
  thanks unto the LORD.
20 This is the gate of the LORD;
  The righteous shall enter into it.
21 I will give thanks unto Thee, for
  Thou hast answered me,
  And art become my salvation.

22 The stone which the builders rejected
  Is become the chief corner-stone.

23 This is the LORD's doing;

It is marvellous in our eyes.

24 This is the day which the LORD hath
  made;
  We will rejoice and be glad in it.

25 We beseech Thee, O LORD, save
  now!
  We beseech Thee, O LORD, make us
  now to prosper!

26 Blessed be he that cometh in the
  name of the LORD;
  We bless you out of the house of the
  LORD.

27 The LORD is God, and hath given us
  light;
  Order the festival procession with
  boughs, even unto the horns of the
  altar.

28 Thou art my God, and I will give
  thanks unto Thee;
  Thou art my God, I will exalt Thee.

29 O give thanks unto the LORD, for He
  is good,
  For His mercy endureth for ever.

A Joyful Comeback

Success is doubly sweet if it comes after a series of failures. This explains the psalmist's ecstatic joy over his people's rise from the ashes of defeat. He had turned to God for help in a time of national catastrophe: "Out of my distress I called upon God. He answered me with great relief" (v. 5). Scholars believe that Psalm 118 was composed as a victory song after many of the Judeans returned from their captivity in Babylon. Overcoming many hardships and attacks by neighboring peoples, they rebuilt Jerusalem and erected a new sanctuary to replace the Temple of Solomon, which had been destroyed. Addressing the enemies of his people, the psalmist exclaims: "You came down hard upon me that I might fall, but God helped me. God is my strength and song and He is my deliverance" (v. 13–14).

The psalmist understands his people's tribulations as chastisement, but not meant for their destruction: "God has punished me sorely, but He has not handed me over unto death" (v. 18). Now the people, having recovered from their humiliation, need no longer feel rejected, but take a leading role in history: "The stone which the builders rejected has become the chief cornerstone. This is God's doing; it is marvelous in our eyes" (v. 22–23).

The psalmist brims with confidence as he exclaims: "I shall not die but live and declare the works of God" (v. 17). He understands his survival as a mission to witness to the works of God. The psalm ends as it begins, with the identical call to thanksgiving: "Give thanks unto God, for He is good; His loving-kindness endures forever" (v. 1, 29).

❦

Reflection: A Sense of Purpose

In a burst of confidence, the psalmist exclaims: "I shall not die but live, and declare the works of God" (v. 17). Is this a boast of immortality? Hardly. All he wants to say is that he expects to survive the immediate threat to his life. But it is not just survival that he is talking about. He hopes to live for a purpose, "to declare the works of God." A sense of purpose gives a powerful boost to the will to live. It energizes our whole life and raises us to a higher level of achievement. A legend about King Solomon tells of an incident during the building of the temple in Jerusalem. One day the king wanted to see how the workmen were doing. He chose to personally inspect the output of the stonemasons. Watching one hammering away on a large block of stone, the king asked what he was doing. He replied that he was doing his daily allotment of stone cutting and pointed to a small heap of square blocks that he had cut that day. The king noticed that the work was only fair in quality. Going to the next worker's place and seeing a large heap of stone blocks all cut to perfection, the king asked the same question: "What are you doing?" This stonemason reared himself up and said: "I am building the temple." The more clearly a person sees the object or purpose of his work, the greater will be his effort to do it well. Without a sense of purpose, we drift. Aimlessness is a disabling condition that makes for chronic discontent, as Seneca wisely observed: "For him who knows not what port to sail to, no wind is right."

❦ PSALM 119 ❦

א ALEPH

Happy are they that are upright in the way,
Who walk in the law of the LORD.

2 Happy are they that keep His testimonies,
That seek Him with the whole heart.
3 Yea, they do no unrighteousness;

They walk in His ways.
4 Thou hast ordained Thy precepts,
That we should observe them
diligently.
5 Oh that my ways were directed
To observe Thy statutes!
6 Then should I not be ashamed,
When I have regard unto all Thy
commandments.
7 I will give thanks unto Thee with
uprightness of heart,
When I learn Thy righteous
ordinances.
8 I will observe Thy statutes;
O forsake me not utterly.

ב BETH

9 Wherewithal shall a young man keep
his way pure?
By taking heed thereto according to
Thy word.
10 With my whole heart have I sought
Thee;
O let me not err from Thy commandments.
11 Thy word have I laid up in my heart,
That I might not sin against Thee.
12 Blessed art Thou, O LORD;
Teach me Thy statutes.
13 With my lips have I told
All the ordinances of Thy mouth.
14 I have rejoiced in the way of Thy
testimonies,
As much as in all riches.
15 I will meditate in Thy precepts,
And have respect unto Thy ways.
16 I will delight myself in Thy statutes;
I will not forget Thy word.

ג GIMEL

17 Deal bountifully with Thy servant
that I may live,
And I will observe Thy word.
18 Open Thou mine eyes, that I may
behold
Wondrous things out of Thy law.
19 I am a sojourner in the earth;
Hide not Thy commandments from
me.
20 My soul breaketh for the longing
That it hath unto Thine ordinances
at all times.

21 Thou hast rebuked the proud that
are cursed,
That do err from Thy commandments.
22 Take away from me reproach and
contempt;
For I have kept Thy testimonies.
23 Even though princes sit and talk
against me,
Thy servant doth meditate in Thy
statutes.
24 Yea, Thy testimonies are my delight,
They are my counsellors.

ד DALETH

25 My soul cleaveth unto the dust;
Quicken Thou me according to Thy
word.
26 I told of my ways, and Thou didst
answer me;
Teach me Thy statutes.
27 Make me to understand the way of
Thy precepts,
That I may talk of Thy wondrous
works.
28 My soul melteth away for heaviness;
Sustain me according unto Thy
word.
29 Remove from me the way of falsehood;
And grant me Thy law graciously.
30 I have chosen the way of faithfulness;
Thine ordinances have I set [before
me].
31 I cleave unto Thy testimonies;
O LORD, put me not to shame.
32 I will run the way of Thy commandments,
For Thou dost enlarge my heart.

ה HE

33 Teach me, O LORD, the way of Thy
statutes;
And I will keep it at every step.
34 Give me understanding, that I keep
Thy law
And observe it with my whole heart.
35 Make me to tread in the path of Thy
commandments;
For therein do I delight.
36 Incline my heart unto Thy testimonies,

And not to covetousness.
37 Turn away mine eyes from beholding
vanity,
And quicken me in Thy ways.
38 Confirm Thy word unto Thy servant,
Which pertaineth unto the fear of
Thee.
39 Turn away my reproach which I
dread;
For Thine ordinances are good.
40 Behold, I have longed after Thy
precepts;
Quicken me in Thy righteousness.

ו VAV

41 Let Thy mercies also come unto me,
O LORD,
Even Thy salvation, according to
Thy word;
42 That I may have an answer for him
that taunteth me;
For I trust in Thy word.
43 And take not the word of truth
utterly out of my mouth;
For I hope in Thine ordinances;
44 So shall I observe Thy law continually
For ever and ever;
45 And I will walk at ease,
For I have sought Thy precepts;
46 I will also speak of Thy testimonies
before kings,
And will not be ashamed.
47 And I will delight myself in Thy
commandments,
Which I have loved.
48 I will lift up my hands also unto Thy
commandments, which I have
loved;
And I will meditate in Thy statutes.

ז ZAIN

49 Remember the word unto Thy
servant,
Because Thou hast made me to
hope.
50 This is my comfort in my affliction,
That Thy word hath quickened me.
51 The proud have had me greatly in
derision;

Yet have I not turned aside from Thy
law.
52 I have remembered Thine ordinances which are of old, O LORD,
And have comforted myself.
53 Burning indignation hath taken
hold upon me, because of the
wicked
That forsake Thy law.
54 Thy statutes have been my songs
In the house of my pilgrimage.
55 I have remembered Thy name, O
LORD, in the night,
And have observed Thy law.
56 This I have had,
That I have kept Thy precepts.

ח HETH

57 My portion is the LORD,
I have said that I would observe Thy
words.
58 I have entreated Thy favour with my
whole heart;
Be gracious unto me according to
Thy word.
59 I considered my ways,
And turned my feet unto Thy
testimonies.
60 I made haste, and delayed not,
To observe Thy commandments.
61 The bands of the wicked have
enclosed me;
But I have not forgotten Thy law.
62 At midnight I will rise to give thanks
unto Thee
Because of Thy righteous ordinances.
63 I am a companion of all them that
fear Thee,
And of them that observe Thy precepts.
64 The earth, O LORD, is full of Thy
mercy;
Teach me Thy statutes.

ט TETH

65 Thou hast dealt well with Thy servant,
O LORD, according unto Thy word.
66 Teach me good discernment and
knowledge;

For I have believed in Thy
  commandments.
67 Before I was afflicted, I did err;
  But now I observe Thy word.
68 Thou art good, and doest good;
  Teach me Thy statutes.
69 The proud have forged a lie against
  me;
  But I with my whole heart will keep
  Thy precepts.
70 Their heart is gross like fat;
  But I delight in Thy law.
71 It is good for me that I have been
  afflicted,
  In order that I might learn Thy
  statutes.
72 The law of Thy mouth is better unto
  me
  Than thousands of gold and silver.

י YOD

73 Thy hands have made me and fashioned me;
  Give me understanding, that I may
  learn Thy commandments.
74 They that fear Thee shall see me and
  be glad,
  Because I have hope in Thy word.
75 I know, O LORD, that Thy judgments
  are righteous,
  And that in faithfulness Thou hast
  afflicted me.
76 Let, I pray Thee, Thy lovingkindness
  be ready to comfort me,
  According to Thy promise unto Thy
  servant.
77 Let Thy tender mercies come unto
  me, that I may live;
  For Thy law is my delight.
78 Let the proud be put to shame, for
  they have distorted my cause with
  falsehood;
  But I will meditate in Thy precepts.
79 Let those that fear Thee return unto
  me,
  And they that know Thy testimonies.
80 Let my heart be undivided in Thy
  statutes,
  In order that I may not be put to
  shame.

כ CAPH

81 My soul pineth for Thy salvation;
  In Thy word do I hope.
82 Mine eyes fail for Thy word,
  Saying: "When wilt Thou comfort
  me?"
83 For I am become like a wine-skin in
  the smoke;
  Yet do I not forget Thy statutes.
84 How many are the days of Thy
  servant?
  When wilt Thou execute judgment
  on them that persecute me?
85 The proud have digged pits for me,
  Which is not according to Thy law.
86 All Thy commandments are faithful;
  They persecute me for nought; help
  Thou me.
87 They had almost consumed me upon
  earth;
  But as for me, I forsook not Thy
  precepts.
88 Quicken me after Thy lovingkindness,
  And I will observe the testimony of
  Thy mouth.

ל LAMED

89 For ever, O LORD,
  Thy word standeth fast in heaven.
90 Thy faithfulness is unto all generations;
  Thou hast established the earth, and
  it standeth.
91 They stand this day according to
  Thine ordinances;
  For all things are Thy servants.
92 Unless Thy law had been my delight,
  I should then have perished in mine
  affliction.
93 I will never forget Thy precepts;
  For with them Thou hast quickened
  me.
94 I am Thine, save me;
  For I have sought Thy precepts.
95 The wicked have waited for me to
  destroy me;
  But I will consider Thy testimonies.
96 I have seen an end to every purpose;
  But Thy commandment is exceeding
  broad.

מ MEM

97 Oh how love I Thy law!
   It is my meditation all the day.
98 Thy commandments make me wiser
   than mine enemies:
   For they are ever with me.
99 I have more understanding than all
   my teachers;
   For Thy testimonies are my meditation.
100 I understand more than mine elders,
   Because I have kept Thy precepts.
101 I have refrained my feet from every
   evil way,
   In order that I might observe Thy
   word.
102 I have not turned aside from Thine
   ordinances;
   For Thou hast instructed me.
103 How sweet are Thy words unto my
   palate!
   Yea, sweeter than honey to my
   mouth!
104 From Thy precepts I get understanding;
   Therefore I hate every false way.

נ NUN

105 Thy word is a lamp unto my feet,
   And a light unto my path.
106 I have sworn, and have confirmed it,
   To observe Thy righteous ordinances.
107 I am afflicted very much;
   Quicken me, O LORD, according
   unto Thy word.
108 Accept, I beseech Thee, the free-
   will-offerings of my mouth, O
   LORD,
   And teach me Thine ordinances.
109 My soul is continually in my hand;
   Yet have I not forgotten Thy law.
110 The wicked have laid a snare for me;
   Yet went I not astray from Thy
   precepts.
111 Thy testimonies have I taken as a
   heritage for ever;
   For they are the rejoicing of my
   heart.
112 I have inclined my heart to perform
   Thy statutes,
   For ever, at every step.

ס SAMECH

113 I hate them that are of a double
   mind;
   But Thy law do I love.
114 Thou art my covert and my shield;
   In Thy word do I hope.
115 Depart from me, ye evil-doers;
   That I may keep the commandments
   of my God.
116 Uphold me according unto Thy
   word, that I may live;
   And put me not to shame in my
   hope.
117 Support Thou me, and I shall be
   saved;
   And I will occupy myself with Thy
   statutes continually.
118 Thou hast made light of all them
   that err from Thy statutes;
   For their deceit is vain.
119 Thou puttest away all the wicked of
   the earth like dross;
   Therefore I love Thy testimonies.
120 My flesh shuddereth for fear of
   Thee;
   And I am afraid of Thy judgments.

ע AIN

121 I have done justice and righteousness;
   Leave me not to mine oppressors.
122 Be surety for Thy servant for
   good;
   Let not the proud oppress me.
123 Mine eyes fail for Thy salvation,
   And for Thy righteous word.
124 Deal with Thy servant according
   unto Thy mercy,
   And teach me Thy statutes.
125 I am Thy servant, give me understanding;
   That I may know Thy testimonies.
126 It is time for the LORD to work;
   They have made void Thy law.
127 Therefore I love Thy commandments
   Above gold, yea, above fine gold.
128 Therefore I esteem all [Thy] precepts concerning all things to be
   right;
   Every false way I hate.

פ PE

129 Thy testimonies are wonderful;
 Therefore doth my soul keep them.
130 The opening of Thy words giveth
 light;
 It giveth understanding unto the
 simple.
131 I opened wide my mouth, and panted;
 For I longed for Thy commandments.
132 Turn Thee towards me, and be
 gracious unto me,
 As is Thy wont to do unto those that
 love Thy name.
133 Order my footsteps by Thy word;
 And let not any iniquity have
 dominion over me.
134 Redeem me from the oppression of
 man,
 And I will observe Thy precepts.
135 Make Thy face to shine upon Thy
 servant;
 And teach me Thy statutes.
136 Mine eyes run down with rivers of
 water,
 Because they observe not Thy law.

צ TZADE

137 Righteous art Thou, O LORD,
 And upright are Thy judgments.
138 Thou hast commanded Thy
 testimonies in righteousness
 And exceeding faithfulness.
139 My zeal hath undone me,
 Because mine adversaries have
 forgotten Thy words.
140 Thy word is tried to the uttermost,
 And Thy servant loveth it.
141 I am small and despised;
 Yet have I not forgotten Thy
 precepts.
142 Thy righteousness is an everlasting
 righteousness,
 And Thy law is truth.
143 Trouble and anguish have overtaken
 me;
 Yet Thy commandments are my
 delight.
144 Thy testimonies are righteous for
 ever;
 Give me understanding, and I shall
 live.

ק KOPH

145 I have called with my whole heart;
 answer me, O LORD;
 I will keep Thy statutes.
146 I have called Thee, save me,
 And I will observe Thy testimonies.
147 I rose early at dawn, and cried;
 I hoped in Thy word.
148 Mine eyes forestalled the night-
 watches,
 That I might meditate in Thy word.
149 Hear my voice according unto Thy
 lovingkindness;
 Quicken me, O LORD, as Thou art
 wont.
150 They draw nigh that follow after
 wickedness;
 They are far from Thy law.
151 Thou art nigh, O LORD;
 And all Thy commandments are
 truth.
152 Of old have I known from Thy
 testimonies
 That Thou hast founded them for
 ever.

ר RESH

153 O see mine affliction, and rescue me;
 For I do not forget Thy law.
154 Plead Thou my cause, and redeem
 me;
 Quicken me according to Thy word.
155 Salvation is far from the wicked;
 For they seek not Thy statutes.
156 Great are Thy compassions, O
 LORD;
 Quicken me as Thou art wont.
157 Many are my persecutors and mine
 adversaries;
 Yet have I not turned aside from Thy
 testimonies.
158 I beheld them that were faithless,
 and strove with them;
 Because they observed not Thy
 word.
159 O see how I love Thy precepts;
 Quicken me, O LORD, according to
 Thy lovingkindness.
160 The beginning of Thy word is truth;
 And all Thy righteous ordinance
 endureth for ever.

161 Princes have persecuted me without
a cause;
But my heart standeth in awe of Thy
words.
162 I rejoice at Thy word,
As one that findeth great spoil.
163 I hate and abhor falsehood;
Thy law do I love.
164 Seven times a day do I praise Thee,
Because of Thy righteous ordinances.
165 Great peace have they that love Thy
law;
And there is no stumbling for
them.
166 I have hoped for Thy salvation, O
LORD,
And have done Thy commandments.
167 My soul hath observed Thy testimonies;
And I love them exceedingly.
168 I have observed Thy precepts and
Thy testimonies;
For all my ways are before Thee.

169 Let my cry come near before Thee,
O LORD;
Give me understanding according to
Thy word.
170 Let my supplication come before
Thee;
Deliver me according to Thy word.
171 Let my lips utter praise:
Because Thou teachest me Thy
statutes.
172 Let my tongue sing of Thy word;
For all Thy commandments are
righteousness.
173 Let Thy hand be ready to help me;
For I have chosen Thy precepts.
174 I have longed for Thy salvation, O
LORD;
And Thy law is my delight.
175 Let my soul live, and it shall praise
Thee;
And let Thine ordinances help me.
176 I have gone astray like a lost sheep;
seek Thy servant;
For I have not forgotten Thy
commandments.

The Glorification of Torah

Torah is the key word in this longest of all the psalms. It occurs 22 times
in its 176 verses, divided into 22 stanzas according to the 22 letters of
the Hebrew alphabet. Literally, the word *Torah* means teaching, referring to the entire body of revelations, the narratives and commandments found in the Bible. In postbiblical times, the term *Torah* came to
mean all of the sacred writings as amplified in the interpretations of
teachers and sages that were passed on from generation to generation.
The entire psalm resonates with the supreme joy the author feels as he
immerses himself in the study of Torah and tries to apply its teachings
to his own way of life.

Stanza 1 (119:1–8): Torah Makes for Happiness

The Torah, with all of its instructions, rules, and commandments, is
not a burden but a source of happiness to the psalmist: "Happy are the
upright in the way who walk according to God's Torah" (v. 1). His love

of Torah comes from the heart: "I will thank You with sincerity of heart when I learn Your righteous ordinances" (v. 7).

Stanza 2 (119:9–16): How to Live a Clean Life

How can a person stay morally pure? The psalmist proposes three steps by which to internalize God's Torah: First, memorize God's words: "I have stored up your word in my heart that I might not sin against You" (v. 11). Second, pronounce the commandments and ordinances aloud: "I repeat aloud all the ordinances You have commanded" (v. 13). Third, keep thinking about God's instructions: "I meditate on Your precepts" (v. 15). Such attention will implant the Torah in his mind: "I will delight myself in Your statutes; I will not forget Your word" (v. 16).

Stanza 3 (119:17–24): God Helps Us Understand His Word

The psalmist wants to be enlightened so that he might appreciate God's Torah: "Open mine eyes that I may see wondrous things out of Your Torah" (v. 18). The disapproval of influential leaders cannot deflect him from the study of Torah: "Even though princes huddle together and speak against me, I study Your statutes" (v. 23).

Stanza 4 (119:25–32): The Comfort of God's Teachings

The psalmist tells of the uplifting effect of Torah study in his personal life. Breaking down under the burden of many problems, he turns to God for guidance: "I am down in the dust. Revive me according to Your word. I have told You of my way and You have answered me. Teach me Your statutes" (v. 25–26). He wants to be morally cleansed through Torah: "Remove from me the way of falsehood and favor me with Your Torah" (v. 29).

Stanza 5 (119:33–40): Curb Your Greed

The psalmist prefers eagerness in the study of God's commandments to the accumulation of riches: "Incline my heart toward Your edicts and not toward material gain" (v. 36). He also wants God's help in the achievement of a sound scale of values: "Let me not pay attention to worthless things but keep me going in Your ways" (v. 37).

Stanza 6 (119:41–48): You May Have to Sacrifice Popularity

Following God's teachings does not guarantee popularity. The psalmist suffers ridicule and insults because of his faithfulness to Torah and asks for help "that I may have an answer for him who abuses me because I trust in Your word" (v. 42; see also v. 21–23 and 39).

Stanza 7 (119:49–56): Undeterred by Ridicule

The psalmist clings to Torah and its way of life despite the mockery of the irreligious, whom he calls "arrogant": "The arrogant made fun of me; yet I have not turned aside from Your Torah" (v. 51). He is infuriated by those who abandon the sacred teachings and observances: "I am enraged by the wicked who forsake Your Torah" (v. 53).

Stanza 8 (119:57–64): The Companionship of Fellow Believers

The psalmist was not always religious, but became so after rethinking his own way of life: "I considered my conduct and turned back to Your instructions" (v. 59). He now performs his religious duties without delay, undeterred by the obstructions of the irreligious: "I hurry and delay not the observance of Your commandments. I do not forget Your Torah despite the wicked who try to entrap me . . . I keep close to all who revere You and observe Your precepts" (v. 60–61, 63).

Stanza 9 (119:65–72): Turned around by Suffering

The psalmist confesses that he had swerved from his faith earlier in life, until affliction induced him to study and observe God's word: "Before I was afflicted, I did err, but now I observe Your word" (v. 67). He recognizes his former affliction as a blessing in disguise: "It is good that I was afflicted in order that I might learn Your commands" (v. 71).

Stanza 10 (119:73–80): Seeking Approval by the Faithful

The psalmist acknowledges God as the creator of his body who can also endow him with spiritual power: "Your hands have made me and fashioned me; give me understanding that I may learn Your commandments" (v. 73). Then he will win approval by those who revere God: "Your worshippers will be glad to see me because I placed my hope in Your word" (v. 74).

Stanza 11 (119:81–88): Observing God's Commandments Despite Affliction

The psalmist resolves to follow the precepts of Torah regardless of adversity. Beset by enemies, he holds on to God's instructions: "They almost wiped me off the earth; but, as for me, I did not forsake Your instructions" (v. 87).

Stanza 12 (119:89–96): Make Torah the Foundation of Your Life

Amidst the insecurities and uncertainties of life, the psalmist looks to God for stability: "Your faithfulness is unto all generations. You have established the earth and it stands" (v. 90). God's Torah has upheld him in the storms of life: "Had not Your Torah been my delight, I would have died in my affliction" (v. 92).

Stanza 13 (119:97–104): Torah, Source of Wisdom and Moral Power

The teachings of Torah have made the psalmist wiser and kept him from transgression: "I have gained more understanding than all my teachers, for I meditate on Your instructions. I have refrained from every evil way in order that I might observe Your commands" (v. 100–101).

Stanza 14 (119:105–112): Torah, a Light on the Pathway of Life

The psalmist's life is troubled by strife. Enemies want to do him harm. In the darkness of adversity, God is his light: "Your word is a lamp unto my feet and a light unto my path" (v. 105). Even when threatened by danger, he remembers God's Torah: "My life is always in danger, yet I have not forgotten Your Torah" (v. 109).

Stanza 15 (119:113–120): God Supports the Faithful

In his struggle for survival, the psalmist feels sheltered by God: "You are my security and defense. I hope for Your word" (v. 114). He will continually occupy himself with God's commands, if only he can be rescued from his attackers: "Support me and save me, and I shall always pay attention to Your commands" (v. 117).

Stanza 16 (119:121–128): A Cry for Help

The psalmist cannot stand up alone against his oppressors. He needs God's help: "Guarantee my well-being and let not the arrogant oppress me" (v. 122). In return for God's protection, he will fight those who violate His commands: "It is time to act on behalf of God, for they have violated Your teachings" (v. 126).

Stanza 17 (119:129–136): Going God's Way

The Psalmist will gladly submit to God's guidance in the conduct of his life, if only he has protection against oppressors: "Order my steps by Your word and let not any iniquity have mastery over me. Deliver me from the oppression of man and I will observe Your precepts" (v. 133–134).

Stanza 18 (119:137–144): Empowered by God's Commands

Sharing with God the nobility of Torah compensates the psalmist for his own powerlessness: "I am just a little and despised person; yet, I have not forgotten Your commands. Your righteousness is everlasting and Your Torah is true" (v. 141–142).

Stanza 19 (119:145–152): Meditation, Day and Night

The psalmist will not neglect his meditation on God's word even when desperately in need of protection against enemies: "Before dawn I cry for help and hope for Your word. I greet the night watches and meditate on Your word" (v. 147–148). Devotion to Torah brings him near God: "You are near, O God, and Your commands are true" (v. 151).

Stanza 20 (119:153–160): Steadfast in Tribulation

Tormented by numerous problems and pressures, the psalmist does not forget Torah: "Many are my persecutors and adversaries, yet I have not turned aside from Your instructions" (v. 157).

Stanza 21 (119:161–168): Fearless in the Love of God's Word

The psalmist is steadfast in his love of God's teachings despite persecution: "Princes have persecuted me without cause, but my heart is in awe of Your words" (v. 161). He feels secure and confident in the study of Torah: "Great peace have they that love Your Torah; they do not stumble" (v. 165).

Stanza 22 (119:169–176): Unswerving Loyalty to God's Torah

The psalmist cries out for help. Whether or not God will answer remains to be seen. But even if he must suffer, he will praise God and His commandments: "Let my lips utter praise because You teach me commands" (v. 171). He associates salvation with God's Torah: "I yearn for Your salvation, O God. Your Torah is my delight" (v. 174). In conclusion, he asks God to seek him out and bring him back to the right path, from which he had strayed: "I have gone astray like a lost sheep; seek Your servant, for I have not forgotten Your commandments" (v. 176).

Reflection: Rejoicing in God's Teachings and Commandments

This extraordinary tribute of devotion to Torah by an unknown poet proves that the study of the scriptures was already entrenched in biblical times. The author did not expect to gain popularity or immunity against adversity through his study and meditation on the sacred Hebrew text. He valued it as the fountainhead of spirituality and moral guidance. Studying it was like thinking the thoughts of God, an act of love through which one might come as close to the Eternal as a human being could ever get. You may wonder what made the psalmist so enthusiastic about studying and fulfilling the commandments of God. There are several possible explanations: The psalmist regards the revelation of commandments as a sign of his people's special relationship with God, the covenant. The belief that God commanded the faithful to do or not to do certain things adds importance to every act in life and proves to the psalmist that God cares for His people. Last but not least, living in response to God's commandments is life with a high purpose. It is life dignified by a portion of God's holiness. Seen in this light, living under the law is not a burden but a privilege.

⁓ PSALM 120 ⁓

A Song of Ascents.

In my distress I called unto the LORD,
And He answered me.
2 O LORD, deliver my soul from lying lips,
From a deceitful tongue.
3 What shall be given unto thee, and
what shall be done more unto thee,
Thou deceitful tongue?
4 Sharp arrows of the mighty,

With coals of broom.

5 Woe is me, that I sojourn with Meshech,
That I dwell beside the tents of Kedar!
6 My soul hath full long had her dwelling
With him that hateth peace.
7 I am all peace;
But when I speak, they are for war.

⁓

The Misfortune of Having Bad Neighbors

If good neighbors are a blessing, bad neighbors are a curse. The psalmist complains about lying and deceitful neighbors: "O God, deliver me from lying lips and a deceitful tongue" (v. 2). He cannot live in peace with them: "Too long have I dwelt near those who hate peace" (v. 6). His efforts to develop a peaceful relationship with them failed. Still, he keeps talking to them: "I am all for peace but when I speak, they are for war" (v. 7).

⁓

Reflection: On Being a Nonconformist

The distress of which the psalmist speaks results from his sharp disapproval of the people surrounding him. He despises them because of their "lying lips" and "deceitful tongue" (v. 2). They are quarrelsome; they "hate peace" (v. 6). The psalmist does not tell us anything about the specific issues of the conflict, but whatever the conflict is about, the psalmist does not fit in his environment. He is a nonconformist. The person who is out of step with the majority of his group or community risks their contempt and hatred. It takes special courage to voice dissent on moral grounds. As he rejects the standards of his neighbors, so do they reject him. The conscientious nonconformist must face the abuse of being called wet blanket, square, coward, traitor, and other uncomplimentary appellations. Thoreau applauded the one who, in obedience to his own conscience, dares to be out of step with the crwod "because he hears a different drummer."

❧ PSALM 121 ❧

A Song of Ascents.

I will lift up mine eyes unto the mountains:
From whence shall my help come?
2 My help cometh from the LORD,
  Who made heaven and earth.

3 He will not suffer thy foot to be
  moved;
He that keepeth thee will not slumber.
4 Behold, He that keepeth Israel
  Doth neither slumber nor sleep.

5 The LORD is thy keeper;
  The LORD is thy shade upon thy right
  hand.
6 The sun shall not smite thee by day,
  Nor the moon by night.
7 The LORD shall keep thee from all
  evil;
  He shall keep thy soul.
8 The LORD shall guard thy going out
  and thy coming in,
From this time forth and for ever.

❧

Look Up to the Mountains

Your body language expresses your mood. By bowing your head and looking down, you indicate discouragement. Looking up suggests hopefulness. The author of Psalm 121 is in need of help. Whatever the problem, one should try to gain a larger perspective on the situation. Stretch your horizons. Don't confine your entire attention to the narrow scope of the problem at hand. That can turn into obsession. Extend your vision as does the psalmist: "I will look up to the mountains; from whence shall my help come?" (v. 1). As he looks up into the immensity of space, he feels reassured: "My help comes from God Who made heaven and earth" (v. 2). Fellow worshippers assure the psalmist that the

God who keeps us alive is not taking naps. He knows and watches all you are doing: "He that watches you will not slumber. . . . God will watch over your going and coming, now and always" (v. 3, 8).

❧

Reflection: God, Our Helper

This is one of the most popular and beloved psalms. It says what you like to hear. It is so very reassuring: God is not only watching you, He is looking out for you: "He will not suffer your foot to be moved; He that keeps you will not slumber. . . . God shall keep you from all evil" (v. 3, 7). How shall we understand this? Remember that these are not the words of God but the hopes of the psalmist. He would like total insurance coverage from God against all mishaps. This may be the psalmist's fond expectation, but God promises no such thing. God will not, like a rescue squad, rush to save us in all circumstances. If a person jumps out of a window, he should not count on God to spread a safety net for him. A person exposing himself to danger must pay the price for folly or carelessness.

In what sense, then, is God your helper and "your keeper"? (v. 5). God in His creation of life endowed the human species with wondrous physical and mental capacities. As is said by another psalmist, "I am wonderfully made" (Psalm 139:14). We have been equipped with the marvelous gift of reason by which we can foresee danger, apply the arts of healing, and guard against the destructive forces of nature. If human beings only used their God-given minds properly, we would have little to fear. God keeps us from evil through the gift of intelligence. Scientists tell us that the vast majority of mankind develop only a small fraction of their potential abilities. Superior physical training and better education would make for a longer, healthier, more productive life and turn our earth into paradise.

❧ PSALM 122 ❧

A Song of Ascents; of David.

I rejoiced when they said unto me:
"Let us go unto the house of the
 LORD."
2 Our feet are standing

Within thy gates, O Jerusalem;
3 Jerusalem, that art builded
 As a city that is compact together;
4 Whither the tribes went up, even the
 tribes of the LORD,
 As a testimony unto Israel,

To give thanks unto the name of the
  Lord.
5 For there were set thrones for
  judgment,
  The thrones of the house of David.

6 Pray for the peace of Jerusalem;
  May they prosper that love thee.

7 Peace be within thy walls,
  And prosperity within thy palaces.
8 For my brethren and companions'
  sakes,
  I will now say: "Peace be within thee."
9 For the sake of the house of the Lord
  our God
  I will seek thy good.

Pray for the Peace of Jerusalem

Few joys can match that of reaching your goal. Psalm 122 reflects the jubilant mood of pilgrims from afar upon their arrival in Jerusalem, the goal of their long and dangerous journey. Now they are about to walk through the Holy City up to the Temple Mount to worship God in the sanctuary: "I rejoiced when they said to me, 'Let us go to the house of God.' Our feet are standing within your gates, O Jerusalem" (v. 1–2). Then the psalmist calls on his comrades to offer a prayer that has been on the lips of countless Jews and Christians ever since: "Pray for the peace of Jerusalem; may they prosper who love you" (v. 6).

Reflection: Jerusalem

The psalmist's words, "our feet are standing within your gates, O Jerusalem," have been recited during the past several thousand years by many millions of Jewish and Christian pilgrims to the Holy City. Every pilgrim sees Jerusalem through the image of his dreams. He sees Jerusalem not merely as a city of streets and houses encircled by ancient walls and towers on the hills of Judah, but as a meeting place with God, a symbol of holiness. Some interpret the word "Jerusalem" to mean "city of peace." The nineteenth-century English poet Gerald Massey thought of Jerusalem as a place of soul purification:

> Jerusalem the Golden!
>   I toil on day by day;
> Heart-sore each night with longing
>   I stretch my hands and pray,
> That mid thy leaves of healing
>   My soul may find her nest;
> Where the wicked cease from troubling,
>   And the weary are at rest!

William Blake even dreamed of transplanting the mystique of Jerusalem to his native England:

> I will not cease from mental fight,
>   Nor shall my sword sleep in my hand,
> Till we have built Jerusalem
>   In England's green and pleasant land.

Jews and Christians the world over look to Jerusalem as the cradle of their faiths. It will remain, for all time to come, a spiritual center for Judaism and Christianity, a reminder of their common origin and of the hope that someday all people of faith will be united in the vision of the one God.

❧ PSALM 123 ❧

A Song of Ascents.

Unto Thee I lift up mine eyes,
O Thou that art enthroned in the
  heavens.
2 Behold, as the eyes of servants unto
  the hand of their master,
As the eyes of a maiden unto the hand
  of her mistress;
So our eyes look unto the LORD our
  God,

Until He be gracious unto us.

3 Be gracious unto us, O LORD, be
  gracious unto us;
For we are full sated with contempt.
4 Our soul is full sated
With the scorning of those that are at
  ease,
And with the contempt of the proud
  oppressors.

❧

Prayer of a Victim of Contempt

Psalm 123 opens like Psalm 121, on a note of expectation. The psalmist looks up, searching for help. But the mood is very different. Instead of the serene confidence that marks Psalm 121, this psalm is full of anxiety. The psalmist, a pathetic victim of contempt and oppression, turns to God with the plea: "Show us Your favor, O God, for we have suffered our fill of contempt" (v. 3).

❧

Reflection: Coping with Insoluble Problems

This psalmist is one of those rare persons who can bear humiliation and insult without responding in kind. He has suffered his fill of contempt: "We are fully sated with contempt" (v. 3). He does not speak a word of hatred against his "proud oppressors" (v. 4), nor does he pray for vengeance. Instead, he humbly puts himself in God's hand "with the eyes of a servant looking at his master" (v. 2). If you find his meekness unappealing, ask yourself, what good would a blast of fury or an outcry of self-pity have done? We all must pass through, at times, certain problems and frustrations for which there are no solutions at the present moment except one, namely to endure it. We are better able to endure hard times if we remember that all things pass, including trying times. Change can happen suddenly. Life is like a kaleidoscope—the slightest turn can completely change the picture. By surrendering himself to God's will, the psalmist testifies to his trust that a good God will help the good prevail, if only we can wait.

❧ PSALM 124 ❧

A Song of Ascents; of David.

"If it had not been the LORD who was
  for us",
Let Israel now say;
2 "If it had not been the LORD who was
  for us,
When men rose up against us,
3 Then they had swallowed us up alive,
When their wrath was kindled against
  us;
4 Then the waters had overwhelmed us,
The stream had gone over our soul;

5 Then the proud waters
Had gone over our soul."

6 Blessed be the LORD,
Who hath not given us as a prey to
  their teeth.
7 Our soul is escaped as a bird out of the
  snare of the fowlers;
The snare is broken, and we are
  escaped.
8 Our help is in the name of the LORD,
Who made heaven and earth.

❧

Salvation at the Brink of Disaster

Despair collides with faith in Psalm 124. We do not know just what sort of crisis it was, but for the author of this psalm, it was a close call: "When men rose up against us, they would have swallowed us alive as their wrath flamed up against us" (v. 2–3). The psalmist and his people felt abandoned and in imminent danger of extinction. At the crucial moment, the peril suddenly vanished and they survived. A dramatic change of mood is reflected in this psalm, comparable to what Jews throughout the world experienced during the Six-Day War of 1967 when the state of Israel, facing catastrophe, turned the crisis into a spectacular victory. Then many Israelis thanked God in the words of the psalmist: "Blessed be God who has not handed us over as prey to their teeth. . . . Our help is in the name of God, Who made heaven and earth" (v. 6, 8).

❧

Reflection: Don't Be Stingy in Thanksgiving

We are much too stingy in thanksgiving. Usually we acknowledge with thanks a gift, a helping hand, and a favor. But far more numerous than these specific occasions when we feel indebted to someone are the unacknowledged benefits that we enjoy without a word of gratitude on our part. When Charles Lamb became aware of how many good things in his life he was taking for granted, he said: "I am disposed to say grace upon twenty other occasions in the course of the day besides my dinner. I want a form for setting out upon a pleasant walk, for a moonlight ramble, for a friendly meeting, or a solved problem. Why have we none for books, those spiritual repasts—a grace before Milton?"

This psalmist reminds us of another dimension of thanksgiving—not for the good we receive, but for the bad we escape. He expresses gratitude to God for having been spared destruction "when men rose up against us who would have swallowed us alive" (v. 2–3). Hardly a day passes on which we might have been injured or killed but for some lucky break, or when we would have been ruined by some mistake had we not caught it by chance. Add to these known escapes from harm the countless unknown dangers from which we emerge unscathed day and night. We might well include in our daily prayers the psalmist's grateful acknowledgment: "Our help is in the name of God Who made heaven and earth" (v. 8).

❧ # PSALM 125 ❧

A Song of Ascents.

They that trust in the LORD
Are as mount Zion, which cannot be
     moved, but abideth for ever.
2 As the mountains are round about
     Jerusalem,
So the LORD is round about His people,
From this time forth and for ever.

3 For the rod of wickedness shall not
     rest upon the lot of the righteous;
That the righteous put not forth their
     hands unto iniquity.

4 Do good, O LORD, unto the good,
And to them that are upright in their
     hearts.
5 But as for such as turn aside unto their
     crooked ways,
The LORD will lead them away with
     the workers of iniquity.
Peace be upon Israel.

❦

Peace Be upon Israel

Psalm 125 was composed by pilgrims to Jerusalem whose successful conclusion of a long and hazardous journey justified their confidence in God, whose protection they must have implored all along the way. Conscious of His presence among them, they feel like mountains that cannot be moved: "They who trust in God are as Mount Zion, which cannot be moved but abides forever" (v. 1). Anyone who has ever seen Jerusalem from a distance, situated high up at the top of surrounding mountains, will appreciate the psalmist's inspired analogy: "As the mountains are round about Jerusalem, so God is round about His people" (v. 2). Trusting that God's justice will reward the good and punish the evildoer, the psalmist closes with a heartfelt prayer: "Do good, O God, unto the good and to them who are upright in the way. . . . Peace be upon Israel" (v. 4, 5).

❦

Reflection: Trust

The mountain is a symbol of reliability. Immovable and unchanging, the mountain stands steady and stable. So are people you would trust. Particularly trustworthy, in the psalmist's opinion, are "they that trust in God. They are as Mount Zion, which cannot be moved but abides forever" (v. 1). You cannot rely on people who are forever changing their minds, moods, and beliefs. The psalmist trusts God because he believes God to be the guardian of order in the universe. In God's creation, nature behaves in a steady pattern. Also, in human affairs, we observe steady patterns of behavior: Love begets love, hate begets hate, abuse provokes violence, and justice makes for peace. People who trust God respect the laws He established for order and stability. They act in ways that are steady and predictable, which makes them worthy of trust.

❦ PSALM 126 ❦

A Song of Ascents.

When the LORD brought back those
   that returned to Zion,
We were like unto them that dream.
2 Then was our mouth filled with
   laughter,

And our tongue with singing;
Then said they among the nations:
"The LORD hath done great things
   with these."
3 The LORD hath done great things with
   us;
We are rejoiced.

4 Turn our captivity, O LORD,
  As the streams in the dry land.
5 They that sow in tears
  Shall reap in joy.

6 Though he goeth on his way weeping
  that beareth the measure of seed,
  He shall come home with joy, bearing
  his sheaves.

❧

A Happy Homecoming

One of the world's mysteries is the millennial existence of the Jewish people, the sole surviving nation of the ancient Middle East and Europe. Superpowers have come and gone, but Israel remains, a vibrant people spread throughout the world. If at times the Jewish people sank into decline, soon enough they would rise again for an even larger role in civilization. Psalm 126 records one of those revivals, the return of Jews from captivity in Babylon to rebuild their homeland, Jerusalem, and the temple, which had been destroyed by the Babylonians in the sixth century B.C.E. Those who returned could hardly believe it was happening: "We were like dreamers" (v. 1). People from other nations were amazed at the revival of a nation believed to have been exterminated: "God has done great things with them" (v. 2).

The psalmist draws a lesson from this experience: "They that sow with tears shall reap in joy" (v. 5). It applies to all of us. Never say, "It's all over." What was can be again. What has been destroyed can be rebuilt. Where there is a will, the way may sooner or later open up for a comeback.

❧

Reflection: No Gain without Pain

The psalmist's words, "They that sow in tears shall reap in joy," have become a proverb in many languages. It states the compelling truth that effort and sacrifice are rewarded. Life is not a lottery. Things don't happen at random. The law of cause and effect applies. What you put in determines what you get out. To be sure, not all efforts are rewarded in the same way, but there is no reward without some kind of exertion. Even those blessed with great talents must work and struggle to achieve, as was well said in Arthur Guiterman's aphorism, "Talent made a poor appearance until he married Perseverance." The financier and counselor of presidents Bernard Baruch, looking back on his long life, acknowledged that success was earned by hardship and struggle: "I was the son of an immigrant. I experienced bigotry, intolerance and prejudice, even as so many of you have. Instead of allowing these things to embitter me, I took them as spurs to more strenuous effort." We can draw illustrations of the same truth from all areas of life, in education, in the arts, even in marriage and parenthood. Learning and growing up is a rocky and bumpy road, with many a tear shed on the way, but the bumps are what you climb on. You can't get around the rule as worded by the psalmist: "They that sow in tears shall reap in joy."

❧ PSALM 127 ❧

A Song of Ascents; of Solomon.

Except the LORD build the house,
They labour in vain that build it;
Except the LORD keep the city,
The watchman waketh but in vain.
2 It is vain for you that ye rise early, and
  sit up late,
Ye that eat the bread of toil;
So He giveth unto His beloved in
  sleep.

3 Lo, children are a heritage of the
  LORD;
  The fruit of the womb is a reward.
4 As arrows in the hand of a mighty
  man,
  So are the children of one's youth.
5 Happy is the man that hath his quiver
  full of them;
  They shall not be put to shame,
  When they speak with their enemies
  in the gate.

Get Off the Treadmill

If you are on the treadmill of an overactive life, trying to keep up with your ambitions, finances, family responsibilities, and social obligations, read and reflect on Psalm 127: "It is vain for you to rise early and stay up late, you who eat the bread of toil" (v. 2). Some of the most precious things in life are not obtained in pursuit, but fall into your lap if only you can sit still for a while. Does your life need a new direction, goal, or purpose? Allow God to show you better ways toward contentment and happiness: "So He gives to His beloved ones in sleep" (v. 2).

Reflection: Take Time for Reflection

Isaac Newton was resting in an orchard when he saw an apple fall from a tree, which sparked his discovery of the law of gravitation. An hour of reflection may open your eyes to things you are otherwise too busy to notice. Also, reflecting on what you said or did today may do wonders for keeping your personal relationships in good repair, at home or at work. Racing breathlessly through the day's routine puts blinders on you. You are so bent on your agenda that you can't see open doors of opportunity, and miss encounters with worthy personalities. Do nothing for a while, and you will be surprised by the good ideas that will pop into your head. God's gifts may come to you unawares: "He gives to His beloved ones in sleep" (v. 2).

❧ PSALM 128 ❧

A Song of Ascents.

Happy is every one that feareth the
   LORD,
That walketh in His ways.
2 When thou eatest the labour of thy
   hands,
Happy shalt thou be, and it shall be
   well with thee.
3 Thy wife shall be as a fruitful vine, in
   the innermost parts of thy house;

Thy children like olive plants, round
   about thy table.
4 Behold, surely thus shall the man be
   blessed
That feareth the LORD.

5 The LORD bless thee out of Zion;
And see thou the good of Jerusalem all
   the days of thy life;
6 And see thy children's children.
Peace be upon Israel!

❧

Prescription for Happiness

The pursuit of happiness is the "unalienable" right of every American under the Declaration of Independence. But what kind of happiness is it, and how do you go after it? The author of Psalm 128 has an answer: Whatever you do, remember that happiness is linked to reverence of God and to living by His commands: "Happy is everyone who reveres God and walks in His ways" (v. 1).

Then devote yourself to two priorities. First, be self-supporting: "When you eat the fruit of your labor, you will be happy and it will be well with you" (v. 2). Second, seek contentment with a loving spouse and the company of children. The psalmist draws an enchanting picture of the home as a refreshing garden: "Your wife shall be like a fruitful vine within your house; your children, like olive plants round about your table" (v. 3).

❧

Reflection: What Makes a Good Marriage?

A person with a happy marriage should be called successful even if he or she fails in everything else. Leo Tolstoy said, "All happy families are alike." How are they alike? There are at least two ingredients shared by happy families: First is the caring love of well-mated spouses. Ivan Turgenev, Tolstoy's compatriot and the author of many novels, deplored the lack of it: "I would give up all my genius, and all my books, if there were only some woman, somewhere, who cared whether or not I came home late for dinner." The other essential quality without which marital love cannot last is well identified in the rhyme by the eighteenth-century English poet William Cowper:

> The kindest and the happiest pair
> Will find occasion to forbear
> And something, every day they live,
> To pity, and perhaps forgive.

No one is perfect. We all get hurt and hurt the other, but lovers find it in their hearts to forgive each other's faults and offenses. The example of such love is the greatest legacy parents can leave to their children. Father Theodore Hesburgh, former president of Notre Dame, said it well: "The most important thing a father can do for his children is to love their mother."

❧ PSALM 129 ❧

A Song of Ascents.

"Much have they afflicted me from my youth up",
Let Israel now say;
2 "Much have they afflicted me from my youth up;
But they have not prevailed against me.
3 The plowers plowed upon my back;
They made long their furrows.
4 The LORD is righteous;
He hath cut asunder the cords of the wicked."

5 Let them be ashamed and turned backward,
All they that hate Zion.
6 Let them be as the grass upon the housetops,
Which withereth afore it springeth up;
7 Wherewith the reaper filleth not his hand,
Nor he that bindeth sheaves his bosom;
8 Neither do they that go by say:
"The blessing of the LORD be upon you;
We bless you in the name of the LORD."

❧

Strength through Hardship

When you are going through a difficult time, you might boost your confidence by remembering former crises you have overcome. You say to yourself, "I've done it before, I can do it again." This may explain the lament of the psalmist at a time of oppression. He reminds his people of earlier times when things were far worse: "Let Israel say, 'Much have they afflicted me from my youth up; but they have not prevailed against me'" (v. 1–2). He offers another thought for the consolation of his people. Israel's new enemies will vanish like those of the past, "as the grass on the housetops which withers before it can be pulled" (v. 6).

∾

Reflection: Stronger through Struggle

The psalmist never heard of Friedrich Nietzsche's remark "We take unto ourselves the strength of that which we overcome," but he expresses the idea in his own words: "Much have they afflicted me from my youth up; but they have not prevailed against me" (v. 2). What do we learn in the school of hard knocks? The challenge of troubles is a trial in the dual sense of the word, as affliction and test. Every affliction is a test not only of how much you can endure but of your strength to overcome. You don't know the full scope of your abilities until you meet with hardship. Adversity introduces a person to himself. More than that, in the process of coping with hardship, you stretch the limits of what you can do; you become more ingenious as you try to solve the problem. The struggle makes you more confident about your own abilities.

> For every hill I've had to climb
> For every stone that bruised my feet
> For all the blood and sweat and grime,
> For blinding storms and burning heat
> My heart sings but a grateful song
> These were the things that made me strong
>
> (AUTHOR UNKNOWN)

Acute suffering tends to make a person self-absorbed. At a later point, however, the experience of suffering may make us more sensitive and sympathetic to the pains and sorrows of others. You feel more for the starving poor if you yourself have suffered hunger. A line from the *Union Prayer Book* says: "We learn to counsel and comfort those who, like ourselves, are sorrow-stricken." The experience of hardship is a unifying force in the fellowship of suffering. Justice Oliver Wendell Holmes went as far as to say "Trouble makes us one with every human being in the world."

Psalm 130

A Song of Ascents.

Out of the depths have I called Thee,
  O LORD.
2 LORD, hearken unto my voice;
  Let Thine ears be attentive
  To the voice of my supplications.

3 If Thou, LORD, shouldest mark
  iniquities,
  O LORD, who could stand?
4 For with Thee there is forgiveness,
  That Thou mayest be feared.

5 I wait for the LORD, my soul doth
  wait,
  And in His word do I hope.
6 My soul waiteth for the LORD,
  More than watchmen for the morning;
  Yea, more than watchmen for the
  morning.

7 O Israel, hope in the LORD;
  For with the LORD there is mercy,
  And with Him is plenteous redemp-
  tion.
8 And He will redeem Israel
  From all his iniquities.

A Cry Out of the Depths

This psalm is an example of crisis religion, that is, the outreach to God impelled by some desperate need or fear. The psalmist is in agony over some problem: "Out of the depths I call You, O God" (v. 1). From the context, it appears that he is tormented by guilt feelings. He suffers under a heavy burden of sin. It has reared a barrier between him and God that can only be removed by repentance. He expresses his remorse, counting on God's mercy: "I wait for God, my soul does wait, and in His word to I hope" (v. 5).

Reflection: The Search for God

Many have embarked upon the search for God, driven by all sorts of affliction, illness, bereavement, defeat, and guilt. Calamity exposes our weakness, our vulnerability, our dependence and insufficiency. The sudden reversal from strength to weakness shows us how precarious our existence is. We recognize that so much of life is beyond our control. In our deepest need, we seek the nearness of God for shelter. As the saying goes: "Man's extremity is God's opportunity." How can we insure God's response to our need? There is no way of compelling God's attention. All we can do is wait, with faith that as we wait for God, God waits for us. This thought was expressed by the twelfth-century Spanish Jewish poet Judah Halevy:

Longing I sought Thy presence;
    Lord, with my whole heart did I call and pray
        And going out toward Thee
    I found Thee coming to me on the way.

PSALM 131

A Song of Ascents; of David.

LORD, my heart is not haughty, nor mine eyes lofty;
Neither do I exercise myself in things too great, or in things too wonderful for me.
2 Surely I have stilled and quieted my soul;
Like a weaned child with his mother,
My soul is with me like a weaned child.

3 O Israel, hope in the LORD
From this time forth and for ever.

The Reward of Humility

It takes wisdom and maturity to recognize one's limitations. Pride is a cruel taskmaster. It is the engine that drives our ambition, the quest for power and prominence, and it gets us into many troubles. The psalmist liberated himself from the tyranny of pride and in his humility found contentment: "O God, my heart is not proud. . . . I do not strive for great things or for what is unattainable" (v. 1). He is at peace and satisfied: "I have stilled and quieted my mind, like a weaned child in his mother's lap" (v. 2). It is the picture of contentment.

Reflection: Humility

A daily reading of this short psalm of only three verses would make excellent training for humility. The psalmist sets aside pride and ambition. He will not shoot for the stars; he will not try to win every race or seek positions of power. Why is he scaling down his expectations? He has come to recognize his limitations. In this sober reassessment of himself, he finds peace of mind: "I have stilled and quieted my mind" (v. 2). Relieved of the pressure of ambition, he enjoys contentment "like a weaned child in his mother's lap" (v. 2). One of the rewards of humility is exemption from fears of failure, as suggested in the Yiddish proverb: "If you lie low, a fall won't hurt you."

PSALM 132

A Song of Ascents.

Lord, remember unto David
All his affliction;
2 How he swore unto the Lord,
And vowed unto the Mighty One of
Jacob:
3 "Surely I will not come into the tent
of my house,
Nor go up into the bed that is spread
for me;
4 I will not give sleep to mine eyes,
Nor slumber to mine eyelids;
5 Until I find out a place for the Lord,
A dwelling-place for the Mighty One
of Jacob."

6 Lo, we heard of it as being in
Ephrath;
We found it in the field of the wood.
7 Let us go into His dwelling-place;
Let us worship at His footstool.
8 Arise, O Lord, unto Thy resting-
place;
Thou, and the ark of Thy strength.
9 Let Thy priests be clothed with righteousness;
And let Thy saints shout for joy.
10 For Thy servant David's sake

Turn not away the face of Thine
anointed.

11 The Lord swore unto David in truth;
He will not turn back from it:
"Of the fruit of thy body will I set
upon thy throne.
12 If thy children keep My covenant
And My testimony that I shall teach
them,
Their children also for ever shall sit
upon thy throne."
13 For the Lord hath chosen Zion;
He hath desired it for His habitation:
14 "This is My resting-place for ever;
Here will I dwell; for I have desired it.
15 I will abundantly bless her provision;
I will give her needy bread in plenty.
16 Her priests also will I clothe with
salvation;
And her saints shall shout aloud for
joy.
17 There will I make a horn to shoot up
unto David,
There have I ordered a lamp for Mine
anointed.
18 His enemies will I clothe with shame;
But upon himself shall his crown
shine."

The Ark, the Sanctuary, and God's Presence

Ever since the idea of God entered the human mind, people have sought to make sure of His presence. They built sacred places to meet with God: altars, sanctuaries, temples, churches, and mosques. The people of Israel refrained from any material representation of God in the form of sculptures or images as was the universal practice among their contemporaries. But they created an ark, not as an object of worship but as a token of God's presence, a place for encountering God. The psalmist glorifies Jerusalem as the Holy City because it houses the sanctuary with the ark as symbol of God's presence: "For God has chosen Zion; He desired it as His seat: 'This is My resting place for ever; here will I dwell'" (v. 13–14).

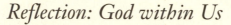

Reflection: God within Us

In postbiblical times, the rabbis began to question the notion that God wants any specific location as His dwelling place. They detected hidden meaning in the original command: "Let them make me a sanctuary that I might dwell among them" (Exodus 25:8). They stressed the scriptural wording, "among *them*," which suggests that God is not in a structure of wood and brick but in the souls, hearts, and minds of His people. Human beings need a place to meet for worship, but God is not confined to any one place.

∾ PSALM 133 ∾

A Song of Ascents; of David.

Behold, how good and how pleasant it is
For brethren to dwell together in unity!
2 It is like the precious oil upon the head,
Coming down upon the beard;
Even Aaron's beard,
That cometh down upon the collar of his garments;
3 Like the dew of Hermon,
That cometh down upon the mountains of Zion;
For there the LORD commanded the blessing,
Even life for ever.

The Need for Community

The harmonious togetherness of kindred people is highly rewarding, according to the psalmist: "Behold, how good and how pleasant it is for brethren to dwell together in unity" (v. 1). The psalm that begins with a call for unity ends with God's blessing of "life forever" (v. 3), as though to suggest that the preservation of life depends on the degree of unity we are able to develop between persons and between nations.

Reflection: Life Is Relationships

"Life is relationships." This is the core of Martin Buber's philosophy. We define ourselves by relationships. Terms such as *parent, son, daughter, spouse, neighbor, worker, citizen,* and so forth all refer to relationships and functions within the community. Life's foremost challenge—and a good definition of "ethics"—is to make all of our relationships mutually beneficial. People want to be included, and feel hurt and resentful when excluded. The poet Edwin Markham pleads for inclusiveness:

> He drew a circle that shut me out—
> Heretic, rebel, a thing to flout.
> But love and I had the wit to win:
> We drew a circle that took him in!

Close personal relations that make for unity are threatened today by our extremely mobile lifestyle, which tends to break up and scatter family and friends hundreds, even thousands of miles apart. The result is a vast number of lonely people, deprived of intimate companionship. Those who are lured by better career opportunities far away from their home communities should consider the price to be paid through the loss of sustaining relationships.

❧ PSALM 134 ❧

A Song of Ascents.

Behold, bless ye the LORD, all ye
   servants of the LORD,
That stand in the house of the LORD
   in the night seasons.

² Lift up your hands to the sanctuary,
   And bless ye the LORD.

³ The LORD bless thee out of Zion;
   Even He that made heaven and earth.

The Neglect of Greeting

According to some interpreters, the three verses of Psalm 134 represent an exchange of greetings between watchmen at the temple in Jerusalem during their nightly change of guards. Those arriving to take their turn of duty would greet their comrades who were awaiting them: "Bless God, you servants of God who stand in God's house at night" (v. 1). The group about to be relieved would answer: "May God bless you out of Zion, He Who made heaven and earth" (v. 3).

Reflection: Communication

The courtesy of greeting is going out of fashion. Neighbors living in the same building pass one another in the hallway or ride together in the elevator without a word of greeting. This is indicative of the decline of interpersonal relations. True, the exchange of greetings most often may be just a matter of routine, but that does not make it worthless. It shows that we pay attention to the other person and care enough to open a channel of communication. That is enough to turn a chance encounter into a more meaningful relationship if we are so inclined.

❧ PSALM 135 ❧

Hallelujah.
Praise ye the name of the LORD;
Give praise, O ye servants of the
LORD,
2 Ye that stand in the house of the
LORD,
In the courts of the house of our God.
3 Praise ye the LORD, for the LORD is
good;
Sing praises unto His name, for it is
pleasant.
4 For the LORD hath chosen Jacob unto
Himself,
And Israel for His own treasure.

5 For I know that the LORD is great,
And that our LORD is above all gods.
6 Whatsoever the LORD pleased, that
hath He done,
In heaven and in earth, in the seas and
in all deeps;
7 Who causeth the vapours to ascend
from the ends of the earth;
He maketh lightnings for the rain;
He bringeth forth the wind out of His
treasuries.

8 Who smote the first-born of Egypt,
Both of man and beast.
9 He sent signs and wonders into the
midst of thee, O Egypt,
Upon Pharaoh, and upon all his
servants.
10 Who smote many nations,

And slew mighty kings:
11 Sihon king of the Amorites,
And Og king of Bashan,
And all the kingdoms of Canaan;
12 And gave their land for a heritage,
A heritage unto Israel His people.

13 O LORD, Thy name endureth for
ever;
Thy memorial, O LORD, throughout
all generations.
14 For the LORD will judge His people,
And repent Himself for His servants.
15 The idols of the nations are silver and
gold,
The work of men's hands.
16 They have mouths, but they speak
not;
Eyes have they, but they see not;
17 They have ears, but they hear not;
Neither is there any breath in their
mouths.
18 They that make them shall be like
unto them;
Yea, every one that trusteth in them.

19 O house of Israel, bless ye the LORD;
O house of Aaron, bless ye the LORD;
20 O house of Levi, bless ye the LORD;
Ye that fear the LORD, bless ye the
LORD.
21 Blessed be the LORD out of Zion,
Who dwelleth at Jerusalem.
Hallelujah.

❧

Prayer Is Not Always Begging

If you think that prayer is just a begging ritual, think again. The Book of Psalms is, with very few exceptions, a book of prayers. Many are petitions, but many are not. They reflect all sorts of moods, needs, and situations: confessions (see Psalm 51), celebrations of love (see Psalm 133), thanksgiving (see Psalm 92), a struggle between faith and doubt (see Psalm 73), reflections on life and death (see Psalm 90), and pure joy in the presence of God (see Psalm 98). Psalm 135 is just praise of God, without a single word of petition.

The psalmist calls on all to "praise God for He is good. Sing praises to His name" (v. 3). He then proceeds to glorify God as creator of the universe: "Whatever God wanted, He did in heaven and on earth, in the seas and in all deeps" (v. 6). The psalmist believes in God's involvement in the history of Israel, in the redemption from Egyptian bondage, and in the conquest of the land of Canaan, which became "a heritage unto Israel, His people" (v. 10–12). The psalm ends with the derisive rejection of all pagan idols, "the work of men's hands" (v. 15–18).

∞

Reflection: What Prayer Will Do

Prayer is almost as much a mystery as is God. Billions of human beings pray, many regularly, and others at various times. Large numbers of worshippers are convinced that prayer accomplishes many things; others wonder if it isn't a waste of breath, but keep on praying just the same.

It is fruitless to speculate just what prayer does to God. We would like to think that God takes notice of every word we pray, but that is an unverifiable assumption. It is possible, however, to recognize what prayer does for the worshipper. Every time we turn to God in prayer, we also turn inward and gain more insight into ourselves. Even as we read our prayers or pray in our own words, we sort out our feelings, anxieties, and needs. Whatever else prayer may be, it includes spiritually elevated reflections.

We see and judge ourselves by God's standards, that is, in the light of God's commandments. Above all, prayer is a call that connects us with God even if we do not perceive a signal that we are connected. C. S. Lewis suggests that when we cannot be sure that God hears us, we should persist in prayer: "The value of persistent prayer is not that He will hear us. . . . but that we will finally hear Him."

❦ Psalm 136 ❦

O give thanks unto the LORD, for
　He is good,
For His mercy endureth for ever.
2 O give thanks unto the God of gods,
For His mercy endureth for ever.
3 O give thanks unto the LORD of lords,
For His mercy endureth for ever.

4 To Him who alone doeth great
　wonders,
For His mercy endureth for ever.
5 To Him that by understanding made
　the heavens,
For His mercy endureth for ever.
6 To Him that spread forth the earth
　above the waters,
For His mercy endureth for ever.
7 To Him that made great lights,
For His mercy endureth for ever;
8 The sun to rule by day,
For His mercy endureth for ever;
9 The moon and stars to rule by night,
For His mercy endureth for ever.

10 To Him that smote Egypt in their
　first-born,
For His mercy endureth for ever;
11 And brought out Israel from among
　them,
For His mercy endureth for ever;
12 With a strong hand, and with an out-
　stretched arm,
For His mercy endureth for ever.
13 To Him who divided the Red Sea in
　sunder,

For His mercy endureth for ever;
14 And made Israel to pass through the
　midst of it,
For His mercy endureth for ever;
15 But overthrew Pharaoh and his host
　in the Red Sea,
For His mercy endureth for ever.
16 To Him that led His people through
　the wilderness,
For His mercy endureth for ever.

17 To Him that smote great kings;
For His mercy endureth for ever;
18 And slew mighty kings,
For His mercy endureth for ever.
19 Sihon king of the Amorites,
For His mercy endureth for ever;
20 And Og king of Bashan,
For His mercy endureth for ever;
21 And gave their land for a heritage,
For His mercy endureth for ever;
22 Even a heritage unto Israel His
　servant,
For His mercy endureth for ever.

23 Who remembered us in our low
　estate,
For His mercy endureth for ever;
24 And hath delivered us from our
　adversaries,
For His mercy endureth for ever.
25 Who giveth food to all flesh,
For His mercy endureth for ever.
26 O give thanks unto the God of
　heaven,
For His mercy endureth for ever.

❦

Thank God, Again and Again

Psalm 136 is an anthem of thanksgiving. Like some other psalms, it lists many reasons for gratitude to God. These can be summarized under two headings: thanksgiving to God for creating an orderly universe, and for guiding and protecting His people throughout their history. Psalm 136 goes beyond all other psalms of thanksgiving by its refrain, repeated twenty-six times: "For His mercy endures forever." There is no limit to God's gifts. As He is eternal, so are His bounties, everlastingly bestowed upon us without cessation.

〰

Reflection: Thanksgiving Makes You Happy

There is a saying that in the Messianic age, when all prayers will become unnecessary, prayers of thanksgiving will still be said. The point is that every creature, every person, is a "given" being and owes thanks to the Giver for having been created and kept alive. Psychologically, every word of thanks, to some degree, cheers us up, whether we are the recipient or the giver of the gift. People with thanks on their lips are happier than those who find nothing to appreciate.

〰 PSALM 137 〰

By the rivers of Babylon,
There we sat down, yea, we wept,
When we remembered Zion.
2 Upon the willows in the midst thereof
We hanged up our harps.
3 For there they that led us captive
   asked of us words of song,
And our tormentors asked of us mirth:
"Sing us one of the songs of Zion."

4 How shall we sing the LORD's song
In a foreign land?
5 If I forget thee, O Jerusalem,
Let my right hand forget her cunning.
6 Let my tongue cleave to the roof of
   my mouth,

If I remember thee not;
If I set not Jerusalem
Above my chiefest joy.

7 Remember, O LORD, against the chil-
   dren of Edom
The day of Jerusalem;
Who said: "Rase it, rase it,
Even to the foundation thereof."
8 O daughter of Babylon, that art to be
   destroyed;
Happy shall he be, that repayeth thee
As thou hast served us.
9 Happy shall he be, that taketh and
   dasheth thy little ones
Against the rock.

〰

Homecoming

Having been dragged into exile to Babylon, and now returning home, after many years on foreign soil, the psalmist is ecstatic about Jerusalem, his native city. The torments he suffered at the hands of his captors are still fresh in his mind as he utters the awesome oath of loyalty to Jerusalem: "If I forget you, O Jerusalem, let my right hand forget its cunning and my tongue cleave to the roof of my mouth, if I remember you not; if I set not Jerusalem above my chiefest joy" (v. 5–6).

Psalm 137 might well be considered the birth certificate of Zionism. For centuries, Jews have been chanting it daily when saying grace at mealtime. The psalm, remembering the bitterness of exile and the oath never to forget Jerusalem, has kept alive the hope for the restoration of Jerusalem and the Promised Land.

❧

Reflection: The Joy of Reunion

How we value an object that has been lost and is found again! There is no greater love than the love for one with whom we are reunited after a long separation. How passionate is the embrace for a dear one who comes back from afar. No truer words were spoken than the proverbial "absence makes the heart grow fonder." Every homecoming to family and friends makes the heart beat faster. Such reunions may involve considerable sacrifices, but are richly rewarded by the renewal and intensification of loving relationships.

❦ PSALM 138 ❦

[A Psalm] of David.

I will give Thee thanks with my whole heart,
In the presence of the mighty will I sing praises unto Thee.
2 I will bow down toward Thy holy temple,
And give thanks unto Thy name for Thy mercy and for Thy truth;
For Thou hast magnified Thy word above all Thy name.
3 In the day that I called, Thou didst answer me;
Thou didst encourage me in my soul with strength.

4 All the kings of the earth shall give Thee thanks, O LORD,
For they have heard the words of Thy mouth.

5 Yea, they shall sing of the ways of the LORD;
For great is the glory of the LORD.
6 For though the LORD be high, yet regardeth He the lowly,
And the haughty He knoweth from afar.
7 Though I walk in the midst of trouble, Thou quickenest me;
Thou stretchest forth Thy hand against the wrath of mine enemies,
And Thy right hand doth save me.
8 The LORD will accomplish that which concerneth me;
Thy mercy, O LORD, endureth for ever;
Forsake not the work of Thine own hands.

❧

"You Answered Me"

At times, when praying to God, you may have the feeling of talking to a wall. But then, quite unexpectedly, you are in touch with God: "On the day that I called, You answered me; You boosted me inwardly with strength" (v. 3). God is far beyond the earth, yet He is aware of His humble creatures and sizes up the arrogant: "Though God is far above, He considers the humble and knows the proud from afar. If I walk into trouble, You keep me alive" (v. 6–7). The psalmist is certain that God has some plan for his life: "God will carry out His purpose concerning me" (v. 8). The Creator Who gave us existence should have an interest in preserving us alive. Therefore, he prays: "Forsake not the work of Your hands" (v. 8).

❦

Reflection: How God Answers

The psalmist rejoices that his prayer was answered, but he does not tell us what he prayed for. Did God grant his request? Whether or not he got everything he asked for, the psalmist is not complaining. Evidently he felt that his prayer was not in vain, for he acknowledges before God "You boosted me with inner strength" (v. 3). Possibly the psalmist had prayed for something else.

❦ PSALM 139 ❦

For the Leader. A Psalm of David.

O LORD, Thou hast searched me, and known me.
2 Thou knowest my downsitting and mine uprising,
Thou understandest my thought afar off.
3 Thou measurest my going about and my lying down,
And art acquainted with all my ways.
4 For there is not a word in my tongue,
But, lo, O LORD, Thou knowest it altogether.
5 Thou hast hemmed me in behind and before,
And laid Thy hand upon me.
6 Such knowledge is too wonderful for me;
Too high, I cannot attain unto it.

7 Whither shall I go from Thy spirit?
Or whither shall I flee from Thy presence?
8 If I ascend up into heaven, Thou art there;
If I make my bed in the netherworld, behold, Thou art there.

9 If I take the wings of the morning,
And dwell in the uttermost parts of the sea;
10 Even there would Thy hand lead me,
And Thy right hand would hold me.
11 And if I say: "Surely the darkness shall envelop me,
And the light about me shall be night";
12 Even the darkness is not too dark for Thee,
But the night shineth as the day;
The darkness is even as the light.

13 For Thou hast made my reins;
Thou hast knit me together in my mother's womb.
14 I will give thanks unto Thee, for I am fearfully and wonderfully made;
Wonderful are Thy works;
And that my soul knoweth right well.
15 My frame was not hidden from Thee,
When I was made in secret,
And curiously wrought in the lowest parts of the earth.
16 Thine eyes did see mine unformed substance,

And in Thy book they were all
written—
Even the days that were fashioned,
When as yet there was none of them.
17 How weighty also are Thy thoughts
unto me, O God!
How great is the sum of them!
18 If I would count them, they are more
in number than the sand;
Were I to come to the end of them,
I would still be with Thee.

19 If Thou but wouldest slay the wicked,
O God—
Depart from me therefore, ye men of
blood;

20 Who utter Thy name with wicked
thought,
They take it for falsehood, even
Thine enemies—
21 Do not I hate them, O LORD, that
hate Thee?
And do not I strive with those that
rise up against Thee?
22 I hate them with utmost hatred;
I count them mine enemies.
23 Search me, O God, and know my
heart,
Try me, and know my thoughts;
24 And see if there be any way in me that
is grievous,
And lead me in the way everlasting.

Where Is God? Where Is He Not?

Even true believers do not always have a sense of the living presence of God. Many, perhaps the majority, can only point to certain moments of inspiration when they had the feeling of being in dialogue with God. Every moment of worship holds out the hope of entering again into communication with God. When it doesn't seem to happen, you may wonder if God is at all reachable. Maybe the human being is too insignificant to merit God's attention? Psalm 139 answers such doubts: Yes, you are worthy of God's attention. Long before you began looking for God, God was looking over your "unformed substance" (v. 16). Your Creator knows all about you: "O God, You have examined me and know me. You know my every move. . . . There is not a word in my mouth but that You, O God, know it altogether" (v. 1, 2, 4). We cannot imagine such knowledge, and neither does the psalmist: "Such knowledge is too wonderful for me; it is a mystery, I cannot grasp it" (v. 6).

Are you looking for God and cannot find Him? The psalmist tells you that you cannot possibly get away from God's presence. There is no place where God is not: "If I go up to heaven, You are there; If I get down to the bottomless depth of the world, You are there. If I take off to the ends of the oceans, even there would You be leading me and uphold me" (v. 8–10). You are never alone. God is with and within you. It is an idea that enhances human dignity. If anyone belittles or despises you, think about how much you matter to God.

∽

Reflection: God's Nearness and Self-Esteem

The psalmist speaks of a most intimate relationship between God and man. God relates to the yet unborn person in the mother's womb: "You have knit me together in my mother's womb. . . . Your eyes did see mine unformed substance" (v. 13, 16). God's involvement with the human being in his prenatal stage bestows dignity and sanctity on every individual.

This thought had a transforming influence on the noted African-American theologian and author of some twenty-two books, Howard Thurman. While working as an adolescent on a Florida plantation, he was treated with contempt and humiliated by the young daughter of the wealthy plantation owner. Fearing loss of his emotional control, he ran to his hut, threw himself on the cot, and sobbed. He tells us what happened next: "There was a Bible in the room. I opened it on Psalm 139 and read: 'O God, You have examined me and know me . . . whether I sit down or rise up; . . . You understand my thought from afar. . . . There is not a word in my mouth but that You, O God, know it altogether . . .'" (v. 1, 2, 4). Assured of his inseparability from God, Howard Thurman recovered his dignity as a man. He repeated to himself over and over again: "You fashioned my inward parts and knit me together in my mother's womb" (v. 13). Wherever he would be in the future, God would be at his side: "There would You be leading me and uphold me" (v. 10). The psalm healed Thurman's shattered self-respect. He felt precious in God's sight. Come what may, his Maker would never leave and forsake him.

∽ # Psalm 140 ∽

For the Leader. A Psalm of David.

2 Deliver me, O LORD, from the evil man;
  Preserve me from the violent man;
3 Who devise evil things in their heart;
  Every day do they stir up wars.
4 They have sharpened their tongue like a serpent;
  Vipers' venom is under their lips.
        Selah

5 Keep me, O LORD, from the hands of the wicked;
  Preserve me from the violent man;
  Who have purposed to make my steps slip.
6 The proud have hid a snare for me, and cords;
  They have spread a net by the wayside;
  They have set gins for me.
        Selah

7I have said unto the LORD: "Thou art
  my God";
 Give ear, O LORD, unto the voice of
  my supplications.
8O God the LORD, the strength of my
  salvation,
 Who hast screened my head in the
  day of battle,
9Grant not, O LORD, the desires of the
  wicked;
 Further not his evil device, so that
  they exalt themselves.   Selah

10As for the head of those that compass
  me about,
 Let the mischief of their own lips
  cover them.

11Let burning coals fall upon them;
 Let them be cast into the fire,
 Into deep pits, that they rise not up
  again.
12A slanderer shall not be established in
  the earth;
 The violent and evil man shall be
  hunted with thrust upon thrust.

13I know that the LORD will maintain
  the cause of the poor,
 And the right of the needy.
14Surely the righteous shall give thanks
  unto Thy name;
 The upright shall dwell in Thy
  presence.

❦

When You Battle Evil, God Is on Your Side

It is only natural to want to strike back at anyone who abuses or
maligns you. The author of Psalm 140 would do likewise. Nobody likes
his persecutors. The psalmist is encouraged by his belief that he is not
alone in this struggle. He is an ally of God: "I know that God will
maintain the cause of the poor and the right of the needy" (v. 13). If
your cause is just, your battle is God's battle, and you may call on Him,
as did the psalmist: "Deliver me, O God, from evil men; preserve me
from the violent" (v. 2).

❦

Reflection: Gossip

Surrounded by malicious people, the psalmist prays: "Deliver me, O
God, from the evil man" (v. 2). In his list of those who would do him
harm, he singles out persons who are wounding him with words:
"They have sharpened their tongue like a serpent" (v. 4). He is a victim
of gossip and slander. Gossip is generally condemned, but most people
enjoy it.

   The Bible and moralists around the world sharply condemn gossip
as a kind of moral assassination. "Do not go up and down as a tale-
bearer among your people," says Leviticus 19:16. The eleventh-
century moralist Rabbi Eliezer ben Isaac compared the person who
gossips to "a fly seeking sore spots." The thing to do, he suggested, is
to "cover up your neighbor's flaws!" The listener to gossip encourages

the defamation of a neighbor and, at the same time, exposes himself to danger, as we are warned by the Spanish proverb: "Whoever gossips to you, will gossip about you." Some rabbis went so far as to caution against all talk about people, even in lavish praise, because it might provoke one of the listeners to contradict you with a recital of all the faults of the person you have just praised. The poet William Blake raises an important point about the damage done by gossip. It is damnable not only when spreading falsehood, but also, at times, by telling the truth about someone:

> A truth that's told with bad intent
> Beats all the lies you can invent.

❧ PSALM 141 ❧

A Psalm of David.

LORD, I have called Thee; make haste unto me;
Give ear unto my voice, when I call unto Thee.
2 Let my prayer be set forth as incense before Thee,
The lifting up of my hands as the evening sacrifice.
3 Set a guard, O LORD, to my mouth;
Keep watch at the door of my lips.
4 Incline not my heart to any evil thing,
To be occupied in deeds of wickedness
With men that work iniquity;
And let me not eat of their dainties.

5 Let the righteous smite me in kindness, and correct me;
Oil so choice let not my head refuse;
For still is my prayer because of their wickedness.

6 Their judges are thrown down by the sides of the rock;
And they shall hear my words, that they are sweet.
7 As when one cleaveth and breaketh up the earth,
Our bones are scattered at the grave's mouth.

8 For mine eyes are unto Thee, O God the LORD;
In Thee have I taken refuge, O pour not out my soul.
9 Keep me from the snare which they have laid for me,
And from the gins of the workers of iniquity.
10 Let the wicked fall into their own nets,
Whilst I withal escape.

❧

Reject the Partnership of Evildoers

The common adage "If you can't beat them, join them" would not be acceptable to the psalmist. Powerful adversaries make a tempting offer if he joins in their enterprise. But he cannot bring himself to become a partner in crime and asks God to help him overcome the temptation: "Incline not my heart to any evil thing, to get involved in deeds of wickedness with iniquitous men, and let me not eat of their dainties" (v. 4). He decides to await the downfall of those crooks and not be entrapped by them (see v. 9–10).

∽

Reflection: Criticism

Unlike most of us, who hate criticism, this psalmist welcomes it, provided that it is given with kindness: "Let the righteous smite me in kindness, and correct me" (v. 5). Such tolerance for criticism is a rarity. "Few persons have enough wisdom to prefer useful criticism to deceptive praise," said the seventeenth-century French writer La Rochefoucauld. The person who shuts his ear to criticism shuts the door to his own improvement. Giving criticism is almost as hard as taking it. The psalmist is exceptional in asking for correction, albeit "in kindness." Deplorably, the critic often aims to embarrass and hurt rather than help the other improve. In that case, criticism is disguised hostility. A Yiddish proverb says: "If you're determined to beat a dog, you're sure to find a stick." A common error in judging others is to generalize, from a single fault, that the other person must be wholly corrupt or inept. It is equally mistaken to believe, on the basis of a single virtue or talent, that the other is superior in every way.

∽ PSALM 142 ∽

Maschil of David, when he was in the cave; a Prayer.

2 With my voice I cry unto the LORD;
   With my voice I make supplication
      unto the LORD.
3 I pour out my complaint before Him,
   I declare before Him my trouble;
4 When my spirit fainteth within me—
   Thou knowest my path—
   In the way wherein I walk
   Have they hidden a snare for me.
5 Look on my right hand, and see,
   For there is no man that knoweth me;
   I have no way to flee;
   No man careth for my soul.

6 I have cried unto Thee, O LORD;
   I have said: "Thou art my refuge,
   My portion in the land of the living."
7 Attend unto my cry;
   For I am brought very low;
   Deliver me from my persecutors;
   For they are too strong for me.
8 Bring my soul out of prison,
   That I may give thanks unto Thy
      name;
   The righteous shall crown themselves
      because of me;
   For Thou wilt deal bountifully with
      me.

When You See No Way Out

The very least a cry to God will do is give you some relief. The author of Psalm 142 finds himself in a desperate situation. His persecutors have him cornered: "I have no way to flee. No one cares for me" (v. 5). There is no sign that his problem is being solved, but he keeps asking God for help: "I cry unto You, O God; I say You are my refuge, all I have among the living" (v. 6). The hope that God may help comforts him: "Deliver my soul from its prison that I may praise Your name. . . . for You will do me good" (v. 8).

Reflection: Ask and You Will Receive

There is only one rule for the art of asking: Don't be shy. If you are in need, come out with it and say, I need your help! Say it to the person capable of helping—and say it to God. Follow the sound advice of the apostle Matthew: "Ask and it shall be given to you; seek and you will find, knock and the door will open to you" (Matthew 7:7). The seventeenth-century English poet Robert Herrick offered similar advice:

> To get thine ends, lay bashfulness aside.
> Who fears to ask doth teach to be deny'd

The psalmist in his need quickly gets to the point: "I cry aloud unto God . . . I declare before Him my trouble" (v. 2–3). Persecutors have brought him very low, yet he is confident that God will help: "You will deal bountifully with me" (v. 8). Why do some people in need hesitate to go and ask for help where it is available? Call it shame or false pride, which is the same. Why not accept in humility the fact that all human beings are utterly dependent on others for their survival? The humble, knowing his weakness, will not shrink from asking for what he needs. The needy who is too bashful to ask should realize that his request in a way honors the one who is in a position to help. A petition for help is not a nuisance but a compliment to the one who has the means and power to assist those less fortunate than he.

❧ PSALM 143 ❧

A Psalm of David.

O LORD, hear my prayer, give ear to
my supplications;
In Thy faithfulness answer me, and in
Thy righteousness.
2 And enter not into judgment with
Thy servant;
For in Thy sight shall no man living
be justified.

3 For the enemy hath persecuted my
soul;
He hath crushed my life down to the
ground;
He hath made me to dwell in dark
places, as those that have been long
dead.
4 And my spirit fainteth within me;
My heart within me is appalled.

5 I remember the days of old;
I meditate on all Thy doing;
I muse on the work of Thy hands.
6 I spread forth my hands unto Thee;
My soul [thirsteth] after Thee, as a
weary land.   Selah

7 Answer me speedily, O LORD,
My spirit faileth;

Hide not Thy face from me;
Lest I become like them that go down
into the pit.
8 Cause me to hear Thy lovingkindness
in the morning,
For in Thee do I trust;
Cause me to know the way wherein I
should walk,
For unto Thee have I lifted up my
soul.

9 Deliver me from mine enemies, O
LORD;
With Thee have I hidden myself.
10 Teach me to do Thy will,
For Thou art my God;
Let Thy good spirit
Lead me in an even land.
11 For Thy name's sake, O LORD,
quicken me;
In Thy righteousness bring my soul
out of trouble.
12 And in Thy mercy cut off mine ene-
mies,
And destroy all them that harass my
soul;
For I am Thy servant.

❧

Why Should God Help You?

You will not find a single psalm whose author claims that he *deserves*
God's favor. This psalm is the petition of a hard-pressed person humble enough to admit that he is no saint: "Do not enter into judgment
with me, for no living person shall be justified in Your sight" (v. 2).
Why should God help him? He is up against a formidable enemy
who "crushed my life into the ground" (v. 3). He does not argue on
grounds of merit, counting only on God's love: "Let me hear Your
loving-kindness in the morning, for in You do I trust" (v. 8).

While asking for help, he submits to God's guidance and humbly
admits that he may be too weak to fulfill God's commandments: "Let
me know the way I must go . . . teach me to do your will" (v. 8, 10). He
is no hero. He has flaws of character. He understands that God's help

will not be a reward for any good he has done, but an expression of God's beneficence: "For your name's sake, O God, keep me alive and, in Your beneficence, get me out of my trouble" (v. 11).

❧

Reflection: The Power of the Will

How much—or how little—depends on our own will? We know deep in our bones how very fragile our existence is, how very dependent we are on all sorts of conditions beyond our control. Events all over the globe and the actions of others determine our health, security, and prosperity.

There is room, to be sure, for our will to steer us through various passages of our life. Our own will may not always be decisive, but it does make a difference. The psalmist has a low self-image. He knows that he has fallen short in many ways and asks God: "Enter not into judgment with me" (v. 2). It is somewhat amusing how he is trying to excuse his own delinquencies by declaring all mankind delinquent: "No living person shall be justified in Your sight" (v. 2). Aside from help to cope with enemies outside, he needs help against the enemy within his own mind. He needs God's guidance for the proper conduct of his life: "Cause me to know the way I should walk . . . teach me to do Your will" (v. 8, 10). He recognizes that knowledge alone is not enough; you need the will to act accordingly. The psalmist wants God to strengthen his will to live by God's commandments. The English poet and playwright John Drinkwater identifies lack of will as our major predicament:

> Knowledge we ask not—knowledge Thou hast lent;
> But Lord, the will—there lies our bitter need.
> Give us to build above the deep intent
> The deed, the deed

How much better our life could be if only we had sufficient will to live up to principles we already know to be right!

❧ PSALM 144 ❧

[A Psalm] of David.

Blessed be the LORD my Rock,
Who traineth my hands for war,
And my fingers for battle;
2 My lovingkindness, and my fortress,
My high tower, and my deliverer;

My shield, and He in whom I take refuge;
Who subdueth my people under me.

3 LORD, what is man, that Thou takest knowledge of him?

Or the son of man, that Thou makest account of him?

⁴Man is like unto a breath;
His days are as a shadow that passeth away.

⁵O Lᴏʀᴅ, bow Thy heavens, and come down;
Touch the mountains, that they may smoke.

⁶Cast forth lightning, and scatter them;
Send out Thine arrows, and discomfit them.

⁷Stretch forth Thy hands from on high;
Rescue me, and deliver me out of many waters,
Out of the hand of strangers;

⁸Whose mouth speaketh falsehood,
And their right hand is a right hand of lying.

⁹O God, I will sing a new song unto Thee,
Upon a psaltery of ten strings will I sing praises unto Thee;

¹⁰Who givest salvation unto kings,
Who rescuest David Thy servant from the hurtful sword.

¹¹Rescue me, and deliver me out of the hand of strangers,
Whose mouth speaketh falsehood,
And their right hand is a right hand of lying.

¹²We whose sons are as plants grown up in their youth;
Whose daughters are as cornerpillars carved after the fashion of a palace;

¹³Whose garners are full, affording all manner of store;
Whose sheep increase by thousands and ten thousands in our fields;

¹⁴Whose oxen are well laden;
With no breach, and no going forth,
And no outcry in our broad places;

¹⁵Happy is the people that is in such a case.
Yea, happy is the people whose God is the Lᴏʀᴅ.

❧

Life Is a Passing Shadow

Regardless of your power or prosperity, your life hangs on a thin thread. The psalmist has David, the most heroic warrior of Israel, speak of life as a "vanishing cloud" (v. 4). David, despite his strength, also needs God's help: "Reach out from on high; rescue me, and deliver me out of many waters" (v. 7). Now the nation enjoys peace and prosperity: "Our storehouses are full with all kinds of goods" (v. 13). For all this God is to be thanked: "Happy is the people whose God is the Lord" (v. 15). But power and prosperity will not prevent death. Whether you are at the top of the heap or the lowest of the lowly, in the end we are all equal: "Man is like a breath; his days are as a passing shadow" (v. 4).

❧

Reflection: The Brevity of Life

In the midst of boasting about his prowess in war, the psalmist suddenly thinks of the utter frailty of life: "God, what is man that You take knowledge of him? . . . Man is like a breath; his days are as a passing shadow" (v. 3–4). It is sobering to remember again and again that all our power, wealth, and the works we are so proud of will vanish even as we must vanish. We are told that the Anglo-Jewish philanthropist Sir Moses Montefiore had his butler knock on his door at the stroke of each hour and say: "Sir Moses, another hour of your life has passed." Every ambitious executive, artist, and achiever in whatever field of endeavor needs to be aware of the brevity of life. Why be so frantic in building our little empires? Soon all of it will turn to dust. Why heap up more and more wealth, none of which will follow us to the grave? Should we not share more generously with the needy while we are still alive? Why be so obsessive in the pursuit of our goals, which will soon be laid to rest with us? Should we not aim at a more balanced life, leaving more time to be with family and friends, to read, to learn, to reflect—and to pray? Next to the Shakespeare statue in London's Westminster Abbey is a tablet inscribed with a slightly modified quotation from his play *The Tempest:*

> The cloud-capp'd towers,
> The gorgeous palaces,
> The solemn temples,
> The great globe itself,
> Yea, all which it inherit,
>   Shall dissolve:
> And like the baseless fabric of a vision
> Leave not a wreck behind.

❧ PSALM 145 ❧

[A Psalm of] praise; of David.
I will extol Thee, my God, O King;
And I will bless Thy name for ever
   and ever.
2 Every day will I bless Thee;
   And I will praise Thy name for ever
   and ever.
3 Great is the LORD, and highly to be
   praised;
   And His greatness is unsearchable.
4 One generation shall laud Thy works
   to another,
   And shall declare Thy mighty acts.

5 The glorious splendour of Thy
   majesty,
   And Thy wondrous works, will I
   rehearse.
6 And men shall speak of the might of
   Thy tremendous acts;
   And I will tell of Thy greatness.
7 They shall utter the fame of Thy
   great goodness,
   And shall sing of Thy righteousness.
8 The LORD is gracious, and full of
   compassion;
   Slow to anger, and of great mercy.

9 The LORD is good to all;
And His tender mercies are over all
His works.
10 All Thy works shall praise Thee, O
LORD;
And Thy saints shall bless Thee.
11 They shall speak of the glory of Thy
kingdom,
And talk of Thy might;
12 To make known to the sons of men
His mighty acts,
And the glory of the majesty of His
kingdom.
13 Thy kingdom is a kingdom for all
ages,
And Thy dominion endureth
throughout all generations.
14 The LORD upholdeth all that fall,
And raiseth up all those that are
bowed down.
15 The eyes of all wait for Thee,

And Thou givest them their food in
due season.
16 Thou openest Thy hand,
And satisfiest every living thing with
favour.
17 The LORD is righteous in all His ways,
And gracious in all His works.
18 The LORD is nigh unto all them that
call upon Him,
To all that call upon Him in truth.
19 He will fulfil the desire of them that
fear Him;
He also will hear their cry, and will
save them.
20 The LORD preserveth all them that
love Him;
But all the wicked will He destroy.
21 My mouth shall speak the praise of
the LORD;
And let all flesh bless His holy name
for ever and ever.

❧

God Is Near to All Who Call upon Him

Many worship God as creator, others as provider, and still others love
God as the eternal companion who is near and hears their prayers. For
the author of Psalm 145, God is all of these. He reveres God for "the
glorious splendor of Your majesty and Your wondrous works" (v. 5). He
praises God because "God is good to all and His tender mercies are
over all works" (v. 9). He revives the ill, invigorates the weak, and sustains all His creatures: "God upholds all who fall. . . . You open Your
hand and satisfy every living thing with favor" (v. 14, 16). Moreover,
He lets us come near Him in prayer: "God is near to all who call upon
Him, to all who call upon Him in truth" (v. 18).

❧

Reflection: The Biblical View of God

Observant Jews recite this psalm several times daily. It comes close to
a confession of the biblical faith. It summarizes the biblical view of God
as creator, provider, and heavenly friend of all who call upon Him. It is
a symphony of adoration of God, whose "kingdom is a kingdom for all
ages" (v. 13). It may be inconceivable to the human mind why the ruler
of the cosmos cares for every one of His creatures: "You give them
their food in due season. . . . You open your hand and satisfy every

living thing" (v. 15–16). But faith goes beyond knowledge and reason. How does God feed all that lives? We should not imagine God running a universal soup kitchen. He feeds us by making nature fertile to grow food for all—and there would be food for all if only mankind used their minds properly and refrained from mutual destruction. God in His majesty is approachable by the humblest of His creatures: "God is near to all who call upon Him" (v. 18). How does God "hold up all who fall and raise up those who are bowed down?" (v. 14). God's help is conveyed to us through the hearts of people in whom God implanted compassion. The helping hand stretched out by one human being to another is to be regarded as the extension of God's saving arm. In the Bible, God's love is always linked to justice and righteousness. The psalmist also, after praising God's mercy, says that people "sing joyfully of God's righteousness" (v. 7).

The nineteenth-century English poet Matthew Arnold commented on the biblical association of moral conduct with joy: "All, or very nearly all the nations of mankind have recognized the importance of conduct. They, however, looked at conduct, not as something full of happiness and joy, but as something one could not manage to do without. No one has ever come near Israel in feeling, and in making others feel, that to righteousness belongs happiness."

❧ PSALM 146 ❧

Hallelujah.
Praise the LORD, O my soul.
2 I will praise the LORD while I live;
I will sing praises unto my God while
I have my being.
3 Put not your trust in princes,
Nor in the son of man, in whom there
is no help.
4 His breath goeth forth, he returneth
to his dust;
In that very day his thoughts perish.
5 Happy is he whose help is the God of
Jacob,
Whose hope is in the LORD his God,
6 Who made heaven and earth,
The sea, and all that in them is;
Who keepeth truth for ever;
7 Who executeth justice for the
oppressed;

Who giveth bread to the hungry.

The LORD looseth the prisoners;
8 The LORD openeth the eyes of the
blind;
The LORD raiseth up them that are
bowed down;
The LORD loveth the righteous;
9 The LORD preserveth the strangers;
He upholdeth the fatherless and the
widow;
But the way of the wicked He maketh
crooked.
10 The LORD will reign for ever,
Thy God, O Zion, unto all
generations.
Hallelujah.

Only God Is Truly Dependable

This psalm and the remaining four that close the Book of Psalms feature the word *hallelujah* (praise God!) at the beginning and end. Being alive is in itself a mandate to praise God: "I will praise God while I live. I will sing praises unto Him while I have my being" (v. 2). The psalmist has lived a long time, and evidently learned from experience how risky it is to rely on people in power: "Put not your trust in princes, mortal men who cannot help" (v. 3). All of a sudden, they may be swept from power or perish. God alone is dependable. The Creator of the universe "keeps faith forever" (v. 6). Those who put their trust in God "Who made heaven and earth, the sea and all that is therein" (v. 6) will not be disappointed.

The psalmist does not elaborate on God's laws, which regulate the cosmos and maintain order in nature. Instead, he stresses God's intimate involvement in human affairs. He provides our food; His healing power restores us; He is the source of justice; He inspires liberation and helps the downtrodden and needy (see v. 7–9).

Reflection: Protect the Stranger

This psalmist is a man of the people. He cares little for the princes, nobles, and oligarchs who rise to power on their wealth. He would not put his confidence in any mortal. Only the God of justice is to be trusted (see v. 7). Echoing the words of the prophet Isaiah (see Isaiah 58:7-9), he trusts in God's concern and care for the hungry, the imprisoned, the blind, the stranger, the orphan, and the widow (v. 7–9). A special comment is in order about the psalmist's concern for the stranger. The command not to oppress the stranger is often repeated in biblical law. There is nothing in other ancient legal codes to match the biblical concern for the welfare of the alien. Modern nations generally would like to keep aliens as far away as possible. Their status often lacks the civil rights and protection that make for freedom and security. The philosopher Hermann Cohen discerned in the biblical protection of aliens the birth of the idea of humanity: "With the law of shielding the alien from wrong, true Religion begins. The alien was protected not because he was a member of one's clan, community or people; but because he was a human being. In the alien, man discovered the idea of humanity."

❧ Psalm 147 ❧

Hallelujah;
For it is good to sing praises unto our
God;
For it is pleasant, and praise is
comely.
2 The LORD doth build up Jerusalem,
He gathereth together the dispersed
of Israel;
3 Who healeth the broken in heart,
And bindeth up their wounds.
4 He counteth the number of the stars;
He giveth them all their names.
5 Great is our LORD, and mighty in
power;
His understanding is infinite.
6 The LORD upholdeth the humble;
He bringeth the wicked down to the
ground.
7 Sing unto the LORD with thanksgiving,
Sing praises upon the harp unto our
God;
8 Who covereth the heaven with
clouds,
Who prepareth rain for the earth,
Who maketh the mountains to spring
with grass.
9 He giveth to the beast his food,
And to the young ravens which cry.
10 He delighteth not in the strength of
the horse;
He taketh no pleasure in the legs of a
man.

11 The LORD taketh pleasure in them
that fear Him,
In those that wait for His mercy.

12 Glorify the LORD, O Jerusalem;
Praise thy God, O Zion.
13 For He hath made strong the bars of
thy gates;
He hath blessed thy children within
thee.
14 He maketh thy borders peace;
He giveth thee in plenty the fat of
wheat.
15 He sendeth out His commandment
upon earth;
His word runneth very swiftly.
16 He giveth snow like wool;
He scattereth the hoar-frost like
ashes.
17 He casteth forth His ice like crumbs;
Who can stand before His cold?
18 He sendeth forth His word, and
melteth them;
He causeth His wind to blow, and the
waters flow.
19 He declareth His word unto Jacob,
His statutes and His ordinances unto
Israel.
20 He hath not dealt so with any nation;
And as for His ordinances, they have
not known them.
Hallelujah.

❧

God, the Cosmic Power, and Personal Being

Is your God a cosmic power, or a personal being with Whom you can
have a relationship? For the psalmist, it is not a question of either or.
He believes in a God Who is both personal and the supreme power in
the universe. Psalm 147 expresses awe and wonder at the powers of
God that control nature, "Who prepares rain for the earth, who makes
the mountains put forth grass" (v. 8).

On the other hand, the psalmist speaks of a personal bond with
God that grew out of his experience in life. The God of the vast oceans

and the mighty mountains and the starry heaven above also cares for the humblest creature: "He heals the broken in heart and binds up their wounds . . . God upholds the humble; He brings the wicked down to the ground" (v. 3, 6). God is unimpressed by athletic champions but "takes delight in people who revere Him and wait for His mercy" (v. 11).

∞

Reflection: Israel's Distinction

The psalmist was among that generation of exiles who returned to Jerusalem from captivity in Babylon. He witnessed the restoration of his people and the rebuilding of the temple. He deeply believes that God is involved in the course of history. The psalm ends with a proud assertion of Israel's privilege of having received God's revelation, implying a special obligation to make God's word known among the nations: "He declared His word unto Jacob, His statutes and ordinances unto Israel. He has not dealt so with any nation; and as for His ordinances, they do not know them" (v. 19–20). The English poet Matthew Arnold agreed with the psalmist's assertion of Israel's distinctive role in mankind's moral development: "As long as the world lasts, all who want to make progress in righteousness will come to Israel for inspiration, as to the people who have had the sense for righteousness most glowing and strongest. This does truly constitute for Israel a most extraordinary distinction."

∞ PSALM 148 ∞

Hallelujah.
Praise ye the LORD from the heavens;
Praise Him in the heights.
2 Praise ye Him, all His angels;
Praise ye Him, all His hosts.
3 Praise ye Him, sun and moon;
Praise Him, all ye stars of light.
4 Praise Him, ye heavens of heavens,
And ye waters that are above the
heavens.
5 Let them praise the name of the
LORD;
For He commanded, and they were
created.

6 He hath also established them for
ever and ever;
He hath made a decree which shall
not be transgressed.

7 Praise the LORD from the earth,
Ye sea-monsters, and all deeps;
8 Fire and hail, snow and vapour,
Stormy wind, fulfilling His word;
9 Mountains and all hills,
Fruitful trees and all cedars;
10 Beasts and all cattle,
Creeping things and winged fowl;
11 Kings of the earth and all peoples,

Princes and all judges of the earth;
12 Both young men and maidens,
   Old men and children;
13 Let them praise the name of the
   LORD,
   For His name alone is exalted;
   His glory is above the earth and
   heaven.

14 And He hath lifted up a horn for His
   people,
   A praise for all His saints,
   Even for the children of Israel, a
   people near unto Him.
   Hallelujah.

〰

The One God Unites the Universe

This psalm is a jubilant vision of cosmic order and unity. All forms of life and all the forces of nature are united in God's plan, fulfilling His commands: "Fire and hail, snow and vapor, stormy wind, fulfilling His word" (v. 6). The heavenly bodies, earth, nature, and all living things join in praising God: "Let them praise the name of God, . . . His glory is above the earth and heaven" (v. 13).

〰

Reflection: God Unifies the World

The conflicts raging in many parts of the world convey the impression of chaotic division. This impression is reinforced by the daily press and news programs, which are filled with violence, conflict, and war. We experience personally the clash of arguments, friction, and division either as witnesses or as contenders. Is the world coming apart at the seams? The author of Psalm 148 has the opposite impression. His psalm is a hymn of cosmic unity. He acts like the world's cheerleader. He calls on the angels, the stars, the beasts, and people of every kind, old men and children, to join in the praise of God (see v. 6–13). In his view, whatever exists, even the elements we have come to fear, has a divinely given purpose. All forms of existence are unified and animated by God. The eighteenth-century English poet Alexander Pope celebrated this cosmic unity in his verse:

> All are but parts of one stupendous whole
> Whose body Nature is, and God the soul.

The psalmist sees the whole universe as though it were one choir chanting God's praises. The call to praise is repeated no less than eleven times, not counting the word *Hallelujah* (praise God) with which the psalm begins and ends. England's poet laureate John Masefield would not have found such lavish praise excessive. He said: "It is a rare, and when just, a noble thing to praise. Few people praise enough; all ought to praise whenever they see something that can be praised."

❧ PSALM 149 ❧

Hallelujah.
Sing unto the LORD a new song,
And His praise in the assembly of the
saints.
2 Let Israel rejoice in his Maker;
Let the children of Zion be joyful in
their King.
3 Let them praise His name in the
dance;
Let them sing praises unto Him with
the timbrel and harp.
4 For the LORD taketh pleasure in His
people;
He adorneth the humble with
salvation.

5 Let the saints exult in glory;
Let them sing for joy upon their beds.
6 Let the high praises of God be in their
mouth,
And a two-edged sword in their hand;
7 To execute vengeance upon the
nations,
And chastisements upon the peoples;
8 To bind their kings with chains,
And their nobles with fetters of iron;
9 To execute upon them the judgment
written;
He is the glory of all His saints.
Hallelujah.

❧

God Wants More Than Lip Service

Enthusiasm, reinforced by passionate militancy, marks this psalm. The people at large—call them the "grassroots" people—and the saints are asked to unite, with song and dance, in praise of God: "Let them praise His name in the dance; let them sing praises unto Him with the timbrel and the harp" (v. 3). The object is not to give the people fun but to rouse their spirits to action: "Let the high praises of God be in their mouth and a two-edged sword in their hand" (v. 6). It is not enough to give lip service to God and to our ideals. We must mobilize material means and willpower to battle against those who would destroy us and our values.

❧

Reflection: Act on Your Beliefs

This psalm begins with joy, in celebration of an important victory—"let the faithful exult in glory" (v. 5)—but soon turns very serious. It is not enough to praise God. The faithful must act on their faith and be ready to defend, even fight for it: "Let the high praises of God be in their mouth and a two-edged sword in their hand" (v. 6). They must put their hand where their mouth is. In every society you will find plenty of idealistic sentiment to go around. but not enough people working to turn good intentions into reality. Wishing does not make it so. Herbert Hoover said: "Words without action are the assassins of idealism." Idealism and enthusiasm have a way of fading into indifference. There is a line of progression that leads from sentiment to conviction, to preaching, and, finally, to realization.

Action on behalf of one's ideals must not be a one-time attempt but a long-term, even lifetime program of systematic learning, teaching, activity, and organization to gain wider support for the cause. The farmer who puts seeds into the ground gets nothing without yearlong cultivation until harvest time. An ideal is like a seed. It will produce nothing without steady cultivation. This is a strong argument for organized religion. Religion is conditioning of the will. The individual needs to be kept on the right path by the community of the faithful. The entire tradition of ritual, worship, and congregational observances serves the purpose of spiritually sustaining and emotionally boosting commitment to the teachings of the faith and its way of life. Religious belief must become religious action.

∾ PSALM 150 ∾

Hallelujah.
Praise God in His sanctuary;
Praise Him in the firmament of His
 power.
2 Praise Him for His mighty acts;
Praise Him according to His abundant
 greatness.
3 Praise Him with the blast of the horn;
Praise Him with the psaltery and harp.
4 Praise Him with the timbrel and
 dance;
Praise Him with stringed instruments
 and the pipe.
5 Praise Him with the loud-sounding
 cymbals;
Praise Him with the clanging cymbals.
6 Let every thing that hath breath praise
 the LORD.
Hallelujah.

∾

The Great Hallelujah

The word *Hallelujah* (praise God) occurs twelve times in the six verses of this psalm. In every place and by every means of expression, the world is called upon to "praise Him for His mighty acts. . . . according to His abundant greatness" (v. 2). The closing sentence, "Let everything that has breath praise God" (v. 6), universalizes the faith of Israel. Not only Israel, but the entire world, not only humans, but all creatures are to join in the praises of God, in the sanctuary or anyplace: "Praise God in His sanctuary; praise Him in the firmament of His power" (v. 1).

∽

Reflection: Praise and Praise Again

The Book of Psalms begins with the words "Happy is the one . . ." (Psalm 1:1) and ends in Psalm 150 with the jubilant *hallelujah* (praise God) refrain, as though to say that happiness depends on faith in God. How is God to be praised? "According to His abundant greatness" (v. 2). How is that possible? Since God's greatness is immeasurable, how can any amount of praise do justice to Him? A prayer that met this challenge was that of a simple, illiterate, but pious Jew who, unable to read the prayer book, stammered out the alphabet and then said: "Dear God in heaven, please, put together the letters I have spoken, to make the right words for Your glory." Maybe the same thinking inspired the psalmist to list all those different instruments, the horn, lute, harp, timbrel, strings, pipe, and cymbals, as though to say that no one of these instruments alone, nor all of them together, could adequately praise God. By whom should God be praised? Not only by the psalmist and his people, Israel; not only by all humanity; but by all living beings: "Let everything that has breath praise God" (v. 6). If you have read the whole Book of Psalms and are now reading the last, Psalm 150, start all over again. The repeated reading of the psalms will open your eyes to the discovery of meaning you have overlooked. Let the Book of Psalms be your companion through life. It mirrors every imaginable human condition: fear, anxiety, sorrow, humiliation, anger, envy, contempt, hatred, love, trust, joy, and thanksgiving. As you read what the psalmists have to say to God, you, too, may find yourself in dialogue with God.

Sources

Beirce, Ambrose. *The Devil's Dictionary*. New York: Oxford University Press, 1998.

Buber, Martin. *Tales of the Hasidim: The Later Masters*. New York: Schocken Books, 1947.

Emerson, Ralph Waldo. *The Complete Writings of Ralph Waldo Emerson, Vol I*. New York: Wm. H. Wise & Company, 1929.

Evans, Bergen. *Dictionary of Quotations*. New York: Delacorte Press, 1968.

Jewish Publication Society. *The Book of Psalms*. Philadelphia: Jewish Publication Society, 1917. Reprint, 1955.

Lewis, C. S. *Reflections on the Psalms*. New York: Harcourt, Brace & Company, 1958.

Morrison, James Dalton. *Masterpieces of Religious Verse*. New York: Harper & Row, 1948.

Stevenson, Burton. *The Book of Home Quotations*. New York: Dodd, Mead & Company, 1935.